Memoirs of
A WONKY—
EYED MAN

The Dad-Knows-Best Years

Jason Byrne

GILL BOOKS

Gill Books

Hume Avenue

Park West

Dublin 12

www.gillbooks.ie

Gill Books is an imprint of M.H. Gill and Co.

9780717194483

Designed by www.grahamthew.com

Typesetting by Jen Patton, Liz White Designs

Edited by Sheila Armstrong

Printed and bound in Great Britain by CPI Group (UK) Ltd,
Croydon, CRO 4YY

This book is typeset in Baskerville, Northern Soul and Venti CF.

The paper used in this book comes from the wood pulp of sustainably managed forests.

A CIP catalogue record for this book is available from the British Library.

5 4 3 2 1

For Daniel and Devin

Contents

Prologue vii

PROLOGUE

Some people say we turn into our parents. Well, here I am, fifty years of age, at the 2022 Edinburgh Festival, and I have actually turned into my dad.

I now have six stents, just like Dad, to add to my list of ailments.

LIST OF JASON'S AILMENTS

1. Born with a lazy eye.
2. Lung collapsed three times.
3. Knee fell off while having a shite.
4. Dislocated arm while surfing.
5. No appendix.
6. Nose bent from sleeping on it all my life.
7. Red hair.
8. Tiny eyes.
9. Small ears.
10. Now six stents in my arteries.

All thanks to my mam and dad's shit genes.

'It's your father's side, you know,' Mam would say, blaming poor auld Dad, whose brothers and sisters lived into their eighties.

'Your signal is dropping, it's defo your end,' Mam would shout from her fuzzy land-line in Ballinteer. Most things were normally someone else's fault.

People have watched me talk about my dad, Paddy Byrne, on stage over the years, saying how well I do his voice and mannerisms. I've even dressed as him and interviewed him, as me, after he passed away on 24 February 2020.

'Just before our birthday, Jay, I'll kill him,' Mam said just after he died.

'Why don't you do a play about him?' a mate said to me.

So I did. I wrote a play called *The Paddy Lama*, all about Dad in his shed in the back garden, the visits I would make and the knowledge I'd get back there. We called him the Paddy Lama due to his amazing life wisdom. He was like a smoking Irish guru that smelt of whiskey. I wanted to do the play so people would know who my dad was. He was a very special type of fella.

I'm pacing up and down backstage now at this tiny venue in Edinburgh. My main room upstairs for the evening show holds 1,200 people a night, but here in the bowels of the venue, it only seats 90, just enough to get the feel of the size of a shed.

I'm thinking about my past life as I pace, the advice I took from Dad to get to this point. Sometimes I listened to him, other times not so much, as it was bullshit advice.

TOP FIVE PIECES OF BULLSHIT ADVICE FROM PADDY

1. When ye know, ye know.
2. If you're looking for the height of the clouds, measure them with the flat of your hand to the horizon.
3. Horses hate pigs, so never bring one near a horse. (Not sure if anybody on Earth has ever done this.)
4. Don't move too much in life. You only get so many heartbeats – be careful or you'll use them up.
5. The Mona Lisa has no lips. (I'm pretty sure he meant eyebrows, but he told everyone she had no lips.)

I smile as I go through the play in my head, thinking of all the sayings he had, the adventures he lived.

I'm fifty. I've done stand-up for twenty-seven years or so. I've lived about six lives, with children, marriage, sickness and now six bloody stents. I've gigged all over the world and made thousands and thousands of people laugh.

I begin to become my dad now, pacing slower, fag in my right hand. I'm wearing his blue jumper for the play, the only bit of clothing of his I use here. I can still smell him from the jumper. I hear the audience. I slow down. I sit like he would sit on a chair backstage.

I wonder how I have ended up here in life, all the decisions, good and bad, that have brought me to this point. Have I done the right things? What if, what if, what if …

To be honest, I'm tired now. I've nearly gigged myself to death. I can hear my dad saying, 'It's time to slow down, son, less of the leaping around on stage.'

I was always a worrier, too. 'If you worry, you die, if you don't worry, you die anyway, so why worry?' Thanks, Dad. Yet again, this slow-talking, whiskey-drinking, smoking guru of a man has put me right. He may be physically gone, but he is still very much alive in my head.

The lights go down and I now hear my mother's voice in the venue. It's a pre-recording of her talking about my dad, how his death has affected us all, how it has made us think about life. How delicate life is. How we should love life.

Mam's voice drifts off. I walk through the small dark curtain, leaving Jason behind. No better way to slow down and take it easy than to become Paddy Byrne …

The man that didn't give a bollix.

CHAPTER 1
THE REAL WORLD
IS SHITE

BASH!

An egg hit the window of the engineering room.

SMASH!

Another egg hit the principal's car. The teachers all ran out of their classrooms to shoo the Leaving Cert year of 1989 away. We then covered the teachers in flour and eggs, as well as each other. This was it: this was the last time we might all be together as children at once.

We cried laughing as we roared goodbye to the school and the teachers, pretending to be delighted. But deep down, I was very sad to be leaving these children behind. We had started out in a sandpit at crèche at the age of three. All the laughter and tears we had been through. The smoking and kissing at the back of the school. The embarrassment of trying to become a teenager as your mates all laughed at your bald mickey in the changing rooms. All spread out over fourteen years and hundreds of housing estates.

I had the best school days ever. I loved walking up the road to school with my mates in hail, sleet and snow, all of us wearing snorkel jackets.

Snorkel jacket

The snorkel jacket was lethal. It was named that because it looked like you were about to go diving in it. It had a hood that zipped up around your face. If, when crossing the road, you looked left or right, the hood stayed looking straight ahead and your head moved inside it, so instead of oncoming cars all you could see was the inside of a fluffy hood. To look left and right, you had to move your whole body as if you were wearing a full-on plaster of Paris coat.

Besides risking death every time you crossed the road, being a schoolchild meant no responsibilities. To be honest, none of us ever thought we'd grow up. None of us ever thought we'd have to leave our parents' houses, the safety of the road we played on. We'd never have to be that parent sitting at the table in the good room opening the bills.

REACTIONS FROM PADDY BYRNE TO OPENING BILLS AT THE TABLE IN THE GOOD ROOM

1. **ESB** ... 'Ah, bollix.'
2. **GAS** ... 'Ye whaaa?'
3. **TV LICENCE** ... 'Don't watch telly that much.'

4. **DOG LICENCE … 'A licence for a fucking dog?' …**
    ripping sounds.
5. **LIFE INSURANCE … 'I'm worth more dead than I am**
    alive, Eithne!' (Shouting to my mam in the kitchen.)

Leaving the school, we all knew that most of us would never see each other again. But you do see some of them. I still see Karl, Ciaran, Brian and Ken. And over time, I have bumped into school friends that weren't from my road, from neighbourhoods much further away. I would see them years after we left school, up to twenty years later, and they are grown men and women – and I mean **grownnn**.

'Terry, Terry O'Neill, it's me – ah, you do remember me, Jason, I was in school with you for years? Miss Allen's class? Terry O'Neill, man, Terry O'Neill, the Neiler, Big T, droopy bollix?' (Named as one of his balls hung lower than the other.)

I love the way Dublin people insist that 'you do remember me, you do', even if you don't. And to shut them up, you'll more than likely lie and say you remember them. Then you're into a whole shitstorm, with them reminiscing about a past you're pretending you know, and all the while you're thinking, 'Who in the name of jaysus is this bloke?'

This is what I do: I look at the man in front of me, the Terry O'Neill. I then draw an imaginary line about five inches in from the outer edges of his body, and I create a smaller person, a bit like editing the edge of a photo and cropping it. Then I widen their eyes, because most of the time, from drink and fags and chippers, their eyes are nearly sunk into their face. Then, hey presto, I've got a Terry O'Neill from 1989. It looks like the child Terry O'Neill is wearing a fat suit to make him look like the adult Terry O'Neill, almost like the child is trapped inside this grown-up body. Which is true for most of us in more ways than one.

'Ah, Terry, now I have ye!'

I was seventeen years of age. I couldn't vote or even have a jar in a pub. Yet I had just been thrown out of school, out of a world that I had known and loved for nearly fourteen years.

'What in the name of jaysus are you going to do with yourself now?' asked Dad while I sat with him in his shed.

TOP TEN THINGS PADDY BYRNE DID IN HIS SHED

1. Smoked.
2. Drank whiskey.
3. Listened to the radio.
4. Called Joe Duffy an auld one.
5. Called Gay Byrne a wanker.
6. Called Gerry Ryan a mad bastard.
7. Called Marian Finucane a clever lady – and she loves a fag, fair play to her.

8. **Pointed at old radios on the shelves.**
9. **Never fixed anything.**
10. **Thought he was Perry Como (about three whiskeys in).**

'You'll have a small one, son.' Paddy offered me a whiskey, as he thought I was old enough now to start my alcoholic journey. I hated whiskey and most alcohol. I would have much preferred a massive bag of milk-teeth sweets.

'Ah, you're no good, son,' my dad said as I nearly choked to death on the whiskey. My dad's way of measuring a human was by how much they could drink or make him laugh. If Dad had ever met Einstein and Einstein refused a drink from him, my dad would say, 'Ah, he's no use, that Einstein.' But he is famous for devising the theory of relativity, Dad. 'Who gives a bollix, the man won't have a drink.'

Once my dad met the mother of one of my girlfriends at a party somewhere. The lady didn't drink, and when my dad found out, he asked me if there was something wrong with her. Dad just assumed that if you didn't drink you had a mental illness.

'I want to go to college, Dad. So my idea is, if I don't get enough points in de Leaving for any of the colleges, I'll go back to school, repeat de Leaving, then get to college,' I announced.

De Leaving ───────────────────────

This is the exam we do at the end of our school journey in Ireland. We study eleven subjects for five or six years, which are whittled down to seven subjects in fifth and sixth year. We then only have two years to prep. Our education system does not know how to prep us properly.

BING BASH WALLOP! And suddenly a thousand students are all in a sports hall trying to listen to a French conversation out of a tape recorder with a tiny speaker that no one can hear. Or filing some metal in shorts and T-shirt, only having an hour to make a stupid moving lock in engineering. Or in an Irish oral, where you tell the examiner that it's a lovely day and what your name is in Irish, because that's all you can speak after fourteen years of shite teaching.

It's called DE LEAVING because we're leaving school, just to remind us all what's happening at the end (we're leaving – get it?) but if you do not do well in DE LEAVING, you can go back to school and leave again by repeating DE LEAVING.

───────────────────────────────

Dad pulled on his cigarette, took a sip of whiskey and squinted at me.

His whiskey glass thudded down on top of his gas heater. 'Well, fair play to you, son, you're only seventeen and you're thinking like a man. I wish I had the opportunities that you lot have now, heading off to college, getting a degree, then seeing the world and coming back to a solid job for life. I'm proud of you, son, proud of you!'

The shed door creaked open. My mam, Eithne, was standing there. 'Will you two come in for your dinner?'

'Jason here was telling me that he's going to repeat the Leaving Cert, then head off to college when he gets the points he needs. Isn't he great, Eithne?' my dad said proudly.

'Oh yeah, Lilly Poland's lad did that. She had to work four jobs to pay the 5,000-pound-a-year fee in Bolton Street for five years,' answered my mam.

'You'll do great son. Sure, I spent most of my life here,' said Dad as we sat in a waiting room in Guinness's. Due to my dad having a minor heart attack from my mother telling him how much it would cost, my life plan had changed rapidly. I was to be an apprentice in the Guinness Brewery in Dublin.

Following in the footsteps of five generations of Byrnes, all coopers, my dad was the last of the Byrnes to work there. His own dad walked him into the cooperage at the age of fifteen, no interview, straight up to the foreman, saying, 'This is my son Paddy Byrne – he starts today,' and bang, my dad was a Guinness's man for life from that moment on.

The room was full of young fellas with their Guinness's dads. A man came out of an office in overalls, he was skinny and wearing a wig. *Oh Jesus, not a wig*, I thought – Dad would not be able to ignore it. You could just see it in his eyes. This man was some sort of supervisor in charge of picking the apprentices, so my dad, as bold as brass, walked me over to him. 'This is Jason Byrne, my son – he starts today.'

'He what now?' asked the supervisor.

'He starts today, he's my son, I'm Paddy Byrne, I work over in the gas plant, I'm from a long line of Byrnes that worked here all their lives,' my dad said, starting to get annoyed. 'So sign him up before I get that rat's nest on your head and shove it up your hoop,' he said, in a posh accent for some reason.

TIMES MY DAD THINKS IT'S A GOOD IDEA TO PUT ON A POSH ACCENT

1. When insulting a priest.
2. When insulting a copper.
3. When insulting a bank manager.
4. When insulting a Guinness's supervisor.
5. When warning us all not to go into the lavatory as 'the shit that one has just done is lethal'.

My dad had never taken notice of the changes in Guinness's. They were about to retire hundreds of workers because they were not needed anymore – modern machinery had taken over. The days of walking your son in were gone. The last time my dad had seen anything like this was in 1954.

'He'll have to do an aptitude test and a bit of practical and then, and only then, will he join the waiting list to see if he'll get an apprenticeship. So which area would he like to go into?' asked the supervisor. Myself and Dad had never discussed this. You had a choice of plumber, electrician or fitter.

My dad looked at my wonky eye. This was so named due to me having a squint as a child where my eye would turn in. Other people called it a cock eye or lazy eye, but Mam said I had a special eye. Dad called it a wonky eye. He always had the funniest names for things.

TIMES MY WONKY EYE WOULD TURN IN

1. When I was tired.
2. When I was hungry.
3. When I told fibs.
4. When I ran too fast.
5. And, in my older age, immediately after sex.

'I suppose nothing where he's measuring or cutting, as that eye of his has a tendency to wander,' said my dad.

'OK then, electrician,' decided the supervisor.

My dad left me with the supervisor and headed back over to the gas plant to finish his shift. 'Ah, amazing, son, you'll be one of us by the end of the day – you'll fly through this.' He pushed open the door to the waiting room, leaving me at the age of seventeen in this shit new world to become an apprentice electrician, when I had never even changed a fuse in my life.

★ ★ ★

'Listen, son, we all make mistakes. Next time, next time,' my poor auld dad said in the car on the way home as he hid behind the steering wheel. I had been run out of the supervisor's workshop, never to return to the Guinness factory ever again. Nepotism, me hoop.

HOW NOT TO BECOME AN APPRENTICE ELECTRICIAN IN GUINNESS'S

1. Wire the neutral wire to the live pin.
2. Wire the live wire to the earth pin.
3. Wire the earth wire to the live pin.
4. Blow up all the bulbs in the ceiling of the workshop.
5. Trip all the trip switches on a board due to blowing all the bulbs.
6. Which then sends half of the Guinness factory into a blackout.
7. Gallons of Guinness lost due to machinery cutting out.
8. Thousands of pounds in costs and damages.
9. Embarrass the Byrne name which has existed there for five generations.
10. Call the supervisor a baldy bollix.

I was not cut out for any of this manual work, be it building, wiring or plastering. I could never do any of these things because Dad was such a bad teacher when it came to DIY.

TIMES DAD TRIED TO TEACH US DIY

1. 'Hold the bloody wood, hold it!' as I tried to hold a huge plank at the age of six while Dad tried to saw it, but it just kept moving.
2. 'Of course you can do it!'
3. 'Why in the name of jaysus would you do that?'
4. 'It's wallpaper on a wall, not the Sistine Chapel!'
5. 'Your mother is going to kill me. Just pull the nail out of your hand quickly – that way you won't feel it.'

I'd have to find another trade.

'Jaysus, I just won a holiday to Spain, to Salou of all places,' announced my dad excitedly. Myself, Eric, Rachel and Eithne were not as excited.

Eric Byrne

The eldest. Five years older than me, battered me when I used his vinyl, battered me when I wore his Iron Maiden jacket, battered me for being in his bedroom. He moved to Sweden in his twenties, married a Swede and became Eric the Phone, as that was all the communication we had with him.

Rachel Byrne ————————————————————

Younger sister by two years. Great fun, full of laughter, very like my mam. In fact, they now live together, spending all their days looking out the living-room window, wondering where this or that neighbour is going, has come from, has been to. Most exciting moments in their lives: when a new car or a stranger pulls up. Rachel's finger is on the phone to call the guards like it's a trigger on a shotgun.

————————————————————

Eithne Byrne ————————————————————

Youngest sister. Nearly ten years younger than me. I babysat Eithne a lot. She would bang her head on the back of the couch to the beat of the music. I would often drag her around the carpet in a sheet, resulting in massive carpet burns on her back. She once fell off a swing, was knocked unconscious and brought to hospital. I was so upset, but at the same time wondered if I could get a puppy if she was dead.

————————————————————

All us kids automatically thought we weren't going. None of us had ever been on a sun holiday with Mam and Dad.

REASONS WHY DAD WOULDN'T BRING US ON SUN HOLIDAYS

1. They wouldn't enjoy themselves.
2. It's too hot for them.
3. They'd be eaten alive by midges.

4. **It's too far.**
5. **We'd need shares in suncream.**
6. **They'd hate to leave their friends.**
7. **They could all drown in the pool.**
8. **They'd be taken out to sea – the currents are mental in Spain.**
9. **They'd eat nothing.**
10. **Sure, have you seen the size of the ants over there? They'd lift you outta your bed.**

What my dad really meant was that he would not be able to enjoy himself with four kids hanging out of him while he was trying to drink and enjoy the sun. So we never went with them. They would put us in neighbours' houses or send us to stay with aunties and uncles in Finglas. Two weeks on couches and floors in smelly sleeping bags, the four of us separated like some sort of World War II babies. Then Mam and Dad would come back all tanned and fresh-looking with massive sombreros on their heads, a figurine of a Spanish lady that was full of booze, and bags and bags of sweets for us.

I'm pretty sure myself and my siblings would have enjoyed ourselves in Spain. It would have been way better than the shite food and accommodation in our relatives' or neighbours' houses. I hated eating outside my house as a kid anyway, so when I returned home, I was always almost see-through. My mam would cry for a week with guilt while my dad just kept telling her how much we wouldn't have enjoyed ourselves.

REASONS WHY JASON WAS MALNOURISHED IN OTHER PEOPLE'S HOMES

1. Their hallway smelt of cabbage or carrots.
2. Their butter was different.
3. Their milk was different.
4. They had no goodies (as in chocolate).
5. Their clothes smelt weird.
6. They all smelt of Lynx at the dinner table.
7. Their nana ate with them, with food and teeth falling out of her mouth.
8. They had egg in everything.
9. The sitting room smelt of farts.
10. They had weird cups and bowls that smelt.

(Deep breath: the above is the reason to this day why I hate eating in other people's houses and especially staying overnight. Your spare beds are shite, your showers are powerless, the food is gack, and still to this day, your houses smell of cabbage, eggs, children and quinoa. So stop inviting me! And I don't give a bollix about your kids' talent show that we all have to clap along to before they go to bed … and BREATHE!)

Paddy Byrne had entered a raffle in work that he had organised. I remember him bringing in all the cash and pouring it out on the good-room table. 'That's a thousand pounds, kids. Take a good look, 'cause you'll never see it again,' said Dad. He obviously had zero aspirations for any of our futures.

It was one pound to buy a ticket and one lucky family would head off to Salou for a week, all expenses paid. So guess who won? Paddy Byrne, the fella who organised it all. A mystery, that.

So we were all going, but none of us was sure about it.

REASONS WHY THE KIDS THOUGHT WE SHOULDN'T GO TO SPAIN

1. We wouldn't enjoy ourselves.
2. It's too hot for us.
3. We'd be eaten alive by midges.
4. It's too far.
5. We'd need shares in suncream.
6. We'd hate to leave our friends.
7. We could all drown in the pool.
8. We'd be taken out to sea – the currents are mental in Spain.
9. We'd eat nothing.
10. Sure, have you seen the size of the ants over there? They'd lift us outta our beds.

'Ah jaysus, where are you getting all that rubbish from? We'll all have a ball, for Christ's sake,' Dad reassured us, shaking his head at Mam. You see, he had to bring us this time because it was a family-holiday prize – only men with children could enter.

So I was seventeen years of age, it was the middle of the summer of '89, and myself, Rachel, Eithne and Eric were all heading to Salou. We were shitting ourselves, thinking we were going to drown or be taken away by giant ants.

Well, we weren't. But Dad was right: it was too hot, we all got burnt to death, and Mam put yoghurt on us all going to bed. Dad had a ball on the holiday because he didn't have to mind any of us. Eric was five years older than me, so he watched me until he went out. I was two years older than Rachel, so I watched her. Then, when I wanted to go out, Rachel watched Eithne because she was seven years older than her. My mam watched my dad.

I met an Irish friend of mine over there, Peter, who was on holidays with his family too. He was a year older than me, so he could buy drink, but mind you so could I. I was tall and looked the age, but in Salou in the '80s they'd sell drink to me baby sister, which I think they did anyway …

Peter had his own apartment away from his family. He was a mad bastard. He had the idea that we would hire mopeds, then we'd get a tray of cans, drink them in his apartment, then head to the local nightclub. We headed down to the bottom of the complex to an Irish bar where all our families were.

PLACES MY PARENTS HAVE BEEN TO IN THE WORLD AND WHERE THEY'VE GONE THERE

1. Spain … Irish bar.
2. Portugal … Irish bar.
3. Sweden … Irish bar.

4. **France ... Irish bar.**
5. **Tunisia ... Irish bar.**
6. **Italy ... Irish bar.**
7. **New York ... Irish bar.**
8. **England ... Irish bar.**
9. **Wales ... Irish bar.**
10. **Ireland ... an Australian-themed night in an Irish bar.**

My own mother came home from a holiday once with the girls, saying, 'Ah, that was great. We found an Irish bar and stayed there for ten days, singing and dancing, and we didn't have to meet one local. Well, apart from Pedro the barman, but your auntie Olive was convinced he was taking the piss with the accent and all – she thought Pedro was from Rialto and had the dark skin from a fella his granny was riding.'

So me and Peter crept by the horde of Irish who were singing along to 'The Fields of Athenry' with Tony and the Two Terrys from Finglas, which consisted of Tony and two female backing singers called Terry. Just as we passed to get to the place where we could rent mopeds, I felt a hand grab my arm.

'I was young too once, you know – be careful and use your head.' It was my dad. He had leaned back on his chair from the crowd of singers to give me the warning. My dad never really had long, heavy chats with me about life. It was normally in short bursts like the above.

PADDY BYRNE'S ADVICE

1. Never say yes unless you have permission to say no.
2. If you worry you die, if you don't worry you die anyway, so why worry?
3. There's always someone somewhere trying to be you.
4. Never get involved.
5. Sign nothing.
6. Never stare at a dog.
7. Only part with your money when you have to.
8. Eat porridge.
9. Trust no one.
10. Never, ever let your kids get in the way of your social life.

'Passport! Passport!' shouted the Spanish fella renting us the mopeds like he was working border control from the telly. We were at SPEEDOS, the shop that rented the bikes. The fella that owned it was called Speedo, some mad nickname that he had no idea rhymed with paedo. He only wore Speedos with a weird bulge – the rest of him was bare-skinned with patches of oil marks on him, all finished off with a flat cap. So we renamed him 'Speedo the paedo in the Speedos'.

He wanted Peter's passport as a type of deposit so we wouldn't steal the mopeds. I couldn't find mine, even though I was sure I had it. Peter handed him his passport and we both gave him around twenty pounds each for a couple of hours. The fella was happy enough with just Peter's passport.

And off we went: no licence, no experience. Sure enough, we were only five minutes on the mopeds when Peter went down in front of me while turning a bend. His moped slid across the road, Peter went the opposite way, and a fecking truck went over the moped. He was so lucky.

I parked mine up on the path and went to help Peter up. One side of his leg was scraped to shite. We managed to get his moped upright then wheeled it back towards the fella we got it from.

Speedo went mental, screaming, 'No passport, no passport!' We left, shitting ourselves. What a disaster. Peter had no passport and I had lost mine.

We headed back to the Irish bar with Peter hobbling along. I managed to find the table both our families were at, still singing, Peter's mam came over to him, screaming when she saw his bloody, scraped leg. Then the dad came out and they both said they were going to kill him while hugging him at the same time.

> PETER'S MAM: Your poor leg, what did you do?!
>
> PETER: We rented mopeds.
>
> PETER'S MAM: You feckin' idiots, I'll kill ye.
>
> PETER: I fell off the moped.
>
> PETER'S MAM: Me poor boy.
>
> PETER: Jason came too.
>
> PETER'S MAM: He's too young, I'll kill ye!

> PETER: Me leg is bleeding.
>
> PETER'S MAM: You poor thing.
>
> PETER: The fella kept me passport.
>
> PETER'S MAM: I'll kill ye!

I too had to tell my mam and dad that I'd lost my passport. We were only three days into the holiday, and I didn't know how I was going to get home without it. Peter's mam and dad went up the next day with a fistful of cash and got Peter's passport back off Speedo the paedo in Speedos.

I, however, had no idea where mine was. My dad made me search everywhere. While they headed to the beach or water-parks, I was properly punished by being left behind to search for the passport.

At night there was no more heading off on our own. Me and Peter had to sit with our parents and be tortured by the singing while my sisters went to kids' clubs.

Big brother Eric drank with the locals and ended up getting a Spanish girlfriend called Maria. He introduced her to Mam and Dad, said he was bringing her home to marry her. My dad laughed so much that sangria came out of his nose and Eric walked off in a huff.

'Sure, why don't we bring her whole family home?' Dad shouted after him.

Come the end of the holiday, there was still the worry of the missing passport. Dad said there was no way he could get me home without one.

On the last night in the bar, Dad had organised with Tony and the Two Terrys for me to be called up on stage to give a final call-out for my lost passport. I was mortified. Up I went in front of hundreds of Irish people to see if any of them had seen the passport.

> TERRY: We have a little boy here (seventeen, six feet tall) and his mammy and daddy say he has lost his passport – is that right, son?
>
> ME: (mortified, had never spoken into a mic before) I had it … then it's gone … (pointing) somewhere … (more pointing) ground …
>
> TERRY: Ah sure, we'll have no probs finding it with all that information. And if you don't find it, you can stay with me and the two Terrys and help us for the rest of the season.

The crowd laughed and clapped as the two Terrys stared at their potential slave.

The next morning, I had knots in my stomach heading to the airport on the bus. Dad said they might just let him take me home because I was his son. Rachel and Eithne didn't care as they were going through the coloured pens and keyrings they had bought their mates. Eric was wearing the face off the Spanish girl, Maria, at the back of the bus. Mam was just looking out the bus window silently …

> MAM (to herself): What if I just jumped off this bus now, stayed here in this lovely heat, let Paddy take the brats home and raise them? I'll meet a lovely Spanish man who will cook me Mediterranean meals while making mad love to me on the beach each night.

'Eithne, look at the mickey on that statue!' Dad shouted for the whole bus to hear as he pointed at a Greek statue on a round-about, and Mam's head was straight back on the bus.

We arrived at the airport. Dad said if they wouldn't let him take me home I would have to stay in the airport in a special cell until he went home, got my new passport and flew back with it to Spain. Dad said not to worry – it would only take about ten days.

Tears were welling up in my eyes as we queued for passport control. Dad and Mam seemed quite calm for a couple about to lose their son. Eithne and Rachel were playing chasing around a disgruntled childless couple, while Eric was inconsolable at the thought of Maria not being in his life.

'Passports, passports,' the guard said.

My dad handed him my mam's and his, then he handed him Eithne's and Rachel's. Eric held his up while trying to dry his eyes and wipe his face with a scarf that Maria had given him, sniffing it at the same time.

Then the guard pointed at me. 'Passport, passport?' This was it: I would have to live in Spain for ten days, all alone in a cell. My life was ending.

'Yep, here it is,' said my dad as he handed the guard my passport. We all walked through and dad couldn't stop laughing. 'The face on ye, son,' he cried.

'Ah, Paddy, you're awful,' said Mam.

'He had to learn a lesson, and he won't fucking do it again, the dope,' announced Dad, the super-fucking-nanny.

'Where was me passport?!' I asked. Even Eric had cheered up a bit now.

'Remember, trust no one, son.' My dad leaned forward and put the passport into my back pocket.

The sly shit. When my dad had grabbed my arm a few days ago when me and Peter were going to get the mopeds, he had lifted my passport from my jeans so I wouldn't hand it over.

'Sure, we all heard about your mission, son. Don't be collaborating near your sisters – they've ears like elephants.'

I looked at Eithne and Rachel. They both had their tongues out at me.

We then flew home to Ireland with Dad hitting the air hostess bell, ordering as much free drink as he could, while telling everyone about the joke he had played on me.

> DAD: Passport?! … yer man here … moped? … on stage announcing it … thought he had to live in the airport! Hahahahaha … jaysus …
>
> DAD (in his posh voice): Another Heineken if you will, my good lady.

That was the last time I ever went on a sun holiday with them. Even when they asked me to come again, I had to say to them, 'Nah, you're alright, I wouldn't enjoy it.'

CHAPTER 2
MR BLEEDIN' POPULAR

'How in the name of jaysus did you manage that?' asked Ken Newman as he looked over at Pamela Flood. She was a six-foot blonde, a tall, smiley lady. Yes, Pamela Flood from the telly. From *Off the Rails*! RTÉ! And all things lovely. And she was my date for the Debs.

The Debs ────────────────────────

The Debs is short for debutante. This is where young Irish adults debut themselves as grown men and women for the first time at an end-of-school dance. In other countries, it's called a prom, a ball, a graduation, etc., which is all very straightforward and easy to follow. None of us had a clue why it was called the Debs, nor did we give a shite. I can only assume the Catholic Church had a hand in this, like they do everything …

BISHOP BIG HAT: They're all children of God, so let them get dressed up to look lovely and they can debut themselves in front of Our Lord to show him the new adults entering his church … mwahahaha! (Added this laugh in as I always see bishops at the top of a castle surrounded by chemistry flasks like in Breaking Bad, *inventing the next Catholic converter.)*

────────────────────────────────

Pamela and I were workmates in the Braemor Rooms. This was a top-class cabaret venue where Joe Dolan, Dickie Rock, the Drifters, Niall Tóibín and the Dubliners, to name a few, played each weekend in the suburbs of Churchtown. My mam was a waitress there, dishing out spoons of mashed potato, veg and meat to massive tables of drunk, singing Irish heads. I had started there a long time ago as a lounge boy, collecting glasses, taking orders and eventually serving pints.

One of the most bizarre things I ever saw there was when Dickie Rock was on. In case you don't know Dickie Rock, he was and still is an Irish cabaret crooner. The women loved him. Even now as I type this I can hear most of Ireland screaming. When he played the Braemor Rooms, there was mayhem, with parallel rows of tables packed full of women. Dickie would come out, they'd shout, 'SPIT ON ME, DICKIE!' and off he'd go crooning.

What Dickie loved to do was walk among the women while he sang. The spotlight had to try to follow him offstage and around the floor. The fella operating the spotlight used to singe his own hair from the heat while trying to get the correct angle. The room wasn't even that big – they could have used torches to pick up Dickie.

In those days there were no wireless mics, so the wire on Dickie's mic needed to be very long. But as he twisted and turned around the tables, the wire would get caught. Dickie would be stuck in the middle of the floor while his wire coiled around some drunk auld one and her G&T.

Dickie had to employ a fella, Willy the Wire we called him, to follow him. He was ordered to stay down on his hands and knees to stay out of the spotlight as he unravelled the microphone lead from tables and chairs and drunk punters.

Every now and again you'd see him, with his thick-rimmed glasses and comb-over, pop up into the spotlight behind Dickie, out again and in again, like a meerkat with an armful of mic lead.

'And I love you soooo,' sings Dickie (Willy pops up, Dickie gives him a belt, down goes Willy), 'the people ask me howww …' It was like something out of *Naked Gun*.

So anyway, Pamela Flood and I were off to the Debs, and Ken was trying to figure out how I'd done it.

'I just asked her straight out – she couldn't refuse the charm of the Byrne,' I said.

JASON MOPPING FLOOR IN BRAEMOR ROOMS; PAMELA STACKING BOTTLES ON A SHELF

JASON (leaning on the mop): Hey, eh, heyyyy.

PAMELA: Oh, how are you, Jay?

JASON: Yeah, yeah, look, I, eh …

PAMELA: Yeah?

JASON: Yeah.

PAMELA: Yeah?

JASON: I have … the lads, we're going …

PAMELA: Going …?

JASON: Yes, yes, we're going – are you going?

PAMELA: Going where?

JASON: Ah, I wouldn't if I was you …

PAMELA: Go where, Jay?

JASON: The Debs, it's shite, you're right.

PAMELA: You want me to go to your Debs?

JASON: I know, it's cool, it doesn't matter, just leave it, I'll head off.

PAMELA: I'd love to go to your Debs.

JASON: Fuck off!

PAMELA: Sorry?

JASON: I mean, fuck, em, sorry, right, that's that then.

PAMELA: That's that then.

Slick as biscuits – sure, no woman in the world could resist that type of smooth-talking charm.

It was freezing, standing outside the school waiting for the bus. We had all just done our Debs photos, which had us all lining up as couples in the gym, like a weird endless wedding fair. I thought of it more like proof in later life that you actually had a date, and that's who you'd be wearing the face off later on that night.

DIFFERENT NAMES FOR KISSING IN IRELAND

1. **Wear the face off each other.**
2. **Frenchies.**
3. **Tonsil hockey.**
4. **Get off with someone.**
5. **Score (I think this is a different thing these days).**
6. **Mooch/smooch.**
7. **Lob in the gob.**
8. **Eat the face off each other.**
9. **Shift.**
10. **Stall the head off ye.**

Pamela was with her mam and dad, and of course I was with mine. All my schoolmates were dressed in hired tuxedos that didn't fit, and the girls were all orange from shite eighties spray tans.

But as me mam said: 'Ah jaysus, you all look massive!'

Well, the boys didn't have much to worry about when it came to how they looked, but the poor girls had lovely dresses that were ruined by literally half a bush pinned to their shoulder in the guise of an orchid, or shite roses that you handed over in a plastic casing that cost a bleeding fortune.

'Massive, the lot of ye, only massive!' repeated my mam.

'Jaysus, she's some ride, Jay!'

'Paddy Byrne!' My mam reacted to my dad's blunt but honest comment about Pamela.

'Just saying you did very well there, son, what with your red hair, no muscles and wonky eye,' Dad said, filling me with encouragement for the night.

Then the bus arrived. These days the kids go to the Debs in limos and Hummers, but we were all heading to The Sands Hotel, Portmarnock, on Murphy's coaches.

The proud parents waved us off, the mammies blowing us kisses, shouting that WE WERE ALL MASSIVE! while the dads were already on the walk to the pub to celebrate that their babies were becoming adults.

The Jewish religion marks this occasion this by cutting willies or something. Us Catholics are not allowed to know about other religions, so I'm quite vague on that. Catholics head off on a Murphy's bus to a hotel to be served a shite dinner by angry waitresses and beer by barmen who know that most of us are still underage.

'Ah sure, you've hair on your bollix, son, that's good enough for me,' a barman said as I collected two pints of lager for myself and Pamela.

I was only seventeen, but it wasn't the beer that was worrying me. It was me having to behave around a lady, to not be an arsehole like us lads were in school. But thank God our school was a mixed school, so a lot of my mates were girls. I was pretty clued in on how to talk to them, except a lot of the girls in BCS (Ballinteer Community School) were tougher than me.

I sat with Pamela after we ate our chicken-and-ham-something dinner. She was great craic. We were mates so the chats flowed, unlike for the rest of the lads who had just asked random girls from different schools to their Debs, girls that they had never talked to before. There was a sea of lads and girls just looking out towards the dance floor, not speaking to each other at all.

But soon the dance floor had a handful of seventeen-year-old boys, a long way off from becoming men, on it. They had abandoned their poor dates at the tables and now couldn't give a bollix anymore. They were hammered on two pints, flashing their bare arses and mickeys to one another, jumping on each other with one lad on another lad's shoulders trying to pull the mirrorball down.

'Leave the mirrorball alone, ye fucking eejits!' screamed the bouncer.

'Fuck off, Moustache – go home and ride your missus,' answered Liam O'Neill while the bouncer dragged him to the ground.

LIAM O'NEILL'S REACTION TO BEING DISCIPLINED

1. Ask me bollix.
2. Shove it up your hoop.
3. Your ma is your da.
4. Do want Mr Sheen for that head?
5. You should buy a bra, ye fat bollix.
6. Get your hands off me, ye paedo.
7. Here, Bugs Bunny is looking for his ears back.
8. Rudolph wants his nose back.
9. The auditions for the munchkins are closed.
10. Who cut your hair, Helen Keller?

You had to love these head-the-balls. I would miss them so much.

Je t'aime, je t'aime, je t'aime … a ne nurr ne naaa, a ne nurr ne naaa, neee naaaa …'

Ah bollix, the slow set had just come on. This was a big game changer in discos across the land of Ireland in the eighties and nineties. The music would slow down, and you then had to bring your date onto the floor and dance with her.

SLOW SET FOR PEOPLE TOO YOUNG TO REMEMBER OR NOT FROM IRELAND

1. The slow, romantic music comes on.

2. **Boy asks girl to dance.**
3. **Pair go in close to each other.**
4. **Girl places head on boy's shoulder, arms around each other's waists.**
5. **Now use your gut, and wait.**
6. **When gut kicks in, slightly put head down (boy).**
7. **Look up towards boy (girl).**
8. **Now hope she comes towards you.**
9. **Now hope he comes towards you.**
10. **Lock lips and wear the face off each other for four full songs.**

'You absolute spa, Jay,' said Ken Newman. 'I can't believe you haven't kissed her.'

I bottled it. I just couldn't kiss Pamela. I really wanted to, but I was afraid she would reject me and then never talk to me in work again. Or even worse – me wonky eye would turn in and stay there, which it had a tendency to do when I was excited in any way.

I once scared off one of the girls we hung around with. She was doing a practice snog on me, and when she pulled back, me eye was turned in with the excitement. She thought she'd broke me.

'There's loads of stragglers around, man,' Ken said to me.

'Stragglers?' I asked.

'Yeah, there's birds everywhere on their own 'cause their dates are mickeys or hammered on the couches,' said Ken.

Mickeys ─────────────────────────────

An Irish penis or an idiot of a man. One usually attached to the other.

─────────────────────────────

'I've snogged at least five girls at this stage,' he said. Ken was the best-looking fella in the class so he could snog anyone. Not me, with me red hair and wonky eye.

The night ended at about 6 a.m. We all got on the bus again and it dropped us back to Dundrum. Not even Ballinteer, where it had collected us from, but Dundrum, a good five miles away from our homes.

But we all had a laugh. Me and Pamela, along with loads of already hungover children, most of us not wearing our jackets cause you had to give it to the girl you were with, went into Bewley's upstairs in the old Dundrum shopping centre. There we all sat in a kind of big classroom for the last time ever. Fuck, I miss them all.

Pamela's mam, Paula, then came to collect her. I gave her a hug and a peck on the cheek. I found out years later that Pamela was wondering why I never kissed her …

'Well, ye made a bollix of that, man,' Ken said to me as he put his arm around my shoulder.

It was freezing. Our parents were never going to collect us. I could hear Paddy Byrne in my head: 'What time? Seven a.m.? Ask me bollix, it's a Sunday! He'll be grand.'

We walked back to Ballinteer in the freezing cold.

I went on to be a Debs connoisseur, though. I was invited to the Debs of my mate from up the road, Brian Roche. A mate of his, Susan, had no one to bring, so she asked me.

On the night, I remember me and Brian on the steps of the venue waiting to bring Susan home. She was inside kissing the fella she actually fancied – she'd just brought me so she wouldn't look desperate. When Brian told me this, we both howled laughing. 'Fair play to her,' I said. 'She's some bollix, that one.'

The third Debs I went to was very odd. It was in Coleraine in Derry, Northern Ireland, and it was called a Formal. I went to a Formal with an actual Derry girl. The girl, Arlene was her name, was a friend of someone off the road who fancied me and asked me to go.

I had to travel to Northern Ireland on my own. I had never been there, and I was only eighteen years of age, shitting myself as all the borders were still up then.

The Dublin bus we were travelling on was stopped at Newry. I had no idea what this was all about. As I looked out my window, a soldier was pointing his rifle at me. I thought, *Holy shit, he's going to shoot me.* Then I saw him aim his rifle along the bus at each passenger.

'He's just using his scope to see who's on the bus. Don't worry, son – he won't shoot you,' a lady said to me in a very strong Derry accent.

Holy jaysus, what an introduction to Northern Ireland.

I eventually got to Coleraine and it was no Dublin. It was literally a different world up there. Arlene and her angry dad collected me. Her family were Protestants and not happy that Arlene had asked a Catholic to her Formal. This type of thinking was a million miles away from Dublin, where all religions mixed in harmony – well, apart from the slight slag. This all felt hostile.

I was thrown into a small room in the house and my eye would not stop turning in with fear. Arlene came in to see how I was before we all got ready. I told her I was fine, but I wasn't. I just wanted to go home. 'I love me local priest and parish, get me outta here,' I was thinking.

Just as Arlene left the room, she asked, 'Oh, by the way, I heard that people from Dublin wear shiny tuxedos with a weird short jacket and a black sash with slip-on shoes. Please tell me that's not true?' she pleaded.

'Oh no, no …' I nervously laughed.

I shit you not, cut back to Dublin two days before.

'Dad, I need the money for a tuxedo. I'm going to a Debs in two days.'

'Well, I need the money for a mickey transplant, but I don't have it. Go away outta that – you've been to two Debs,' slagged me dad.

'Gary O'Sullivan down the road owns his own tux. I'm sure he'll let you borrow it,' screamed my mam from upstairs.

Gary O'Sullivan was a real dude. He had been invited to so many Debs that he thought it was better to own the tux instead of renting it all the time. If you actually owned a tux in those days, it was like having a Ferrari in your driveway. You were the man. So I borrowed it.

'Arghhh, what the fuck?!' screamed a voice in a Derry accent. Arlene gazed at my very shiny Dublin tuxedo with a short jacket, accompanied by Brian Roche's slip-on shoes, which he used as a lounge boy in the local pub.

All I had in my head was Gary O'Sullivan holding me by the shoulders, looking into my eyes and saying, 'The ladies love the shiiiine.'

Arlene burst into tears. Her dad walked into the room, looked me up and down and said: 'Fucking Catholics.' I was in an episode of *Derry Girls* years before it was created.

That was the last Debs I ever went to, thank God. This wonky-eyed man had had enough emotion for one year.

'I was fixing a socket in the living room when you were smaller. We didn't have any trip switches then to isolate the socket – you know, to kill the electricity in the wall. I opened out the socket, was moving around loads of bare wires …'

I was in Paddy Byrne's shed again. The Paddy Lama, sitting out in this garden shed like some sort of Zen master that you would visit, except this wasn't Tibet: it was a garden in Ludford Drive, Ballinteer. Dad was telling me one of his stories from the past – you know, the ones where he nearly kills me or himself.

'I had to reach in and touch the live wires, so I was getting little belts left, right and centre,' Dad continued.

FIZZZZ … 'Oww' … **FIZZZZ** … 'Jaysus!'

BUZZZZ … 'Bastard!' … **BANG!** … 'Wanker!'

'I was getting so many that the fag in me mouth was lighting up every time I was shocked. So enough was enough. I headed off to get a phase-tester screwdriver that would stop me getting these little shocks,' Dad explained. 'I had no idea that you were in the room at the time. You had been playing behind the couch – you must have been around five or six. When I went to get the screwdriver, I left all the live bare wires sticking out of the socket. You went over, saw the coloured wires, grabbed them and …'

'Your mother heard the noise and ran into the sitting room. You had gotten a belt and were lying on the ground … Your mother was about to grab ye, but thank God I had just come in behind her. I pulled your mother back away from ye,' he said.

> DAD: Jesus Christ, Eithne, I wouldn't touch him for five minutes or you'll end up down there with him – look at him, he's still glowing.

'I know what you're thinking, poor Jason on his own on the ground, but I could see your chest going up and down, so you were fine. I'd seen lads in Guinness's get belts like this and they were fine,' said Dad, trying to justify me basically dying on the ground of the living room. Comparing me, a five- or six-year-old, to a grown man in Guinness's getting the same shock, who would have a mound of fat to stop the electricity flowing around his body …

> MAM (screaming): Jesus Christ, Paddy, he's grabbed the wires!

'I then said the best thing ever to your mother, and this is a lesson to you when you have kids. I looked at your mother and I said … WELL, HE WON'T DO IT AGAIN, WILL HE?!'

He continued: 'And you didn't, you never, ever touched a single bare wire in your life again, cause you knew that it would hurt you. Parents have to let kids out now, take them off their leashes, let them run free the way I let you all out. Children need to find their own danger, damage themselves enough to know not to do that thing again.'

THINGS WE DID WHEN WE WERE KIDS THAT NEARLY KILLED US. MOST LIKELY DARES FROM OUR MATES

1. Cycled as fast as you could into a wall.
2. Tried to clear the riverbank on your BMX.
3. Looked into a fire.
4. Put a banger up your arse at Halloween.
5. Called your teacher Mr Haze a bollix.
6. Licked the top of a battery.
7. Touched an electric fence (Go on, it doesn't hurt!).
8. Smelt someone's finger (Here, smell that).
9. Sneaked up on a dog.
10. Licked a rat's hole (arse, bum, anus).

Dad was right, though: **YOU WON'T DO IT AGAIN, WILL YOU?**

'So, I heard ye made a bollix of the Debs, son,' said Dad. The news had spread everywhere that I brought the best-looking girl to the Debs and didn't kiss her.

'Jaysus, just leave it, Dad,' I moaned as he lit up another fag and poured a 'small one', as he called it, into his whiskey glass.

It was early September 1989, school was over and, thank jaysus, no more Debs.

I had barely passed the Leaving Cert. I was a clever kid when I put my mind to it, but I discovered girls and messing in fifth year, and my grades dropped. I even remember burning my maths book in the field with Brian Roche before the exams because we thought this was hilarious.

Anyway, the day I got my results up at BCS, it was very different to now. These days, parents are in school-groups online, and if your child sneezes you'll know about it. In 1989, my dad had never been to my school. My mam was only in it once, when I forgot me lunch or something.

Our Leaving Cert results were handed to us in a brown envelope by the headmaster. I opened mine and had just about passed. Did I go home to tell me mam the good news? Did I bollix. I went to Simple Minds in the RDS with me results in me back pocket.

I opened the door later that night to a whack on the head. Mam had no idea if I'd passed or not. When I told her, she was delighted, and Dad too. They didn't really give a bollix, as it wasn't a big thing in our house. 'As long as you're happy, son, that's all that matters,' Dad would say.

'So what do you want to do now? We couldn't get you into Guinness's cause you nearly burnt the place down,' he reminded me.

'Eh, college?' I replied.

'No way – you can ask me bollix, son! I can't afford that. Well, maybe I could but I'd have to give up the drink and use that money, or even give up the fags – sure, me own life would be over, so no way, we can't afford college.' He looked at me. 'But again, if you're talking to anyone, we can, but only if I give up the drink and fags, which I'm not doing, but if anyone asks, I would, 'cause I love me son, but if anyone were to ask, me own son wouldn't put me in that situation … open brackets and close them again, subject matter over,' Dad ranted, while puffing on his fag like a gangster in a movie.

I agreed with Dad that I loved him too much to make him give up fags and booze for my education. I had found a tech college in Dundrum, the College of Commerce – or a pretendy college as me mates called it. I was good at accountancy in school, so I thought, feck it. The deal was: you had to go to a pretendy college for two years and pass the accountancy course, and then a real college like UCD or DCU would let you in. And the best thing was, it cost nothing.

Dad cheered up. 'Go there, son, the College of Commerce in Dundrum – sure, that's a great idea, a *great* idea. I'm so proud of ye, me own son heading to college, even if it is a pretendy college, for free, which is not the point, as discussed earlier.'

We were now back in the living room with Mam, Eric, Rachel and Eithne.

'Your brother is going to college, lads,' shouted Dad with glee.

'A spa's college!' said my brother.

WHACK!

'Shut up, you, at least he's trying,' said Mam, after giving Eric a classic clip on the back of the head.

'You're all spas.' Eric then left the room and went upstairs to continue painting an Iron Maiden album cover onto the back of his denim jacket.

'Oh no, I'll miss you so much, Jason,' cried my eight-year-old sister, who had seen college on the telly in a movie where all the kids were waved off at a train platform.

'No, he's only going to Dundrum,' Rachel clarified.

'Dundrum, that's miles away!' Eithne ran upstairs bawling her eyes out.

'Well, this is a cause for celebration!' announced my dad.

In normal households, when someone says this is a cause for celebration, the man will rub his hands together, head to the drinks cabinet and organise a drink for everyone, while the mother of the house brings in a huge cake in the shape of a mortarboard, with WELL DONE, SON iced on the top.

'Let's celebrate,' me dad roared as he put his coat on, opened the hall door and disappeared up to the pub on his own.

'I think he's celebrating the fact that your college is free, son, as opposed to you actually entering a college. I'll start the dinner,' my mam said, while putting on her apron and fixing the rollers in her hair. They seemed to be in her hair every day, but she never went anywhere. Most mammies on the road did this and never went anywhere.

TIMES IN MY DAD'S LIFE WHEN HE WOULD CELEBRATE

1. New car.
2. New telly.
3. New child.
4. New wallet.

5.   **New coat.**
6.   **New medals from school sports day.**
7.   **New pet.**
8.   **New carpet.**
9.   **New windows.**
10. **New pub.**

I think you get the idea. Dad was celebrating every day.

Myself and Brian Roche walked down to Dundrum. It was only a twenty-minute walk and we had spent most of our childhood in this area. Brian Roche was more or less a plasterer at this stage. He had been helping his dad plaster since he was a kid, so I had no idea why Brian was joining an accountancy course. I think his family heard the title 'accountant technician' and assumed the tech bit was some sort of electrics and thus would help Brian in the trade of plastering in case he needed to move plug sockets on a wall or something.

The college ran like a school. We didn't need to wear a uniform, but we had to be in on time and there was a headmistress. Notes were needed if you were absent. We moved from class to class and had a lunch break. It looked, felt and smelt like a secondary school. It was not very different to BCS, but a million miles away from a real college like UCD or TCD, so, YEP, it was a pretendy college.

Subjects were accountancy, tax, law, typing and something. We had big old manual typewriters on desks. Our typing teacher was a lovely old doll. She had grey hair and always dressed in an office-type uniform, as if she worked for Churchill during the war. She was old enough to have done it.

She would walk up and down the classroom, shouting the keys we had to press in her finest Blackrock 'what the feck am I doing here teaching these little shites' accent.

'Fingers on the keys, children, left hand on A-S-D-F … a gap for G-H … and right hand on J-K-L-;' (I don't know what this last one is called). 'Now: T-H-E … and T-H-E!'

The whole class clunked down on their keys. It sounded like a really slow loom that took a year to weave a rug.

There was nothing funnier than watching Brian the plasterer in typing class. His massive plastering hands were unable to navigate the keys. Instead, he would say, 'This is a load of me bollix,' and walk out of the class.

It was a hard course, but we had fun. We would head to the Dundrum Bowling Alley for our lunch, which was chicken burgers and chips for a whole year.

The Dundrum Bowling Alley was the coolest place ever. Ken Newman and I came third and fourth in the all-Ireland school championships. This was made up of me and Ken, Tommy

Hanlon, who came second, and the winner, John Keys, who basically lived there. That was it: the four of us representing the whole of Ireland.

It also had pool tables, snooker tables and arcade games. This was where I actually had to feed my best friend Karl McDermot burgers and chips into his mouth while he got to the last stage of Donkey Kong. Twenty pence for two hours was not bad. He had a crowd around him like a rock star and his fingers were numb for days after.

Soon the Dundrum Bowling Alley was to be no more, as the Dodder river decided to make a detour through the complex and it was buried forever. You could see bowling bowls floating down the Dodder for days after.

February came, and this was to be the best and worst time ever. I turned eighteen so I could legally drink. On our break, now that the bowling alley had gone, myself and Brian decided to head to the local pub beside the college.

We went back to class pissed. I sat down – well, fell down – into my seat before our accountancy teacher, Miss White, came back. She arrived in and settled us all, but Brian was missing. He then came stumbling through the door with a big red face on him.

The teacher looked at Brian and most likely smelt the waft of beer entering the classroom. She said to him … and this should be on a T-shirt to this day …

'Are you alright, Mr Roche?' she asked angrily.

'Yes, I'm alright – are you alright, miss?' replied Brian.

'Yes, I'm alright,' answered Miss White.

Now here comes the T-shirt …

'Well, if you're alright and I'm alright, then we're all alright.'

Brian then turned around and left the class. He hadn't much time left in this college – he was a plasterer, for God's sake. Neither did I, in fact. I was to be guided away from the world of accountancy on work experience of all things.

Near the end of the year, we were sent to different accountancy firms. This was 1990, so there were no computers, no spread-sheets, only ledgers that needed to be written into all day. The accountants were doing everything by hand with pencils and pens, balancing sheets with their heads.

I was sent to an old office in town near the canal. The office was grim, with filing cabinets everywhere, stacks of files along the walls, no radio or music, just total silence. I had to wear a suit my dad gave me, and I looked like Tom Hanks at the end of the movie *Big* when he turned back into a kid and was left in a man's suit as he waved goodbye to that lady. His adult girlfriend. I'm sure she needed counselling after that.

I was teamed up with a guy called Declan. I'd say he was only in his late twenties, but he looked like he was in his late fifties. These men were everywhere when I was younger. You went up to the pub with your dad and there was a line of beer-bellied, highly unhealthy, slow-moving men up on bar stools with their arses sticking out of their grey suit trousers. I thought they were at least in their seventies. I later found out that this crowd of OAPs were wrecked by drink and smoke and they were only in their late twenties.

So this fella, the accountant chap, was balding and must have had no blood in his veins because he was this off-grey colour. Declan was a drinker and a smoker for sure – he always had a fag hanging out of his mouth and was constantly brushing the ash deposits off his paperwork. He wore a cheap dark suit. I only remember the dark suit because his shoulders were covered in dandruff from the bits of hair he had left. He coughed and sneezed a lot too. I could have taken a shortcut here and told you he basically looked like a modern-day Scrooge.

He took out a ledger and handed me a box of chequebooks with just the stubs. My job was to painstakingly go through each cheque number and enter it into the ledger. I did that for a week. Towards the end of the week, I watched Declan pull open one of his drawers. He had a small bottle of vodka in there. He took it out, had a quick sip and looked at me in the most miserable way. 'Don't ever become an accountant …'

And that was that, in more ways than one.

At the end of the first year, myself and Brian Roche were called into the principal's office with a string of offences under our belts. Brian had said 'If I'm alright and you're alright, then we're all alright' a little too much to too many teachers. He had also been missing for most of the year, as he was plastering with his dad. Also we had brought a lot of pupils to the pub at lunchtime, never to return to class.

So the principal looked at myself and Brian and said, 'Not only have you two been disrupting your class, you have been disrupting the college. So I think it's best for everyone if you both do not return next year. Alright?'

Oh no, not the A-word in front of Brian …

'Yeah, I'm alright, and are you alright, Jay? You alright, miss?' asked Brian.

I couldn't help it. I looked at the principal and said, 'Well, if Brian's alright, and I'm alright, and you're alright, then we're all alright.'

Cut to Brian and me being escorted to the gates, crying laughing. Brian turned out alright – he's still a plasterer.

And me? Well, let's see, shall we … ALRIGHT?

CHAPTER 3
COME ON, YOU BOYS IN GREEN

It was 1990. The Italian World Cup.

Now, I'm not a massive football buff. I try my best, but some comedian friends of mine are geniuses at it – Barry Murphy, Karl Spain, Ardal O'Hanlon, Kevin Gildea, and many, many more – they know everything there is to know about football.

I was once sat beside Barry Murphy (*Après Match* and Gunther) watching a match in a bar. Something happened, and Barry turned to me to say something footbally. Then he went, 'Oh, not you, you know fuck-all about this,' and turned to Karl Spain for top football chats about the 1976 FA Cup Final. In fairness, Baz was right. But I have somehow managed to bullshit my way through footbally things.

I was very good at playing it, would you believe – thanks to Ciaran Tallon and his brother Brendan from Ludford Drive. We played football non-stop for years in the field, and I got all my skills playing with those lads. Our mothers would call us in for dinner at six, halfway through a game up to a hundred – I shit you not, a hundred. We would then wolf the dinner into us, get back out into the field and play well into the darkness, in summer and winter.

I have been on *Soccer AM*, a football show on Sky, eight times, and I have managed to steer away from soccer chat by messing. They then run out of time and never make it to the soccer talk.

I assume I get this bullshitting skill from my dad. We didn't have a definitive sport in our house. The houses on my street were Liverpool houses, Man United houses, Shamrock Rovers houses, some were Dublin GAA, and there was even a Kerry house. In our house, my dad watched whatever sport fed him drink.

SPORTS DAD FOLLOWED HAVING NO IDEA OF THE RULES, LINGO OR NAMES OF PLAYERS

1. RUBGY ... 'Sure, I love rucks and scums.'
2. FOOTBALL ... 'Come on Brazil for the premiership.'
3. DARTS ... '180! That deserves a pint, lads.'
4. SHOWJUMPING ... 'Love the RDS – yes, another gin, please.'
5. TENNIS ... 'Ah, you have to have a drink with your strawberries.'
6. GOLF ... 'See you in the clubhouse, lads! What do you mean, I only played nine holes? The bar is right there now.'

7. **BASKETBALL ... 'Love American basketball on the telly. Eithne, another red plastic cup of beer! Sure, it's like you're there.'**
8. **CRICKET ... (While in London, ended up in Lord's.) 'I fucking love this game. Another beer, Charles? Don't mind if I doooo.'**
9. **BOG SWIMMING IN MONAGHAN ... 'Go on, Malachy! There's a pint and a small one waiting for you after this.'**
10. **SCHOOL SPORTS DAY ... 'It's cold today – I'm glad I brought me whiskey flask.' (Mother mortified.)**

For years we were a rugby house. Not because my dad loved rugby – sure, he hadn't a bog what the players were called – but because his mates in work loved the rugby. They often went to Wales to hook up with mates of theirs to watch the Six Nations – my dad only knew Ireland, England, Wales and Scotland; he didn't even know the other two teams.

We, as in the children, never went with Dad to the rugby matches. As he said, we wouldn't have enjoyed it – it was very cold in those stands and there was lots of hanging around. It was no place for children. Again, in true Paddy Byrne form, the truth was we would just interfere with his drinking. But we didn't really mind, because when dad went, he would bring home presents for us all out of guilt.

He once, and I still have them, brought me home massive earphones that had a radio in them with a huge aerial. On my roller skates, I looked like an American child TV star. Another time my dad brought home a Kermit the Frog puppet, but he must have been hammered when he bought it. He said the Welsh man in the shop said it was Kermit the Frog, but it was in its hole – it looked more like a long green lizard. But Dad kept saying, 'It's the frog off the telly, I'm tellin' ye.'

Those rugby trips were full of stories. Paddy told me once in his shed that he hated flying unless he had to, so the Irish mates going over with him agreed to do every second trip on the ferry. As I said before, Dad made all these outings drink-related, and boy did he make this particular one drink-related.

On this occasion, Dad apparently arrived at Dublin port with a small keg of Guinness, along with a gas bottle and a tap. He said it was for the journey in case they got thirsty. When asked where he got it all from, Dad replied, like he always did, 'Ah, sure, it was just lying around in a warehouse in Guinness's – nobody wanted it, so I popped it in the boot for the trip.'

Dad, Paddy Mc, Tony and Gay dock in Wales and drive the car off the ferry. Dad then drives down the Welsh motorway, says to the lads that they'd better stop and make sure the Guinness is OK. They finally find a layby and pull in. Dad then takes out the keg of Guinness, the gas and the tap, hooks it up, and the lads all sit on the grass verge, downing pints of Guinness.

Suddenly, a cop car turns up. Now, again, this is in the nineties. Two Welsh policemen get out of the car, walk over to my dad and the boys all holding pints of Guinness. My dad, Paddy Mc,

Tony and Gay all stand up as the Welsh police walk towards them.

'You can't be drinking at the side of the road, Paddy, it's not Ireland,' says the Welsh copper. He wasn't talking to my dad or Paddy Mc – he was talking to the group as a whole. Paddies.

HOW TO SPOT PADDIES ABROAD

1. Wearing a GAA T-shirt on a beach in Australia.
2. Drinking anywhere and everywhere.
3. Passed out on the ground thinking alcohol is 'hydrating' your body in 30-degree heat.
4. Singing hymns, prayers or 'Ooh Aah Paul McGrath' at locals through a loudhailer.
5. Climbing shit.
6. Falling off shit.
7. Laughing loudly in groups or screaming laughing if it's girls.
8. Fake tan everywhere.
9. Men's upper bodies looking like a red-and-white Marlboro box.
10. An Irish flag hanging out of a flat, car or bus window.

Just as Paddy Byrne was about to think up one of his excuses, the other Welsh cop asks, 'Is that Guinness you're drinking? Guinness from James's Gate in Dublin?!'

'It is indeed, son,' answers my dad.

Well, cut to something you just would not see anymore because of all the rules, dash cams, body cams, satellites and phones. We'll soon have invented ourselves out of existence. It's good to have rules, but rules were made to be broken, and no better people than the Irish to break the rules, again, and again, and again.

There they were: Paddy Byrne, Paddy Mc, Tony, Gay and two Welsh cops with their hats off and their sleeves rolled up, all drinking the Arthur Guinness at the side of the Welsh motorway together. No wonder us Celts all got on in the past. After a while, they pack up and go their separate ways. No fines, courts or tickets, just a great memory. An illegal memory, but great all the same.

Dad and his pals headed to the game, full of drink. I remember asking Dad how they got to the loo, because in those days there were no seats in the stands they ended up in. Dad said he and the lads brought a bicycle tube each, cut it in half and put one end on their willies. The other end stuck out the end of their trouser legs, and they would relieve themselves onto the steps. Dad said Paddy Mc needed a tractor tube and laughed a lot.

I'm pretty sure this was bullshit, as they defo would have been arrested trying to fit bicycle tubes onto their knobs in the toilet.

★★★

Accountancy college was way behind me now. I had gone back to the Braemor Rooms, this time as a part-time barman.

As we all know, Ireland was in the Italia '90 World Cup under the management of Jack Charlton. People were taking their photos of Pope John Paul off the wall and replacing them with Jack Charlton pics. God bless St Jack.

We showed the matches on the big screen in the lounge of the Braemor Rooms. The first match up was England v Ireland. I mean, of all the rivalries …

We had all the flags at the ready. I had been eighteen since February so could now serve pints. Dad arrived in with his mate Pat. Both wearing green. Again, knowing nothing about football, but defo knowing that it would involve loads of pints.

He also knew that Mam wouldn't be able to moan at him for going to the pub again …

> MAM: Are you going to the pub again, Paddy?
>
> DAD: But me country needs me, Eithne.
>
> MAM: What in the name of jaysus are you talking about?
>
> DAD: We're fighting the English today and every man is needed to support our boys in Italy.
>
> MAM: In the pub? Now don't be getting into fights, Paddy Byrne.
>
> DAD: It's a football match, for pox sake.
>
> MAM: You don't know anything about football.

DAD: I do, I love it, always have, me own father played for Shamrock Rovers.

MAM: You don't, and your father had a kickabout with Shamrock Rovers one day after work with his Guinness's football team. Name anyone on the Irish football team, go on.

DAD: Eh, Jack Charlton and Packie Haughton. Listen, does it matter? Napoleon didn't know the names of all his men when they went into battle. It's the heart that matters, the love for your country … (Dad kissing the crest on his green top leaving the house.)

MAM (shouting after him): That's a Lacoste top you're kissing, love!

DAD (in the distance): It's the only green top I own. Don't wait up …

The pub was packed with the Irish army. Jack's Army, they were calling themselves, all ready for battle in their green tops – a mixture of jerseys, T-shirts from Penneys (Primark for the British lads) and one Lacoste top.

The double standards were hilarious in the bar, and they still flow through Ireland to this day. 'We hate the English, boo, hope they lose.' You will hear this whenever England are competing in any sport or song contest, even a boat race or tiddlywinks. You name it, the Irish want them to lose.

And yet …

THINGS THE IRISH LOVE MORE THAN THE ENGLISH

1. I love Liverpool football club, my heroes. (Irish tears in their eyes.)
2. Why isn't RTÉ more like BBC – it's so much better!
3. I'd never miss *EastEnders*.
4. I'd never miss *Coronation Street*.
5. Did you see *Emmerdale*? Me heart was in me mouth.
6. *Fair City*? Sure, that's written with crayons.
7. Oh, I'd only shop in Tesco.
8. Ant and Dec are so funny.
9. *The Late Late Show* is shite – Graham Norton is much better.
10. The queen was a lovely woman. We'll miss her dearly.

Well, the reason is mainly this: England is kinda like our big brother that we love to hate. He will help you out if you're in trouble outside the home, with bullies etc., but at the same time, he would have kicked the shit out of you in the past (i.e. British rule). When your bigger brother falls over, you break your bollix laughing. If he's in trouble with your mam and you're in the clear, you can jeer him from afar.

That's how we are with England. We love them, and we also love to tease them – but never to their face, always from a distance. We Irish think the funniest thing in the world is to watch England fail at something.

It was everywhere in the last World Cup in 2022 too. Irish people were praying for an England v Brazil World Cup Final. The English might think, 'Oh, that's nice – good on you, Ireland.' But the real reason we wanted England in the World Cup Final was so they would fall at the last fence. It's like a cat (Brazil) playing with a mouse (England) until it kills it in the end.

But this was Ireland v England. There was no love for England on that day in June 1990.

'Two specials there, son.' Dad winked at me as he ordered.

The main reason why Dad was not in his local pub, The Beavers, which was beside our house, and instead down in the Braemor Rooms, which was a twenty-minute drive, was that on these match days the place was packed, and I was able to give Dad free drink all night. This was like the everlasting gobstopper in *Willy Wonka* for Dad, except it was everlasting Guinness.

We drew with England, and the bar was happy enough with that. The whole pub was chanting away.

> THE PUB: OOH AHH PAUL MCGRATH, I SAY OOH AHH PAUL MCGRATH!

My dad had his arms around a load of supporters, joining in with the chant.

> DAD: OOH AHH PAUL MOGGAA, I SAY OOH AHH PAUL MOGGAA.

All the while, he was constantly pulling the Lacoste crest on his shirt towards his lips to kiss it. What a great supporter he was. Jack Charlton would have been lost without Paddy Byrne in his Lacoste green polo shirt, celebrating the defending of Paul Moggaa.

The pub eventually emptied. Dad said goodbye, but not before he nearly got me sacked by laughing and shouting, 'DO UP MY BILL, GOOD MAN,' while pointing and waving at me. 'SURE, I DIDN'T HAVE TO PAY A THING – THAT'S MY SON. SEE YA LATERS, JAY!' while the bar manager Brian squinted at me.

I was the youngest barman and I had had a good day. Fistfuls of cash were shoved into my shirt pocket. 'Sure, have one yourself, son – come on, Ireland!'

That was all well and good till Brian handed me the mop and bucket, a massive kitchen roll, another bucket with a small shovel, a face mask, goggles, Dettol spray and the long stick with the plunger on it. All with a look that a commander would give a man in a World War I trench before sending him over the top with his whistle in his mouth. He nodded towards the door of the jacks …

I HAD TO CLEAN THE JACKS.

Jacks ————————————————————————

Jacks is the slang word for the toilet in Ireland, most likely named after a toilet inventor called Jack Power …?

————————————————————————

'Oh, mind out for Pat Connors too, son,' Brian warned me.

I stood in front of the door to the lounge jacks, terrified. I had me mop, paper towels and sprays. My stomach churned as I looked at the small shovel in the spare bucket, with the face mask and goggles hanging off it.

I'm a Celebrity … Get Me Out of Here! hasn't a patch on the trial I was about to complete – for no stars, by the way.

I placed the face mask on, then the goggles. I pushed open the door, and as I did, Pat Connors fell out towards me. 'That fucking door is bollixed!' screamed Pat as he staggered off towards the bar door. Pat was always last in the toilet. He could never work out that you pulled the door open from the inside, instead of pushing it. He'd spent hours in there before, leaning against the door, hammered, trying to push it open.

Behind him was a horror movie. A war zone. A murder scene where only people's arses were killed or, it looked like, blown up. It was like an arcade game where you lasered the aliens and they blew up into a goo on the floor.

I once went to the zoo as a kid. We visited the hippos, and I watched one of them actually spray shite out of their hippo arse and paint the enclosure wall with their own shit. This was way worse, I thought.

I'd try to clean the basin area first, I decided. Toilet paper all over the floor, puke in the sinks ... I was in hell. I took out the long stick with the plunger on it, stood in the corner and tried to unblock the puke-filled sink from a distance. I pushed the mask tight to my face as I did this and made sure the goggles were on well. Eventually, after lots of gagging, the sinks were unplugged.

Then it was the cubicles' turn. I lifted my spare bucket, pushed open the doors with my small shovel ...

Now, I'm not going into detail here, but all I'll say is I had to clear the toilet floor with the shovel as if you were clearing the drive on a heavy snow day. Except the snow was brown.

I came out of the toilet like a US marine who had just been down rat holes in Vietnam looking for the enemy. I guess I was in shock. Brian came over to me, took the equipment off me, handed me a pint and sat me down. I now knew what war was like. As I stared into the abyss, I wondered how a grown man could conjure up such evil from his arse.

IRELAND HAD GONE MAD.

'We're doing it, Eithne, we're actually doing it,' Dad shouted as he came in from the pub.

Ireland had drawn with England 1–1, drawn with Egypt 0–0, and drawn with the Netherlands 1–1. (*Thought you didn't know anything about football, Jason?* Calm down, reader, I looked it up. Ha! Remember in the *Beano* and the *Dandy*, the characters always referred to us as 'reader'? Anywayyy ...)

We were into the last sixteen of the World Cup. Ireland had already won in our eyes, so anything from here on in was a bonus.

We had Romania to beat to get to the quarter-finals. Jesus Christ, this was unheard of in Irish sport in those days. I remember exactly where I was on 25 June 1990. I was in the small lounge of the Braemor Rooms. My dad and Pat, of course, were there, having their Willy Wonka everlasting free pints. My dad was still wearing his green Lacoste top – he wouldn't change it or wash it (jaysus) until Ireland were knocked out of the World Cup.

The lounge had the local butchers, barbers and builders, all in their uniforms and work clothes. Nothing was getting done in Ireland that day. Apparently a fella ran out of a pub and quickly took a photo of O'Connell Street in Dublin. Not a soul was there, on the busiest street in Ireland, because we were glued to the telly: man, woman, child, dog, you feckin' name it. You can still see this picture online.

It was full time, so it all came down to penalties. Not a pint was pulled. We stared at the screen as Dave O'Leary walked up to take what we hoped would be the winning goal.

'Ah Jesus Christ, not Dave O'Leary' was heard around the bar more than once. You could see even Jack Charlton was shitting himself as Dave O'Leary walked up to the spot.

'Yeah, not Dave Gearey' was also heard from a man in the corner wearing a green Lacoste top.

BANG!

'He shoots, he scoooores!'

He had done it. Dave O'Leary scored the peno and put Ireland into the quarter-finals. The pub went mental. I was hugging Pat Connors, who had managed to make his way around behind the bar, along with other locals who were just pouring themselves pints and handing them out to everyone else.

My dad leaned in and grabbed one, pointed at me and said, 'Put it on me tab, son. In fact, put all these on me tab.' All the lads cheered me dad and he laughed, falling heavily back into the happiest crowd I have ever seen.

I'd say the only unhappy people that day were the owners of big corporations abroad, the Chinese, the English, the Americans. They knew from then until the next match that nothing was going to be done in Ireland. 'You can ask me bollix or gee' was repeated to bosses all over Ireland that week.

Ireland actually officially closed from the minute Dave O'Leary scored that peno.

'I'm going to Italy, Eithne, the lads need me,' screamed my dad as he fell in from the pub again.

This time there was no match on, but these poor men were exhausted celebrating. It was the day after the penos, around five days to go until we met Italy in the quarter-final.

> MAM: You are in your shite going anywhere, Paddy Byrne.
>
> DAD: Listen, I have to go, all the lads in the pub are going.
>
> MAM: We don't have the money to go to Italy.
>
> DAD: Again, not we, just me. I don't even want to go but the lads said there wouldn't be enough supporters in Italy for our boys in green.
>
> MAM: No, Paddy, we don't have any money, not a chance, and don't be thinking up any of your schemes either.

The next day, I jumped in the car with Dad. He told Mam he was getting some bread and milk. We then took a detour to the credit union in Dundrum …

Credit union ——————————————————

A type of bank, but it isn't a bank. The idea is that if you save with them, they give you good rates on loans – two fingers up to the main banks, if you will. But it's still a loan company – it's just a smaller two fingers back at us when they charge us fees.

——————————————————————————

Holy shit, the queues of men outside the credit union were hilarious. Some of them had Irish flags wrapped around them, and some were in shorts and T-shirts with bags packed, ready to head straight to the airport with their loans.

My dad parked and we both joined the queue.

'Now, don't tell your mother, son,' Dad warned me.

A fella came out of the door of the credit union. He was the manager. He stood up on the bonnet of a car with a loudhailer in his hand and began …

'Is anyone here to lodge money?'

Total silence, with a few coughs and shuffles of feet.

'Is anyone here applying for a loan?'

The whole crowd cheered.

'Is anyone here applying for a loan that is not related to Italy?'

Again, total silence.

'OK, who is here for a loan to go to Italy?'

The whole place went mental.

'OOH AHH PAUL MCGRATH, I SAY OOH AHH PAUL MCGRATH,' the crowd chanted as they lifted the manager off the bonnet of the car and danced him into the credit union. 'OOH AHH CREDIT UNION, I SAY OOH AHH GIVE US A LOAN!'

I was crying laughing. The peasants had literally taken over. If they could, they would have wheeled out the safe and started throwing the money to the waiting crowd.

Unfortunately, or fortunately, my dad did not get a loan. We didn't even get inside the credit union. They locked the doors after two hours with a sign reading NO MORE LOANS. Lads fled the scene to see where else they could get money.

STUFF IRISH FANS DID TO GET TO THE WORLD CUP

1. Re-mortgaged their houses.
2. Sold their cars.
3. Sold their wedding rings.
4. Ten lads chipped in and bought a small van to drive to Italy.
5. Went on cargo ships.
6. Went on cargo planes.
7. Motorbiked.
8. Cycled (ah, sure, if Stephen Roche can do it).
9. Hitched.
10. I think some lads just walked.

'Olé, Olé, Olé Olééé!' screamed the bar in the Braemor Rooms, the crowd in the stadium in Italy, people all around Ireland, Irish people in bars all over the world, all wrapped in the tricolour waiting for Ireland v Italy.

My dad was not in Italy, thank God. He'd tried his best, though. He'd been up in the attic, digging out what he thought were valuables to take to the pawnbroker's.

ITEMS DAD THOUGHT WERE 'WORTH A BLEEDIN' FORTUNE, I'M TELLIN YE ALL' AND BROUGHT TO THE PAWNBROKER'S

1. First edition Isle of Man pound coins, five of them, worth, guess ... yes, five pounds.
2. 1950s wooden pinball machine ... a tenner.
3. Three old clocks, worth three old clocks.
4. A gramophone. (No, Paddy, it's not the first one I've ever seen.)
5. Costume jewellery. (It's for dressing up, Paddy, worth nothing.)
6. Old tellies.
7. Old radios.
8. Old guitars.
9. Old phones.
10. 'A handwritten letter from the queen to me, Paddy Byrne, as a boy when I congratulated her on her coronation.' (I'll give you a fiver and a fake Rolex for it.)

The first whistle blew and we all cheered. The bar was packed. We were playing the Italians, one of the best teams in the world, but we had a great team over there. And the best fans that ever lived, even though when the camera went on them they were all sunburnt, hammered and exhausted. I imagine when the camera went on a load of those fellas' faces, their wives went mental, thinking they were at their mate's house or in the pub.

'Holy feck, Ma, Dad's in Italy,' the kid of the house must've shouted. The wife would've looked out the window to a carless driveway, as the fella had sold it to get to Italy. 'I'll fucking kill him,' she'd have said.

'Oh and Schillaci scores!' roared the commentator. That was it: we were out of the World Cup. The bar fell silent.

'Thank fuck I didn't end up over there,' said a voice in a green Lacoste top.

'Shut up, Paddy, you know nothing about football,' answered another random voice.

'Sure, we got into the quarter-finals,' roared another in the bar.

'Olé, Olé, Olé, Olé, OOH AHH PAUL MC GRATH!' Well, off they went, celebrating all over again.

'Ooh ahh Paul Moggaa,' was also faintly heard.

★★★

My dad brought me into town when Jack Charlton and the lads returned. There was a sea of people and the bus couldn't move. Thousands and thousands of people were rammed into Dublin, the whole country celebrating one of our greatest moments in history.

'Can you image this lot if we won?' Jack Charlton was heard saying.

Jesus Christ, if we had won the island of Ireland would have been lifted into a heaven unknown for us all to celebrate for eternity.

THANK YOU JACK CHARLTON AND THE 1990 IRISH TEAM FOR SOME OF THE BEST MOMENTS IN OUR LITTLE IRISH LIVES.

'I say OOH AHH PAUL MOGGAA, I SAY OOH AHH PAUL MOGGAA!'

Good man, Dad.

CHAPTER 4
'I ... AM ... NOT ... IN ... THE ... IRA!'

'I'm in love. I'm in love and I'm moving to Sweden!' announced my brother Eric to the living room.

It was still the early nineties and I was around nineteen, sitting on the sofa beside my little sister Eithne. She was around ten years of age and I was her best pal. Dad sat quietly listening with his feet in a basin of water with Dettol in it.

Dad always asked Mam to get him a basin of warm water and pop some Dettol in it. It soothed his feet after a very long day in work/sitting in the pub in his overalls. The basin was normally the one Mam used for the washing up. Quite often when Mam brought dinner in to us in the living room on trays, it would smell of Dettol.

My other sister, Rachel, who was eighteen, came into the room with the iron in her hand. 'Mam, where's the ironing board? I need to straighten me hair and do me make-up before town,' she yelled. She was sporting an array of scars on her forehead from ironing her hair on the ironing board.

'Your brother has just said he's moving to Sweden. You're only a child, Eric!' cried my mother.

'Where's that, is that in London?' asked Rachel. 'Will you be long in Sweden? Anyway, the girls are coming soon. If you're back tomorrow, Eric, I'll see you then.' Rachel left the room to straighten her hair and cover up her scars for the fellas.

'Sweden, Eric – I mean, feckin' Sweden,' continued my mam.

Then my dad burst out laughing. 'Bwaaahaaahaaa, fucking Sweden.'

'Daaaddd,' moaned Eric.

'You insensitive man, Paddy Byrne. What is so funny about your son Eric heading off to Sweden forever?!' said Mam crossly.

'Eric, his name is Eric! You and me are geniuses, Eithne, we named our son Eric,' laughed Dad.

'And so what?'

'Sure, Eric is the most popular name in Sweden. He'll fit in no bother!'

My mam began to quiz Eric. 'Why Sweden? Is it a job? Or is it …?'

In the early 90s, people were heading to London, Australia and America for work. But here was Eric, twenty-three years of age, the world was his oyster, and he picks Sweden.

'Fanny, it's defo fanny. I can smell it off him,' shouted Dad, while he paddled his feet in the Dettol. We all laughed except for Mam.

'Fanny!' shouted little Eithne. 'Fanny, fanny, fanny!' she kept shouting, thinking it was funny because we were all laughing.

'Yeah, shut up the lot of ye. Yes, Dad is right, it is fan—I mean, a lovely girl. I met her on holiday in Greece there in the summer. I love her very much and I'm moving to Sweden away from this awful country for a better life,' announced Eric.

There was silence in the room.

Of course, my dad cannot deal with emotional moments. Like all our old dads, they were so badly brought up that they weren't allowed to cry. They weren't hugged, and when they fell they were told to stand up and walk it off. So they used humour to defuse these situations.

'Burrrr dee burrrr deee duuuu daaa daaaa …'

'You're an arsehole!' Eric screamed as he ran out of the living room and out the door. My dad continued to impersonate the Swedish chef from *The Muppets* ...

'Duuuu daaaa daaaa, duuuu daaaa daaaa, it's good that, isn't it?'

Myself and Eithne were laughing. 'I've married an arsehole,' Mam said as she left the room.

DIFFERENT TYPES OF PADDIES MY MAM MARRIED

1. An arsehole.
2. A clown.
3. An eejit.
4. A fool.
5. A terrible human.
6. A cold bastard.
7. A selfish man.
8. A lazy bastard.
9. A mé féiner.
10. Hitler.

Mé féiner ⸻

Pronounced MAY FAYNER. In Ireland, we use this phrase for someone who only looks out for themselves. A dick, basically. I think that's the direct translation, as I only have thirteen years of learning the Irish language in the shittest way possible. It was never taught as a conversational language.

We had to write it down, read it, but never actually speak it. Most of us in Ireland have the weirdest skill with this language. We can't speak it or understand it when it's spoken in front of us. But we all can read it no bother and write it. (So we're fucked if we need to ask where the nearest library is in Irish.) I went to Italy in the summer and learnt enough Italian to get by in a week. 'Tá an Irish government gobshites!' I think you can work that one out yourselves.

'SUMMARISE, PLEASE!'

This is a great phrase to say to someone if they're going on and on with a story. I once sat in Ryan Tubridy's house with himself and his older brother, Professor Niall Tubridy. Ryan began a story about interviewing Kathleen Turner. He got about five minutes in and Niall brought it all to a halt by screaming, 'Summarise, summarise, please, we don't have all fucking night for this shit.'

So as the night went on, Ryan and myself continued different anecdotes, only to be stopped mid-flow by 'Oh for fuck's sake, summarise, man, summarise!'

So, in tribute to Professor Niall Tubridy, I'll summarise the next part of the story.

We all drove Eric to the airport on the day of his move to Sweden. Dad missed the hugs at the gate as he said he would finish his pint off and meet us all there. It was an excuse not to let any emotions out while hugging my brother and watching

him go through the gate. My dad would rather miss his eldest
son leaving than let us all see him cry, so …

'SUMMARISE, MAN!'

Jesus, OK, I'm trying. We all got back in the car to drive home.
Not a word was said except for 'Hitler', murmured under Mam's
breath as she looked out the car window, furious with Dad.

Eric went off to Sweden to his bride to be, Gittan, or to give her
her full name, Birgitta Wilhelmsen. The lucky, lucky girl was to
become Birgitta Byrne. The only female Byrne in Sweden.

★★★

'Oh Jesus, you can see her bump through the wedding dress,' my
mam muttered as Gittan was led up the aisle by her dad.

'Shotgun wedding, whaaa?' whispered my dad to myself and my
sisters sitting behind him in the church. 'Is the father of the bride
packing, whaaa?!'

We were all in Gothenburg, Sweden, at my brother's wedding,
and as you have already guessed, there was a baby in the bride's
belly heading up the aisle.

My mother was mortified. 'I mean, what will Jesus think, a child
out of wedlock. And where in the name of jaysus is Jesus in

here? There's no sign of Mary either. Is my son being married by Satan?' My mam could not handle this church.

'It's a Lutheran church, Mam,' I said into her ear from behind.

'Luther who? A feckin' what? Where's all the guilt? The suffering Our Lord put his son through for our sins? Not a statue in sight of Jesus and his mammy. It doesn't look like a church – it looks like a posh garage with an altar,' she said.

'They're kinda Protestant, Mam,' I told her.

'PROTESTANTS!' she roared.

All the Swedes looked around at my mother.

'Mam!' Eric scolded her.

'She … means … pro … testing … she's pro … test … ing … for *(long pause)* … AIDS.' My dad said this in broken English as he thought no one spoke English when, in fact, they all spoke it fluently. Well, except for Gittan's dad. The Swedes just looked at him with an isn't-he-a-cute-Irish-fellow look.

My mam was livid. Being married by Satan might have been alright, but marrying into a Protestant church? No way.

To make matters worse, I had to go up and do a reading from a letter from some Protestant to another Protestant. My mother squinted at me as I walked by her to the top of the Posh Garage with an Altar.

I was shitting myself. I was only around nineteen, and the last time I spoke into a microphone was in Spain to ask the crowd if they had seen my lost passport that wasn't lost at all.

The priest, or 'the fella with the funny robes who probably has a wife and kids', as my mother described him, called me up. I stood at one of those Prod pulpits, and 'the fella with the funny robes who probably has a wife and kids' turned the mic towards my mouth.

I began to read. 'Hmmm mufff hmmm mufff hmmm mufff ...'

'We can't hear ye, son!' shouted Dad.

'Thank the real Jesus we can't – who knows what pagan stuff he's saying,' said Mam.

It was so nerve-wracking. I couldn't get the words out and no one understood a word. I said to myself: *I will never speak through a microphone again for as long as I live.*

Afterwards, 'the fella with the funny robes who probably has a wife and kids' married my brother and Gittan and the bump.

The whole church clapped. Gittan's side, her family and friends and all the Swedes clapped politely and quietly. Our side –

granted, it was only me, Rachel, Eithne and Dad – all cheered and whooped, much to Eric's embarrassment. Mam made no noise at all, as she was rummaging in her handbag for something.

As Eric and Gittan passed us, we threw confetti at them. My mam had taken out a large bottle of holy water, blessed by the proper Jesus, and literally covered the happy couple as they walked down the aisle. She followed behind them, splashing holy water as if she was in a chipper drowning the chips with vinegar.

WHAT SWEDES ARE LIKE COMPARED TO THE IRISH

1. Very quiet.
2. Never say hello to each other in the street.
3. Never shout at each other.
4. Never think someone is an arsehole.
5. Don't know what an arsehole is.
6. Never talk behind each other's backs.
7. Encourage others to do well.
8. Walk around in the nip a lot.
9. Don't go to pubs.
10. Drink heavily in their houses.

WHAT THE IRISH ARE LIKE COMPARED TO SWEDES

1. Never shut up.
2. Would say hello to a passing tree.
3. Always roaring at each other.
4. Think everyone is an arsehole.
5. Ask everyone, 'Do you know who's an arsehole?'
6. LOVE talking behind people's backs.
7. Biggest begrudgers on earth.
8. Hate being naked.
9. Live in pubs.
10. Drink heavily in their houses.

'Oh, I love an atmosphere … *plink plonk* … I love a little party with an atmosphere … *plink plonk plink* …'

We were at the wedding reception. A man with a mic sat on his own in the corner of a small function room playing a Casio keyboard on low volume. He was singing in a Swedish accent, 'Oh, I love an atmosphere!'

'What bleedin' atmosphere?' said Dad.

BELT!

'Shut it, Paddy,' Mam whispered through gritted teeth.

This was odd. Everyone was sitting at long tables, eating dinner, literally whispering to each other. My dad had no idea what to do, so he drank heavily while having a chat with Gittan's dad, Falka, who had no English. Because the two of them were pissed, they kinda understood each other's drunk chat.

I sipped on a beer while one of the Swedish cousins, a beautiful girl by the name of Freda, was chatting me up. I had no idea what to do. All I'll say is that she was very forward. Rachel and Eithne were over on the other side of the room, rubbing Gittan's bump.

'Thank you.' Small clap from the audience as the most boring man in the world finished another dreadful song on his keyboard.

'Ah, fuck this!' Dad yelled as he leapt up out of his chair and headed towards the poor fella with the Casio. 'Here, do you know any Perry Como? Do you know "Tie a Yellow Ribbon Round the Old Oak Tree"?'

The Casio man said he didn't. So my dad then grabbed the mic and began. 'Just follow me, son …'

Well, that was that. My dad managed to turn a quiet, respectful Swedish wedding into a full-on Irish party. The Swedes were soon up dancing and drinking as my dad kept singing. It was amazing to see a room full of Swedes singing 'Tie a Yellow Ribbon Round the Old Oak Tree', all losing their shit. My mam was even dancing with 'the fella in the funny robes who probably has a wife and kids'. And he did, because they were dancing with my sisters.

Eric had a great wedding. We all did, thanks to Dad. I even saw Dad give Eric a big hug and a kiss, with a little tear coming down Dad's cheek ...

Ah, you'd all love that, wouldn't ye!

Paddy Byrne, a kiss and a hug ... me bollix. At the end of the night, my dad had to be pulled down off the stage by the hotel security. He thought he was Elvis. All the Swedes clapped him to his room, accompanied by Mam and my two sisters, while he sang 'YOU AIN'T NOTHING BUT A HOUND DOG' into the security guard's face.

I stayed behind to learn more about Sweden from Freda and her lashing tongue.

★★★

It was time to leave Sweden. This was the bit my dad was dreading the most. He had some metal in his body from an old leg operation and hated going through the metal detectors in the airport, even though he had a card stating this fact. Going out of Ireland was not too bad, but leaving a country to go back to Ireland was the worst.

'They'll think I'm in the IRA, lads,' Dad said to me, Mam, Rachel and Eithne.

We were queuing up to go through security. Dad and Eric had just had a moment at the gate where they embraced each other. Dad didn't want to leave his eldest son in a strange country, but knew he had to, so he kissed my brother and said he loved him …

Ah jaysus, you didn't fall for it again, did you?

While we were hugging Eric and Gittan to say goodbye, Dad went ahead in the line and waved from a distance, mouthing the words, 'I can't go back, I'll get in trouble.'

Another emotional moment avoided. We caught up with Dad in the line.

> ME: They'll what now, Dad?
>
> DAD: They'll think I'm in the IRA because when I go through that metal detector it'll set the metal off in me leg. The machine will go **BEEP BEEP BEEP** and they'll think I'm a terrorist with a bomb in me jocks!
>
> MAM: Don't be a fool, Paddy, they're used to the machine going off, what with all the old people riddled with foreign bits and pieces inside them.

Dad was called forward to walk through the machine. He was sweating and nervous, and in fairness, he looked like he had something to hide. Dad was also full of whiskey, as he refused to fly without a few small ones inside him …

BEEP! BEEP! BEEP!

> DAD (shouting, arms flailing everywhere): You see, you see, I knew it, I knew it, I am not in the IRA, I am not a terrorist, I am an ordinary citizen of Ireland!

All the security staff could understand were the letters IRA and the word 'terrorist'. The guards wrestled Dad to the ground.

> DAD: I am not in the IRA, I am not in the IRA!

> MAM: Will you shut up saying IRA, Paddy!

If you had a dad like mine, moments like this were not unusual. Dad had gotten into many scrapes before, and they were all self-inflicted.

AWKWARD MOMENTS PADDY GOT HIMSELF INTO

1. Being arrested in Sweden on suspicion of terrorism.
2. 'Are you pregnant long?' (To a big lady at a bus stop.)
3. 'Of course he won't mind.'
4. 'Of course she won't mind.'
5. Jumping out on the wrong woman, thinking it was my mother in the shopping aisle (black eye from the whack of a handbag).

Rachel and Eithne just stared at all the commotion as if watching a dog rolling around on the floor, even if it was their dad in handcuffs.

We were then all escorted out of the security line and into a holding office. We sat along one wall, while Dad sat at the opposite wall, handcuffed. Beside him was a man with a long black beard in white robes, and a security guard at a desk watching us all.

'I told ye, Eithne, didn't I, that they'd think I'm in the IRA?' said Dad.

Mam just rolled her eyes to heaven (proper heaven, not the 'fella in the funny robes who now most definitely has a wife and children' heaven).

Dad looked at the man sitting beside him with the beard and white robes, also in handcuffs. 'You lot get it just as bad as us Irish – we're like brothers in arms. They think I'm in the IRA, can you believe that? And you, my good man, I bet they think you're in IKEA?' he said embarrassingly.

'What? It's Al-Qaeda, Paddy, not fecking IKEA,' corrected my mam.

Oh Jesus, this just couldn't get any worse.

Mam stood up and went over to the bearded man in the white robes. 'I'm very sorry. This man is a feckin' eejit.' Mam then turned to the guard. 'You can shoot this fella' – pointing to my dad – 'but this poor fella is not in IKEA. My gobshite of a husband means he is in Al-Qaeda.' My mam then sat down, thinking she had put the world to rights.

Cut to us all flying home. Dad was handcuffed to a flight security officer all the way until he was handed over to the Irish police.

'Paddy Byrne, can you believe it?' said Paul Ryan, one of our neighbours who was a retired cop, now working security at the airport. He uncuffed Dad.

'Paddy, we need to go home,' pleaded Mam while we all sat on suitcases waiting for Dad to finish his few pints in the airport with Paul Ryan.

'I have to thank the man for not putting me in jail, Eithne,' explained Dad.

Which was never going to happen. But Dad still told everyone when he got home all about him being falsely arrested in Sweden and that he knew how the Birmingham Six felt.

Now that Eric had moved out, there had to be a major shift around of rooms in the house. When an eldest child leaves a home in Ireland, it's literally like the 'Ten in a Bed and the Little One Said' song. Everybody has to roll over, roll over.

There's a metaphorical meaning to this song: as a new child comes into the house, the eldest must leave to make room. Death is very like this: when one person dies, we are simply making room for a new life.

Ah jaysus, now I'm turning into my dad.

Anyway, Rachel and Eithne went into the big room upstairs. Mam and Dad stayed in the other double bedroom upstairs.

YES!

I got a room to myself.

NO!

I was given the boxroom, where children were sent to freeze to death. This was the coldest room in the house and the smallest. It was like a prison cell: a bed rammed against an outer wall the length of a single bed, while the other wall was the window. All the other bedrooms only had one outer wall, but the box room was on the corner of the house and was freezing.

You had to try to lie in the middle of the bed and not move all night. To your side was the mould on the wall, which was to be avoided at all costs, as it would slowly grow onto your PJs while you slept if you weren't careful.

('What about breathing it in?' I hear you all roar.

'Don't mind that lot, son – they know nothing,' I hear my dad say.

I ended up with a collapsed lung when I was twenty-one, that's all I'm saying. I'll get to that later.)

The bottom of the bed was to be avoided too. If your feet hit the bottom wall, they would stick to it, as if you were licking a lamp-post on a minus-degree day.

Builders had never installed the window properly. It was most likely fitted by an apprentice with marla and glue.

Marla ───────────────────────────────

Marla is also pronounced maw-la if you're from Dublin. Marla is a type of playdough that we had in school. I think Marla is Irish for playdough, but I haven't a bog. But mála is also the Irish for bag. This confused the bollix out of primary school kids.

─────────────────────────────────────

The window had a constant whistling noise coming from the gaps. This is also known in Ireland as THE DRAUGHT. This is an accepted defect in all our houses, an actual breeze that moves through them.

'The house needs to breathe – it's designed that way,' Dad would tell us, with his *Grand Designs* knowledge.

Bollix. All our houses were built by the shittiest builders ever. No insulation in the walls and plastering all over the shop. Watching my dad trying to wallpaper was hilarious because he had to cut a crooked line along the paper's edge to fit the hanging crooked ceiling.

'Whuuu, whuuu, whuuu' went THE DRAUGHT. It was like the room was fucking haunted.

But the mad thing is that Irish people actually like this sound now. We fall asleep to noises like this. While other people around the world ask Alexa for birdsong or gentle lapping waves, we Irish on the other hand …

THINGS IRISH PEOPLE ASK ALEXA TO PLAY TO HELP US GO TO SLEEP

1. Loud whistling breezes.
2. Storms.
3. Heavy rain showers.
4. Hailstones instead of snow hitting the car window.
5. Sunshine then torrential rain five minutes later.
6. A busy pub.
7. A couple arguing downstairs.
8. Dogs barking next door.
9. An auld one talking non-stop to the shopkeeper while we all wait in line with our heavy baskets.
10. Confession-box doors opening and closing.

The boxroom was so cold that my mother used to set her trifle in there. I slept in a room cold enough to set a trifle.

I recently spoke to other victims of the boxroom ...

ITEMS KEPT CHILLING IN A VICTIM'S BOXROOM

1. Trifles/jelly/anything that needed setting.
2. Xmas turkey under the window.
3. Slabs of cans.
4. Ice cubes on the windowsill.
5. A crying child ('They'll soon cool down').

My beautiful nana, who we also called Joe 90, came to live with us for a bit because she could no longer live on her own. We called her that because she moved so fast in her earlier days. Joe 90 was a cool secret agent on the telly, and the phrase 'she moves like Joe 90' was a very Dublin phrase.

My nana had one son and three other daughters in all corners of Dublin. She would visit each one every day, taking two buses. I would be playing in the field and I'd see her walking speedily up the path and into the house. Nana, or Joe 90, would then have one cup of tea, give us all Macaroon bars (which I still eat), get her mac back on, handbag in hand, and I'd walk her straight back to the bus stop at top speed. Bus arrives, off she goes, all within an hour.

My grandad had died way back in the eighties, so my nana had been more or less on her own since then. One day in town she walked out in front of a bus on O'Connell Street. She was OK, it just clipped her, but that was enough to start her downward slide into dementia.

So everyone took turns looking after her. We made a makeshift bedroom for Nana downstairs so she wouldn't have to climb the stairs to go to the loo and bed.

When she lived with us she wasn't too bad. There was a bit of memory loss, which sometimes could be heartbreaking, but on the flip side, it could be funny too, situations where you just couldn't help but laugh.

One night just before Christmas, Mam was sitting on the couch with Nana, watching the telly. It was just after dinner, and I was on the floor and Dad was in his chair. We were all having jam sandwiches for dessert.

ODD DESSERTS IN THE BYRNE HOUSEHOLD

1. Jam sandwiches.
2. Doughnuts, cut open, with butter on them.
3. Bread with butter and sugar.
4. Ice cream with custard-cream biscuits broken into it.
5. Turkish delight with wafers.

Then Nana began …

'You know who's a mean auld bollix?' she said in the middle of *Antiques Roadshow*.

We all burst out laughing as Nana never, ever swore.

'Who?' I asked her.

'That Paddy Byrne fella, he wouldn't give you the steam off his piss. He's that mean, that bloody man,' Nana revealed.

We couldn't stop laughing. Even Nana began to laugh. In that moment, she thought she was in someone else's house.

'You're dead right there, Mam – he's as mean as they come, that Paddy Byrne fella,' teased my mam.

'Here, Nana, I'm in the room you know,' moaned Dad.

'Well then, you're still a mean auld bollix,' said Nana.

'Nice one, Nana. Ye mean auld bollix, Dad,' I shouted.

Nana kept laughing with us as she chewed her jam sandwich. I'm pretty sure she had copped on to what she had said but was now continuing to pretend that the Alzheimer's had gotten the better of her. She kept it up.

'And the blow-offs coming out of that man, his arse could run a small country. I'm surprised the farts have room to come out, he's that tight-arsed,' she reeled off.

'You're a genius, Mam, don't stop now, what else?' coaxed my mam. She was loving this.

'Ladies and gentlemen, please welcome to the stage, Nana Carberry!' I screamed, laughing. This was the best gig ever.

'Oh, I'll leave it there. I'm off to the loo, but it's freezing cause Paddy Byrne wouldn't install a heater in there. You'd need a crowbar to open his wallet,' said Nana as she stood up from the couch.

But as she stood up, she let a rasp out of her ancient bottom. Then, as she left the room, she farted on every step …

LEFT … rasssppp … RIGHT … rasssppp …

LEFT … rasssppp … RIGHT … rasssppp …

… all the way out into the hall.

My nana farted whenever she moved. Sure, it's started to happen to me now and I'm only fifty. Sometimes when I reach for something, I fart. If I stand up too quick, laugh or shout, I fart, so I understand it now.

'I'm not the only noisy thing in the house. You could keep the ships off the rocks with that foghorn, Nana!' Dad yelled after her.

'Paddy Byrne,' said Mam.

'Well, she started it,' said Dad.

'She has no idea where she is.'

'Of course I do, and Paddy is still as tight as a jam-jar lid from Quinnsworth,' shouted Nana.

When that Christmas Day rolled around in the Byrne household, Nana was with us too. This was great, as it was the first time we didn't have to get out of our pyjamas to go visit Nana. People were coming to us instead.

The only people dressed were my mam and baby sister Eithne, and Nana of course. They were all going up to Mass. Myself, Rachel and Dad didn't want to.

'So, you little bastards aren't coming to Mass then?' said Mam.

'They don't want to; they don't believe in all that rubbish,' said Dad.

'The reason they all have presents this morning is because of the baby Jesus, Paddy!' Mam replied.

'Ah yeah, and God said, on Christmas Day, go forth and get yourselves a BMX, Barbie dolls and roller skates. Does God pay for those? No, I do.'

'I've never gotten a BMX,' I challenged.

'Shut up, you!'

'Well, I'll be lighting a candle for you, Paddy Byrne,' said Mam.

'You'd be better off with a flamethrower, Eithne, if you're trying to repent for all my sins.'

Mam, Nana and Eithne all went up to Mass, leaving Rachel, Dad and me to watch *The Muppet Christmas Carol.*

Later on, on Christmas night, I thought I was going to have a heart attack laughing. If I had been able to record this and post it on YouTube, I would be able to retire now.

My mam had the idea that we'd switch the telly off and try some Christmas games. Now, to switch the telly off in the Byrne household was like muting us, as we talk through the telly. Imagine a telly on in a corner of a room in a semi-detached house. All the people in the room are facing the telly – they never take their eyes away from the screen as they talk to each other. They literally use it as a source of connection.

Sounds weird? Well, studies today say that if you want to have a serious conversation with your child, put them in the passenger seat of the car while you drive. That way you won't have to make eye contact if the conversation gets heavy. The Byrnes were psychotherapists without even knowing it.

The game that Mam had decided on was ...

TWISTER!

I shit you not – she rolls out Twister onto the floor. This is a world-famous game, so no need to explain it. If you don't know what Twister is, you're probably ... Nana?

'Or have a bucket of shite for a brain.'

Thanks, Nana.

So myself, Dad, Mam, Rachel, Eithne and Nana were all playing Twister. Little Nana was well up for it. Dad had the job of spinning the wheel and telling us what foot or hand had to go on what colour dot. Of course he did – this meant he didn't have to move.

I went: left foot to red dot; Rachel: right foot to green dot; Mam: left hand to yellow dot; Nana: right hand to red dot ...

PARRRPPPPP!

Nana let off the biggest fart as she bent down to put her hand on the red dot, and I was right behind her. I'm pretty sure her dress did a little flap as it came out.

Well, we all lost it. We were in tears. Dad kept making Nana move. 'Nana, left hand to blue dot.'

PARRRRPPPPPP!

'Stop it, Paddy,' Mam tried to say while laughing.

'What? I'm just playing Twister with me family. Right leg to yellow, Nana,' Dad said, crying laughing.

PARRRRRRPPPPPPPPPP!

'Why am I the only one moving?' asked Nana.

'Right hand to green, please, Nana,' Dad said.

'Paddy, stop!' Mam pleaded, drinking her tears.

PARRRRRRRPPPPPPPPPPPPPPPP!

We were now all rolling around on the floor. The laughter had become infectious at that stage.

Dad lifted the phone beside him and pretended to dial 999. 'Hello, I need an ambulance here, I can't stop fucking laughing, I'm going to have a heart attack, come quickly,' he screamed.

This was, I'd say, one of the funniest and simplest moments in my life. I have written, performed and seen comedy all over the world, but I can tell you now that I have never laughed louder and harder than that Christmas night playing Twister with Farting Nana.

Dedicated to my amazing, loving Nana May Carberry, or the great Joe 90.

CHAPTER 5
THE HOTEL MANAGER

'A very good friend of mine, Liam O'Connor, runs the place. I'll see what I can do.'

We were back in Paddy Byrne's shed in the garden on Ludford Drive. I was nineteen and I still had no idea what to do in life. There was no chance of a proper college and the pretendy College of Commerce hadn't worked for me. And, of course, I nearly put Guinness's out of business by shutting the whole operation down for a few hours.

Dad had this idea in his head that I was a nice fella, good with people, so I should try to work in the public eye somehow. Maybe hospitality, due to my years as a lounge boy and mostly illegal underage bar work. Dad thought that if I trained as a barman, waiter or chef, I could become a hotel manager in New York. But I think this was Dad futureproofing. If he had a son running a hotel in New York, he could retire into the hotel, with free accommodation and booze for life.

'Yeah, so it's like AnCO,' explained Dad.

AnCO stood for An Cummarigh Obair, or some bollix like that. It was set up to train people in different trades in Ireland and was mostly auld fellas with brown flared trousers trying to show young fellas how to use a lathe or a furnace without killing themselves.

'You go down there, do a little interview with Liam O'Connor, tell him you want to do the waiter course. Sure I was a waiter for years and I loved it,' said Dad.

Now, no matter what job you did, Paddy Byrne always said that he had done it. But he either never had, or he did it for one day, or saw a fella doing it, or accidentally fell into something for an hour or so.

THINGS THAT PADDY BYRNE SAID HE DID FOR A JOB

1. Radio host. (When he was a teenager himself and his mate had gotten hold of a microphone and a tape machine. They recorded themselves on it for five minutes. This then turned into Dad telling me he hosted a radio show for months with his best friend Terry Macken.)
2. Waiter. (Apparently, one day Dad helped a waitress carry an extra tray to a table on his way back from the jacks while having dinner with my mam in a restaurant.)

NERRRR NERRRR NERRRR NERRRR!

We interrupt this list for a reader update. Sorry, but a pack of lies has just been told.

Paddy Byrne had never in his life sat in a restaurant with my mother on his own. Most likely with a gang of friends, but never on his own with her. 'Sure, what would I say to your mother on me own? There'd be no telly to communicate through' would be Dad's answer.

Now, back to the list …

3. Mechanic. (This meant he paid a mechanic to service his car in the driveway.)
4. Plumber. (This meant he paid a plumber who ran drainage pipes under the house and flooded it. We didn't know – we were wondering what the smell was for weeks. Dad opened the floorboards, looked under the house and there was two feet of water from a leaky pipe.)
5. Drainage expert. (This meant he brought in drainage people. After thousands of buckets were passed along a line of friends and neighbours, we managed to clear the water.)
6. TV presenter. (Walked behind a fella in town who was reporting for the news. Dad was called over for an opinion on the government.)
7. Political correspondent. (After being seen by all the lads on the telly in the pub.)

8. First-aid instructor. (Apparently a lady had fainted on the bus. Dad, in his bravery, not wanting to touch the poor lady, instructed the whole bus on what to do while waiting for the ambulance. I can only imagine – I'd say the lady had her knees in her chest while breathing into a paper bag. 'If the bag is going in and out, it means we haven't lost her, people. I've seen this on the telly – I watch telly all the time. It's OK, I know what I'm doing, I watch telly,' roars Paddy.)

9. Pilot. (Sat in the jump seat once on his way to Spain with my mam. Without us, of course, 'because you wouldn't enjoy yourselves'.)

10. Carpet fitter. (While in Des Kelly's: 'So how much do you charge if I fit the carpet myself?' Cut to weeks of us all having to slowly move furniture around the rooms while Dad tries to fit the bloody carpets.)

I watched my dad walk out of Liam O'Connor's office. On Liam's table was a crate of Guinness. Oh, so that was how Dad was going to get me into this college, course, whatever the feck it was.

Dad came over to me. 'Go ahead in, son. Liam is expecting ye.'

I walked into the office.

'Sit down there, Jason. So, you're Paddy Byrne's son,' said Liam as he lifted the crate of Guinness off his desk and onto the floor. 'He's a good man, your dad.'

I knew that my dad had never met Liam O'Connor before. I'd say he was a friend of a friend of a friend of the fella in the pub that knew a friend of my dad's friend. But somehow, Dad had found out he was fond of the drink.

'We run a tight ship here. This is the top waiter course in the land,' explained Liam.

I looked around at the run-down office, which had highly suspect diplomas on the wall behind him.

'You'll be joining the course tomorrow, Jason. It's a six-week term and our expert waiter instructor Mr Stint, who has many, many years' experience, will be training you,' said Liam.

A waiter instructor, what the fuck is a waiter instructor? I thought you started working at a restaurant and that was where you learnt your trade. I did not have a good feeling about this.

The next day, I got the bus into town to begin my new career as a hotel manager. First up, though, was my waiter course with Mr Stint.

I can't even remember exactly where it was, it was so traumatic for me – some sort of run-down school. It smelt of damp and wafers and it was freezing. It looked like a school for a certain type of person, and I don't even know what that means, but you know what I mean.

I headed in the door and along an old, dark corridor. Other students walking around were heading into different courses in different rooms. As I walked along, the students disappeared till I was alone. Oh Jesus, no, don't tell me I'm going to be doing this course on my own.

I got to a door that read: Mr Stint's Waiter Course. I opened the door into the classroom and there were about three people sitting at the desks.

'Hello, and you are …?' said a man with big curly orange hair, dressed in a pin-striped suit. He actually looked like a hotel manager. He also had a name tag with Mr Stint written on it and, get this, the biggest or worst or even best turned-in eye I have ever seen. I mean it was looking at his nose.

I tried not to look at it but I couldn't help it. The worst thing is, when I concentrate on one spot for too long, my own fucking eye turns in, so at that moment it must have looked like I was slagging him off for having a turned-in eye by turning my own eye in.

Mr Stint blinked. His eye was turning even harder now as he tried to focus on *my* eye, which was also turning madly in while focusing on *his* eye. It was like a beautiful meeting of the wonky eyes.

'Eh, Jason Byrne,' I answered eventually, after my eye calmed down.

'Ah yes, Jason Byrne, here you are.' Mr Stint marked me off the list. 'Have a seat – we're just waiting for the others.' He pointed me to a desk.

I walked past the three other people. One girl, half asleep on her bag, a cool-looking Fonzie-type fella, and a lovely man, who I befriended later, from Sri Lanka called Mohammed. He was so positive and smiley – I loved him.

We all sat and waited for the others.

Then I heard a commotion on its way down the corridor. A man in uniform with a hat and all, who looked like a security guard, entered with a clipboard. 'Morning, Mr Stint, they're all here for ye,' the man said as he handed Mr Stint the clipboard.

Then about twenty pupils, girls and boys, all around sixteen, seventeen or eighteen, entered. They came quietly in a row into the classroom. It was as if they were in a regiment. They looked terrifying, as if they wanted to rip our heads off.

The security man stood at the top till they all took their seats. 'Right then, I'll leave this lot with you, Mr Stint,' he said as he left the room. He looked at the children he had just brought in. 'Behave, I'll only be down the hall!' he roared. This was not a good sign. I hadn't heard anyone shout like that since primary school.

Mr Stint closed the door behind the security man. Myself and the other three people from earlier looked at each other, looked around at the new additions, then looked back at each other, as if to say, 'Where the hell are we, and who are these guys?' Even Mohammed, and that's saying something.

What had my dad gotten me into?

Mr Stint began in a posh accent: 'Hello all, I am Mr Stint, your waiter instructor for the next six weeks. I have worked everywhere from the Ivy to the Dorchester, in palaces and embassies. I have served the rich and famous, from movie stars to politicians to Gay Byrne, who I know personally. I will teach you all you need to know about being the best waiter ever. Just listen and you will learn. Let the teacher make the decisions.'

We then moved to a weird hall with round tables placed all around it, like it was a big ballroom getting ready for a massive banquet. It was four of us to a table: ours was me, Mohammed and two of the strange children.

'First up, we will be setting the table, then serving from trays. I will teach you all how to do this and become the best waiters ever!' announced Mr Stint as his eye flew around in his head.

Mohammed was smiling and trying his best while the other two boys with shaven heads just looked at us.

'OK, get your knives and forks and begin setting the tables. The map is on the wall here.' Mr Stint pointed at a 'how to set a table' diagram on the wall. I quickly grabbed the knives before the two serial killers could, Mohammed got the forks and, thank God, Ted Bundy and his mate were left with spoons.

We then set the tables as best we could. Mr Stint walked around shouting 'No! No! No!' as he rearranged cutlery on the tables of the strange children, which was brave as they were now all holding knives. Mr Stint then came to my table.

'Well done, Mr Byrne, well set,' he half praised, as I think he enjoyed roaring No! No! No! like some medical lecturer in UCD overseeing his classes doing autopsies on dead bodies. But this was just setting tables – how hard could it be? Six weeks of this shit?

'Kill me,' I said out loud by accident. One of the strange children looked at me with raised eyebrows as if it was some sort of invite.

'OK, now we are going to serve the tables, but in a very special way,' shouted Mr Stint.

'Yes!' said Mohammed gleefully.

'The way of the apple.' Mr Stint held an apple over his head in one hand like it was some sort of holy chalice. It was an apple, for jaysus' sake. 'It's all about balance, people. When you manoeuvre around tables in a restaurant, you will have to be able to do it with one hand, as chairs will be in your way, and people, and children, little bastard children that shouldn't be in a restaurant as it's a place of work and ART! …'

Mr Stint paused at that last bit as it looked like he was having a bit of PTSD. 'Watch carefully.' We all watched as he took out a sizeable rectangular wooden tray and placed an apple in the centre. 'The trick is to keep your apple centred. Do not let this apple roll off the tray, or you have lost your duck à l'orange into somebody's lap.'

We all stood to the side as we watched the comedy show unfold. Mr Stint held the tray above his bushy red head with the apple in the centre. He then began to move between the tables and the chairs. His eye was now in super-turned-in mode. The apple rolled around on the tray. This was fine for a while, but then he began to bump into all the tables and chairs. We were all trying not to laugh.

'Ah Jesus, owww, fucking chair, owww, bastard, owww, should have stayed in the Dorchester, owww!' Mr Stint banged into every table and table – his turned-in eye was not his friend – but the apple never fell off the tray.

He finally came to the end of his comical obstacle course. 'OK, people, grab your trays and your apples and begin your walk into your future.'

We all grabbed our trays and placed our apples on them. This task alone was hard, as some of the strange children were dropping their apples and getting angry at this, banging into each other as they tried to walk with their trays.

'Trust yourself, feel the apple, feel the apple and control it!' roared Mr Stint as he tried to guide us. The room was now complete mayhem.

'FUCK THIS!' roared one of the strange children. He got his tray and whacked it over another strange child's head. Well, this set off an insane reaction. All the strange children began to beat the shite out of each other with the trays. There were apples flying everywhere.

Mohammed and I got under a table for shelter.

'Stop it, guys, stop it!' roared Mr Stint as he got several apples fecked at his head.

Then the door of the hall flew open. It was the security-guard fella with three other fellas dressed the same way. They were all blowing whistles, grabbing the kids to try to control them, hitting them with sticks and roaring at them to stop.

Suddenly, two arms reached under the table and pulled myself and Mohammed out.

'No, wait, no, I'm just – and this is Mohammed,' I tried to explain. 'We didn't do anything!'

'Mr Stint!' I roared as I was being pushed out of the room along with Mohammed and the unruly strange children.

But Mr Stint was sitting on a chair, rocking back and forth while chomping wildly on an apple, saying something about 'the Dorchester' and 'Gay Byrne'.

'Hey, what the fuck, no, I'm Jason, I'm not with these guys,' I tried to explain to one of the security guards as he pushed myself and Mohammed – who was still smiling, by the way – onto a bus with all the strange kids. The bus doors then locked and off we went.

★★★

'I'm very sorry, Mr Byrne, and of course Jason, for the unfortunate mix-up,' said the governor of the juvenile prison, which I had been driven to along with the rest of the …

'Prisoners, Dad! Prisoners! You sent me on a course with prisoners! And I ended up on a bus to their PRISON, DAD!'

Dad was driving me home. 'Look, a fella in the pub just told me that this fella Liam O'Connor ran courses for the state. He'd do anything for a drink, so between the jigs and the reels, I thought this would be perfect for ye.'

I didn't know what career I was going to end up doing, but at this rate it was only going to be stand-up comedy. So-called funny shit would not stop happening to me. I wasn't enjoying life right then – this growing-up stuff was utter shite – but I think my dad was definitely enjoying it.

'Here, Eithne, will you stick bars on that boxroom to make Jason feel at home tonight?' Dad shouted from the living room into Mam in the kitchen. 'Will I pop in *Escape to Victory* or *Escape from Alcatraz*? Up to you, Nelson Mandela,' he teased.

The slagging was to go on all night. Even as I got into bed, I heard my dad shout, 'Lock up number six! We've a fugitive among us, Eithne, a fugitive.' Dad cried laughing as he went to bed.

★★★

'Another interview, another day. Remember, son, Rome was never built without its spirit.'

This was another one of Dad's sayings. It was like he played a game of Chinese Whispers with himself, because each time he attempted one of these idioms …

'An idiot!'

'An idiom, Dad, they're called idioms,' I corrected.

'Idiom, me bollix,' was Dad's opening and closing argument on this topic.

… they simply changed.

OTHER IDIOMS DAD CHINESE WHISPERED TO DEATH

1. Don't beat around the hedge.
2. Two birds in a stone are better than one.
3. Better late than clever.
4. I'll cross that bridge when it's built.
5. Don't worry, son, I've the four of hearts up me sleeve.
6. Red sky at night, shepherd's good weather.
7. You can lead a swan to a lake, but the water will just slide off its back.
8. It's not rocket work.
9. Heard that straight from the pony's lips.
10. The orange doesn't fall far from the bush.

We were on the way to Jurys Inn in Ballsbridge. The waiter course was a no-go, as the whole thing was shut down due to an inquiry and numerous cases of assault with trays. I believe Mr Stint had left the teaching course and was trying to find work elsewhere. To prevent me putting in a lawsuit.

Liam O'Connor had set up an interview for me for a job as an apprentice barman. (There was no such thing as an apprentice waiter. Surprise, surprise, Dad.) This was before there were Jurys Inns popping up all over the camp. There was just this one big one in a very posh area in Dublin.

I left my dad in the car park and made my way into the bar …

'SUMMARISE! We don't need to know all the ins and outs of you getting an apprenticeship in Jurys, the job interview, uniform, locker rooms or any of that bollix!'

OK, I got the job, as I already had tons of experience from doing illegal bar work in the Braemor Rooms. My mam and dad were delighted when I told them. My mam especially, as she could go to Mass now and do some fine bragging outside the church.

> MAM (in a posh accent): Oh yes, Jason? Oh he's an apprentice in Jurys Inn in Ballsbridge, being trained by the best.

Mass in Ireland is not what you think. People reading this that are not Catholic may think that Irish people go to Mass to listen to the priest, reflect on what he has to say and try to make themselves better people in the long run.

WRONG!

Mass is for the women and auld-one men, as me dad used to call them, to gossip. (In Ireland, an auld one is an old woman (a gossip) and an auld fella is normally just an old fella. But an auld-one man is a man who loves gossip just as much as the women.)

They couldn't give a hoot about the religion. They live for the end of Mass so they can all get outside, with the gossip horn on them, to see who's wearing what and what's going on in each other's household. They couldn't be told this directly – that would be useless. It has to be behind someone's back.

Example: Mrs Farrell v Mrs Murphy outside the church.

> MRS FARRELL: So how is everything at home, Mrs Murphy?
>
> MRS MURPHY: Oh great, Mrs Farrell. Declan, the husband, is doing great in work, the eldest has just left for college, middle fella doing great in school, and the youngest has just taken her first steps.
>
> MRS FARRELL: Oh, that is lovely to hear, Mrs Murphy. See you later.
>
> MRS MURPHY: And God bless you.

Mrs Murphy heads off. Mrs Kelly joins Mrs Murphy.

> MRS KELLY: Was that Mrs Murphy?
>
> MRS FARRELL: It was indeed, Mrs Kelly.
>
> MRS KELLY (with a small horn on her): And how is Mrs Murphy and the family?

(Meaning she wants the bad shit – shoot me up with that dirty shit, girl.)

MRS FARRELL: She says they're all good, but that's not what I heard, Mrs Kelly.

(Fucking yes! The reason Mrs Kelly got up for Mass today: some heart-racing, horny, juicy … GOSSIP!)

MRS KELLY: GO!

MRS FARRELL: Well, you know her husband, Declan, she says he's doing well in work. But I know for a fact he has drank himself out of that job. He went in hammered one day and smacked the boss in the head …

MRS KELLY: Go away!

(NOTE: Mrs Kelly does not want Mrs Farrell to go anywhere right now. In auld-woman conversation, 'go away' simply means 'you're joking' or 'this can't be true'. As does 'go on outta that' and 'you're pulling me leg' and 'you're having me on'.)

MRS FARRELL: No, I'm telling ye the truth. Then the middle fella, the one going to college? Not at all, he had to get a job in town to keep the family going and isn't going to college at all – he's working in a shoe shop in Henry Street. Mrs Canning said she seen him there last week.

MRS KELLY: Stop it!

(NOTE: 'Stop it' does not mean stop it: it means do not stop this, this is gold.)

MRS FARRELL (a concerned hand over the heart area on her good blouse, as if this wagon actually gave a shit): The youngest one is here in the school but is seeing a … (mouthing the words) … a counsellor!

(This word couldn't be spoken out loud, as there are certain things in Irish gossip that are far too serious to be heard.)

MRS KELLY (wide-eyed, mouthing back): A counsellor?

(Fucking jackpot, she thinks, her knickers nearly falling to the floor like a wet tea-bag.)

MRS FARRELL (confirming, still mouthing): A counsellor.

OTHER THINGS THAT HAVE TO BE MOUTHED IN IRELAND BY AULD WOMEN

1. Anything to do with the vaginal area. Her 'downstairs' would be mouthed instead.
2. If someone is mentally ill. 'His' (said out loud) 'head' (mouthed) 'is at him' (out loud again).
3. The price of something, if it's a high one. 'It was' (out loud) '17,345 euros' (mouthed with lips and teeth here).
4. All terminal illnesses, without exception, are to be mimed.
5. 'Separated' – a massive mouthing here for this word.

★★★

The Dubliner was the name of the bar I worked in at Jurys in Ballsbridge. I hated it. It was a way bigger operation than the Braemor Rooms in Churchtown. It had loads of different sections to it. Restaurants, different smaller bars and a five-star section of the hotel called The Towers where I had to do the most humiliating job ever.

I was told to get the trolley dolly, a trolley very similar to the one on a plane. I had to stock it with drinks, then go over to The Towers and wait at the lift, offering five-star customers a complimentary drink on their arrival.

You see, in the Braemor Rooms, my bar-brain was working in one mode only: mischief and taking the piss. When the bar manager asked me to get the trolley dolly and wait by the lifts, I immediately told him to 'ask me bollix', as I thought it was one of those pranks they were trying to pull on me.

Cut to me, red-faced, stopping people getting out of a lift and asking them if they would like a complimentary drink. Most of them just ignored me and walked on. Others took the drink with a grunt. Very rarely I'd get a thank you.

I learnt then that working-class people say thank you all the time, no matter what, and are way more grateful than any of these posh fucks. I assume it comes from our upbringing.

TIMES YOU WERE FORCED TO SAY THANK YOU FOR SOMETHING OR YOUR MOTHER WOULD KILL YOU

1. Ringing all your different aunties to say thank you for birthday cards. 'You sit there and say thank you to each of those brilliant women, you ungrateful little bastard.'
2. 'Say thank you to the man ... I SAID, SAY THANK YOU!'
3. 'Thank the doctor for the injection,' while you were in floods of tears.
4. 'What do you say?!' 'Thank you for the Mass.' 'He loved it, Father.'
5. 'Go back and say thank you!' 'I did!' 'I didn't hear you, neither did the lollipop lady, so cross back over and say thank you!'

We were frightened into thanking and saying sorry for every move by our mental mothers.

I assume, and I only know a few, that middle- to upper-class people just didn't have to say thank you, ever. Their mother or nanny just didn't care enough about their kids to make them thank others.

In Jurys, the place was full of wankers. Wanker customers all the time. I remember a man one lunchtime reading a newspaper at the bar. As I passed him, he raised his fingers above his paper and clicked his fingers at me. He didn't even put the paper down: he clicked over the top of it. I, of course, ignored the wankbag.

I passed a second time; he did it again. I went to the shelf of the bar, got the first-aid kit and handed it to him over the top of his paper. He asked what I was doing. I told him that it sounded like his fingers had a weird clicking noise in them and that maybe he could find something in the first-aid kit to stop the clicking.

I sat at home later that day after being let go early because I called the CEO of Bord Gáis or Bord Something 'a wankbag' and said, 'I couldn't give a fuck who he is, clicking his fingers at me.'

Dad was in the living room with me and said, 'That's the difference between old and new money, son. That wankbag is new money. New money people are always desperate to stay at the top, so they'll do and say anything to stay there. They have delusions of grandeur. Old money, well, they've always had money. They came in at the top with nothing to prove. That's why you'll always find they're nicer.'

Dad was right. I'd meet Lord Grey of the Greys and he'd be walking around with holes in his jumpers, drinking G&Ts, laughing and hugging everyone. But the CEO of the yacht club? Wankbag.

Jurys Inn wasn't a great time for me, so let's summarise.

1. **Served mainly wankbags for six months.**
2. **Missed the Braemor Rooms.**
3. **Worked in the cocktail bar for a week. Barmen in there thought they were superior to the other barmen.**
4. **Served thousands of wankbags when rubgy was on in Lansdowne Road stadium.**
5. **My lung collapses, thank Christ, for the first time.**

CHAPTER 6
DOCTOR
PADDY BYRNE

'Yes, yes, I see,' said Dr Paddy Byrne as he looked at the chart at the end of my hospital bed, pretending he knew what it all meant.

Why people do this is beyond me. There is always a visitor who lifts the clipboard off the end of the bed and flicks through it while rubbing their chin.

YOU'RE NOT A DOCTOR. PUT IT BACK DOWN – YOU HAVE NO IDEA WHAT IT ALL MEANS!

This was another of my unfortunate Byrne aliments: a collapsed lung. I had already been born with the wonky eye and had to wear an eyepatch and glasses. Now my lung had collapsed for no reason at all, really.

One night, while working in Jurys Inn, I didn't feel well. The top of my back was sore and breathing felt a bit weird. The job sent me to A&E, where they did X-rays and announced I had a collapsed lung. How? Well, the doctor said that because I was tall and thin, the lung had stretched, forming air bubbles at the top, and it had burst like a balloon.

I was sitting up in the hospital bed with a chest drain. They had put what looked like a siphon pipe in me – you know, the one you use to rob petrol out of a neighbour's car – that went down into a bottle to drain air off the top of the lung. It had all reinflated now.

'He'll stay here for another day or two, then we'll remove the chest drain and let him home,' explained the real doctor.

'Absolutely, doctor, I'm happy enough with that. I'm off for a little while, so I'll make sure he gets a bite-sized piece of rest,' said the non-doctor, Paddy Byrne.

'Yes, respite,' corrected the doctor.

'I concur,' said Paddy non-doctor.

'Pardon?' said real doctor.

'Yes,' continued Paddy non-doctor.

They stared at each other for a good twenty seconds. Then the doctor left, confused.

'Sure, they know fuck-all these days, God help them,' Dad said. He had come in for a visit while Mam collected the girls from school. He told me he was on a two-week holiday from work so this collapsed lung couldn't have come at a better time.

I found out later that Dad wasn't on holiday from work – he was smack bang in the middle of an investigation in Guinness's.

Technology had made its presence felt big-time in Guinness's. Gone were the days of turning the oats and barley by shovel. Coopers no longer made wooden barrels; they were all machine-made metal. In fact, machines had taken over most tasks in Guinness's.

My dad was now in the gas section, along with loads of other lads the same age as him. Dad told me that six of them oversaw one button. They had nothing else to do, but Guinness's had to keep them all on because of their contracts. All Guinness's workers had signed contracts years ago up to the age of sixty-five. One button meant that they didn't need to be all there at once, so they took turns. One would watch the button while the other five went to the pub in their overalls.

While Dad and his mates were in the pub one day, an explosion occurred right where they were supposed to be. There was a power surge that resulted in a blast that blew out the side of a wall in the brewery's gas plant area.

My dad and his mates returned to work, oblivious of the news, stinking of pints. They stood behind the firemen and rescue crew as they fought off the blaze. Dad asked the firemen what was going on. They said they were looking for six fellas that most likely were buried in the rubble.

My dad, as bold as brass, said, 'Do you want a hand looking for them?'

The fireman apparently said sure.

Then my dad pointed to himself and the four other lads. 'One, two, three, four and meself, five,' he said.

The fireman was gobsmacked.

But then: 'Austin Tallon!' Dad shouted suddenly. Remember, there were six fellas around one button. 'Austin Tallon is in there!' he screamed at the fireman.

Just then, Austin Tallon came walking up the road with a newspaper rolled under his arm. Apparently, Austin had been off in a completely different part of the brewery having a shit. The gas explosion happened because nobody was watching or working the button.

Here's the best (and very Irish) bit: the six of them received compensation for the trauma of nearly being in a blast.

Trauma! Five of them were in the fucking pub having pints, and the sixth fella was having a shit, all while they should have been watching the gas gauges. But their union rep said that they would suffer PTSD from what might have happened to them if they had been on site, DOING THEIR JOBS, while said explosion occurred.

My dad dined out on this for years. He told people he had to drag other workers out from the rubble, that he was lucky to be alive, that he could have lost a limb or even worse. Of course, when they returned to work afterwards, a special lunch was put on to honour the six brave lads that survived the explosion. Guinness's did it to humour them and keep the union off their back.

'Breathe in and blow!' Dad was shouting at me as I did my lung exercises. He was taking all this way too seriously.

'For God's sake, Paddy, you don't need to be in a tracksuit. And when in the name of jaysus are you going back to work?' asked Mam.

We all sat in the living room. I was now home about a week from hospital. They had given me this thing to blow into. The idea was to get the red ball to the top of the plastic gadget, which would help me strengthen my lung. But Dad was treating it like a training camp. He even had a whistle.

FWEEEEEEEET!

'YAAHHH!' cheered Rachel and Eithne, my two little sisters, encouraging me as I blew. They even used mop heads as pompoms. 'Gooooo, Jason!'

'I'll kill the both of you, me good mop heads,' Mam complained. They weren't even mop heads – they were strips from old tea towels that Mam had cut to save money.

WAYS MAM HAD SAVED MONEY

1. Covered our schoolbooks in woodchip wallpaper.
2. Put tinfoil behind the radiators to push the heat towards the room.
3. Put any leftovers into a pie – I mean, anything.
4. Did all her own sewing, knitting, etc.
5. Covered everything in plastic – lampshades, couches, tables, even the hall had a plastic mat.

'Go, son!' Dad said. 'I'm not back in work for a while, Eithne, as I am suffering from TCP. You're lucky I got up this morning at all.'

'What? And it's PTSD not TCP, ye feckin' fool, and how do you get PTSD from being in a pub while there's an explosion in a completely different place?' asked Mam.

'It's the coulda been, Eithne – I coulda been there, I was nearly there. Now stop disturbing me while I look after Jason here,' Dad moaned.

'Coulda … sure I coulda been at the crucifixion, but I wasn't,' said Mam.

'Jesus Christ, Eithne, what in the name of jaysus are you on about now? You're bringing me TCP up from the deep where I had it buried,' philosophised Dad.

RING! RING! RING!

'The phone's ringing,' my dad said, looking at Mam and the two girls. 'I can't get it, I've got TBA and I'm looking after Jason here, who can't get it 'cause his lung blew up,' he explained.

RACHEL: Hello, oh yeah, hang on.

Rachel then gave the phone to me.

ME: Hello?

ERIC: Yeah, it's Eric.

ME: Oh hi.

ERIC: I heard your lung collapsed – are you alright?!

ME: Yeah, I'm grand, all home now.

ERIC: So you're alright then.

ME: Yeah.

Phone hangs up.

'How's your brother? He sounded good. It's nice of him to check in like that,' said Mam.

'Yeah, he's a real hero,' I replied.

FWEEEEEEEET!

'And again, Jason, go for it, blowww!' screamed Dad.

'Go, Jay, gooo!' cheered the girls.

I never had to go back to Jurys Inn, thank God.

'Everything happens for a reason, Jason. You were meant to get a collapsed lung,' said Mam.

Meant to? I don't think so. It was more likely the shite genes I've inherited from both sides of the family.

'I'm so excited!' screamed Mam in the kitchen. She was heading off with her friends to Spain for a week. Leaving me at home with Dad, his whistle and the two girls. We all always dreaded this when we were younger. Leaving Dad in charge was a disaster when we were smaller, but now myself and Rachel could cook, it wasn't so bad.

STUFF WE'D HEAR WHEN DAD WAS MINDING US

1. 'Why don't you like fish?'
2. 'The brown meat is the best part of the chicken, for Christ's sake!'
3. 'Black bananas means they're ripe.'
4. 'What time is your bedtime normally?'
5. 'The pub is literally up the road, I won't be long.'

My lung was feeling better too. But now I had no job, no college, no waiter course. You name it, I didn't have it. I didn't have a bog of what to do.

But who cared: listen to this.

THE STORY OF EITHNE BYRNE AND THE FLIGHT TO SPAIN AS TOLD BY EITHNE BYRNE HERSELF

(This story may be exaggerated to shit, as it is told by Eithne Byrne. However, I have got it from good sources that most of it is true.)

EITHNE BYRNE: Well, I was all ready for the holiday. It was myself and the girls, or the Virgins on Tour as we liked to call ourselves. The girls had gone ahead to Spain. Salou, it was, we loved Salou – it always had loads of Irish bars. We would stay there for the week, singing and drinking, just with Irish people. We wouldn't even meet a single Spanish head.

The idea was that I was to follow them over, as your dad had some shite to do with work after the gas explosion, a hearing of some sort. He loved this as he could say PTSD a lot that day.

Anyway, I'm going on here. I eventually get to the airport, all on me own. It's great, though, no kids or a husband, bliss! No offence, Jason, but as your dad always said, 'Never let your children get in the way of your social life.' And by God, did we not.

So I'm having me half of Guinness at the bar in the airport, and I look at the telly-screen thingy that tells you when the flights are leaving. Mother of jaysus, there was my gate closing, so I knocked back me half of Guinness and pegged it.

I made it to the gate, out of breath, and I sat into me seat. I got all settled and was talking to a lovely lady beside me. I asked if she was looking forward to Salou. The lady said she'd love to go there one day.

'What?' I said to her. 'Sure you're going there today – this plane is for Salou.' Well the lady hopped up and the air hostess came over, asking what the problem was. I told her that this poor lady beside me had gotten on the wrong plane, that this plane was for Salou.

'No, love, this plane is for Malaga. *You're* actually on the wrong plane,' the air hostess said to me.

Well, it was mayhem. The air hostess ran up to the pilot to stop the plane and they radioed the other plane, the one for Salou, on another part of the tarmac, to tell them to stop.

They get me out of my seat, open the plane, and I walk down the steps to a waiting car.

'Jaysus, missus, you're famous, the whole airport is watching,' said the fella in the car.

I looked over at the airport and thousands of people were watching me along with the two stopped planes. They got my luggage out of the hold, and over we drove to the other plane.

Halfway there, now you won't believe this, the bloody car breaks down. The fella who was driving it had to lift me in his arms, then ran with me to the other plane. Actually carried me. It was like something out of *An Officer and a Gentleman*. Both planes watching, the whole of the airport clapping as I boarded, but not before I turned to the airport and waved at the people cheering me.

Well, I got onto the right plane, I was clapped and cheered into me seat, and they gave me champagne for the rest of the journey.

It was all over the news that night.

'Irish lady boards wrong plane. Officer and a gentlemen gets her to the right flight on time.'

EITHNE BYRNE, OVER AND OUT.

ACTUAL STORY, AS ME MAM LOVES TO EXAGGERATE

TRUE … She defo got on the wrong plane.

FALSE … People in the airport had no idea what was going on.

TRUE … A man drove her to the other plane.

FALSE … The car did not break down.

TRUE … She made it to the other plane.

FALSE … Nobody carried her anywhere.

TRUE … She waved (to no one) at the top of the steps.

FALSE … The people cheered her on.

TRUE … They all wanted to kill her, as their flight was now late.

FALSE … Not a drop of champagne passed her lips.

TRUE … She made it to Salou.

FALSE … It never made the news.

But in my dad's words: 'Ah sure, leave her alone with it.' In other words, when someone tells you a story, especially if it's a story they have been telling for years, just leave them with it, don't question them or say it's not true. It's a story that they've probably convinced themselves is true, as they've told it so many times. It's their own bit of stand-up.

'Isn't he nifty on his Honda 50?'

'Shut up, Dad,' I said.

My little mam had bought a small moped so she could head down to the Braemor Rooms on it. It wasn't a Honda 50 – my dad just loved that song. It was called a Honda Vision, and it was red and white, and tiny.

But Mam wasn't working in the Braemor Rooms anymore, due to my dad telling her he couldn't look after the kids while she worked and deal with his TCP at the same time. So, no more Braemor Rooms for now for Mam, and Dad went back to suffering with PTSD in the pub with his mates every night … God bless him.

So Mam let me have her Honda Vision. I looked like a clown on one of those tiny bikes they cycle across the circus ring, but I loved it. There were no major career moves on the horizon, I was roughly nineteen at this stage, and it was summer. What the hell, I thought, I may as well go back to the Braemor Rooms.

I got a lot of slagging when I went back. 'Oh, here comes the Jurys Inn boy, too posh for us, Jason?' or 'Once you pop you can't stop, eh, Jason? How's the lung? Will I get you a bicycle pump?'

Bastards.

I was back with Pamela, my great friend Greg Larkin, Gary Donaghue, Greg Dunne, Rocky (RIP) and all the ladies who worked the floor too. It was so much fun. I was serving as a barman full-time and I loved working there, in the lounge, bar, main cabaret room and the small bar.

The first night back, I parked the Honda Vision outside the pub. I then pushed open the two main doors where they would later let the punters through.

'You fecking gobshite ye,' I heard.

Niall Tóibín (the Irish comic and actor) stood in front of me, all dressed in a white suit. They were recording his show in the cabaret room that night, and he was in the hall doing little intros. I had walked into his shot while they were recording. I then walked, red-faced, all the way down the lit-up hall, past the cameramen.

'Gobshite, utter gobshite!' I heard Niall in the distance as I walked away.

Years later, I did a gig with him. I was on before him and blew the stage apart, and he struggled after me. He never remembered calling me a gobshite back then.

Another one of Dad's sayings: 'Be careful how you treat people on your way up, as you'll meet them on your way down. They could own half of Ireland one day.'

'That's why I'm always nice to butchers,' he explained once, to total confusion on all our faces.

PEOPLE DAD WAS NICE TO, AS HE THOUGHT THEY'D OWN HALF OF IRELAND ONE DAY

1. Postman ('Sure, he'll own half of Ireland one day').
2. Lollipop lady ('Sure, she'll own half of Ireland one day').
3. Milkman ('Sure, he'll own half of Ireland one day').
4. Barman ('Sure, he'll own half of Ireland one day').
5. Farmers ('Sure, they already own half of Ireland').

I saw amazing people perform in the Braemor Rooms. Al Bannan, Sil Fox, Brendan Grace, Shaun Connors, Twink, just loads of comics. I remember watching them, at the start of the show, discussing what gags they were going to do that night. They were incredible. Brendan Grace's father of the bride was genius.

Then we had the Dubliners in there for months on end. Just heavy, heavy drinking. I had to keep their dressing room full of booze, the stage full of booze, the room full of booze. It was amazing to watch them play – the place would go mad as they sang 'The Irish Rover'. Best sight of my life.

Shane MacGowan came in to play with them one night. There was nothing better than watching the Dubliners singing with Shane MacGowan. Oh wait, yes there is: Terence Trent D'Arby, a friend of Shane's, once came into the venue, as he had been playing a gig in town. So now we had the Dubliners, Shane MacGowan and Terence Trent D'Arby all singing 'The Irish Rover'. None of us worked when they played. I think the barmen were as pissed as the crowd. What a life.

Now, as I said, many acts from all walks of life appeared there. One night we had the Drifters. There was a meeting with the staff and their manager, a big American guy in a white suit and hat who looked like the Kentucky Fried Chicken fella. He warned us all not to give booze to any of the Drifters, as it would ruin their performance. He had locked them in their dressing room and we were only to bring food to them. It was 5 p.m. and they were due to go on stage at 7 p.m. He really did this, locked four grown men in a dressing room. We didn't question it.

I brought them food backstage. When I opened the door from the outside, there sat four sad-looking Drifters. One was an original Drifter, the other three had replaced missing or dead Drifters, and the original Drifter looked like he was about to drift off at any moment.

'Any bourbon with that steak, son?' one of them asked. I just left the food on the table then locked the door behind me. It was like something out of *Shawshank*.

And you'll never guess who was the Drifters' biggest fan – only Paddy Byrne himself. He was so excited. I had gotten himself and Mam tickets.

'So, what are they like, son, did you meet them?' Dad asked as he sat at the bar in the lounge, waiting to go in to see the band.

'I'm sure they're like any other person, Paddy,' my mam answered.

'Not at all, Eithne, these are heroes, geniuses,' Dad defended them.

I told Dad that I had met them, brought them food to their room and locked it again.

'Why in the name of jaysus are you locking them in, son?' Dad looked as if I'd tried to punch his pet rabbit in the face.

'They're not allowed to drink before the gig.'

'WHAT?!'

Now I really had punched Dad's pet rabbit in the face.

'That's a fucking disgrace, they're in Ireland, they can't remember Ireland this way! Locked in a room with no drink – no drink, Eithne! No drink, Jason! No drink, Seamus!' Dad said to a very drunk Seamus sitting on the other side of him.

'Bastards!' roared Seamus.

'Bastards is right, Seamus!' Dad roared back. He calmed down a bit, took a sip of his pint, then looked at me. 'Bring us down to say hello.'

'No way, Dad, I'm not allowed to do that!'

'Look, son, I have TCP, I've been through a lot. The doctors said that happy moments like this could help me forget about the gas explosion!' he pleaded.

'You weren't even there, Paddy!' moaned Mam.

'Not the point, Eithne. Remember, I was nearly blown up and buried alive in rubble. If it wasn't for the fast-thinking lads, I'd be dead,' explained Dad to Mam and drunk Seamus.

'You nearly died – you're a lucky man, Paddy,' Seamus agreed.

'Bang on, Seamus, bang on. So come on, son, don't be a bollix.'

I opened the door to the dressing room. The four Drifters sat up like meerkats. 'Eh, this is …' I mumbled.

'Paddy Byrne, lads, massive fan, massive fan, just had to meet you. The son works here, he's the manager,' lied Dad. 'Leave us now, son, there's man talk to be done. Come back for us in thirty minutes.' He pushed me out of the dressing room, which I then locked, left and went back to work.

Thirty minutes passed and I left the very busy bar to let my dad back out of the room. As I approached the door all I could hear was Paddy Byrne and the Drifters singing:

'Kissing in the back row, of the movies, on a Saturday night with youuu!'

I unlocked the door. Dad came out quickly.

'See you, Paddy, you're the man, Paddy, we love you, Paddy!' the Drifters howled as he left. I locked the door again and we both headed back to the lounge.

'Thanks, son, it's going to be the best gig ever!' said Dad.

LADIES AND GENTLEMEN, THE DRIFTERS!

The Drifters came onto the stage to a packed room, which included my dad and mam.

They got to their mics, sniggering and a bit wobbly. They got words wrong all night and had to start songs again. I mean, they were locked, but the crowd loved it, as did the Drifters.

How were they locked? Yes, you've guessed it. I have never seen my mam or dad pay for a drink in the Braemor Rooms. Dad had always smuggled in booze in his coat.

Well, apparently, he had celebrated in the dressing room with a large bottle of Jameson straight from his coat, got the Drifters locked, then left.

The gig ended and the place went mad. At the end of the night, Dad was leaving. He was in the hall where Niall Tóibín had called me a gobshite. 'Best night ever, son,' he said, as he and Mam passed a very angry Kentucky Fried Chicken American manager roaring at the actual manager of the Braemor Rooms, Leonard.

'We'll never come here again – who gave them booze?!' the Kentucky Fried manager screamed.

Dad stood outside the door with four Drifters hugging him before they got onto their bus. 'Best gig ever, Paddy, thank you so much!'

I continued to work throughout the summer in the Braemor Rooms.

Then a girl with long blonde hair down to her rear that bounced as she walked came into my life. Rachel Gerrard was the newest lounge girl. I was nineteen, she was twenty-one. When I spoke to her, my wonky eye would not stop turning in. I tried my best to control it, but love had taken over my ever-wonky eye.

When I eventually straightened my eye out, I offered to walk Rachel home one night. She bounced along beside me with the biggest smile, and smiley eyes to match.

I stopped outside her house in Churchtown, only metres from the Braemor Rooms.

SNOG!

Oh my God, that was it. I fell in love, my first actual love. I walked home to Ballinteer; my wonky eye must have been rolling around in my head with excitement.

I even lost my virginity to Rachel. I remember it well. I told her I had done it before at a Debs in Northern Ireland. Remember that, everyone: the Debs I brought the shiny suit to and where I was nearly chased out of Coleraine by the Protestants. The only thing I lost that night were Brian Roche's slip-on shoes, which I left behind in a room. Rachel said she knew it was my first time as my eye was literally jammed in as I faced her.

We were now steady boyfriend and girlfriend. She was two years older than me and I loved it. Her dad Tony, mam Nora and brothers Colm and Gavin were so much fun, especially her dad. When I would leave at night after having kisses on the couch with Rachel, Tony would come back from the pub and abruptly put a halt to myself and Rachel's kissing.

He would then show me to the door and say: 'Go on there, young fella, you pole vault home with that in your pants, you'll get back quicker.'

I could hear him laughing as he closed the door on me.

It was to be my last night in the Braemor Rooms, but I had no idea. Fate, I suppose, definitely took over here.

Dickie Rock was back, as was Willy the Wire, but the fella who normally operated the spotlight was nowhere to be seen. The soundman, Terry, who owned and operated all the tech stuff at the gigs, asked me to do the spotlight for the night. He asked my bar manager, who said OK, so I hopped up and followed Dickie all over the room for the night with the beam, while also trying to avoid Willy the Wire crawling between chairs and auld ones' legs at the same time.

The night ended. Dickie did an amazing job – he was such a hero, that man. Terry loved how I operated the spotlight. I remember the conversation afterwards in the bar with him clearly.

He told me that a mate of his, Dieter, had opened a lighting company, and they were looking for people to work in the warehouse, load trucks, fix lights and get orders ready. He gave me Dieter's number. I rang it the next day. He asked me to come into Long Lane in Dublin to Lighting Dimensions for an interview.

I put the phone down.

BOOM.

This was the start of the rest of my new life.

CHAPTER 7
5-4-3-2-1

'OK, so this is the warehouse, here are the cable racks, these are all the lighting racks, and down there is all the trussing that the lights go on. Your bench will be here, where you'll get orders ready for bands, fashion shows and conferences. We hire lights out to all walks of life,' explained Dieter, one of the bosses of Lighting Dimensions, as he walked me around the warehouse.

BANG! 'Bastard!'

'Oh, and that's John down in the corner there. He's a type of genius, our electronic engineer, but he tends to blow himself up a lot working on side projects.'

BANG! 'Bastard!'

'Morning, John!' Dieter shouted down to a long-haired hippie-looking fella, with glasses and a fag in his mouth, as he went in on a live, open electronics board with a soldering iron.

'This is Jason,' howled Dieter.

'Couldn't give a fuck,' mumbled John, fag in mouth, long hair hanging either side of his face, waiting to be set on fire by the fag.

BANG! 'Bastard!'

'Don't mind him, he's a good soul, really. He's had too many shocks, that's all,' explained Dieter. 'We call him Electron John.' Dieter continued, 'These Portakabins are the offices. As you can see, in here we have Bernard, lighting designer, and Andrew, also a lighting designer. They are also bosses of Lighting Dimensions. And Angie, our secretary.'

I got a wave from Angie. Andrew was looking intense on the phone. Bernard had some sort of design out in front of him, with a *Times* newspaper laid out on top of it. It looked like he was designing a lighting rig but at the same time doing a crossword. Two Great Dane dogs lay by his feet. They were called AC and DC, and Bernard brought them everywhere with him.

'So, do you want a job?' Dieter asked there and then.

I said yes and we shook hands. I was now a full-time employee of Lighting Dimensions, a company that wanted me to test lights, repair cables and do all sorts of electronic work. All without a single qualification or piece of paper in electrics.

BANG! 'BASTARD!'

Dad decided to drive me in on the first day. 'Very good, very good, Jay, this job sounds great. Of course, I know a lot about electrics, so if you need any tips, Paddy Byrne is your man,' Dad advised.

THINGS THAT DIDN'T WORK OR DID WEIRD SHIT BECAUSE DAD GOT HIS HANDS ON THEM

1. The downstairs hall light switch operated the upstairs landing lights.
2. The main wall switch for the cooker killed all sockets in the living room.
3. The fuse board would go on fire twice a week if you boiled the kettle too much.
4. Immersion switched to bath would heat the sink, switched to sink would heat the bath.
5. All Mam's hairdryers, straighteners, irons, you name it. Mam had her rosary beads in her hand each time she used one.

'Dad, no, it's me first day,' I pleaded as he walked into the warehouse with a box of broken lights.

He plopped them down on my bench. 'Look, just get to them when you get to them.' Off he ran out of the warehouse like Fagin from *Oliver Twist*.

'Man, welcome to the bench, weeellcome,' a soft, slow voice said to me.

'Yeah, welcome, my name is Steve and this is Eoghan.' Eoghan had a ciggy hanging out of his mouth and Steve was sucking on an old man's pipe. These were my new co-workers. Steve and Eoghan were roughly the same age as me, both around twenty or so, and also had no experience in electronics. And also had just been interviewed the day before. I was beginning to think that not much qualification was needed for this job. It took a certain type to work here, especially for sixty pound a week after tax!

Eoghan was a rocker-type character, a lovely, gentle man. The other was a good-looking, posh-voiced, floppy-haired dude. Steve had a heart of gold but was as slick as a fox – he always had other stuff going on outside the warehouse. He always had money and always smoked his pipe with a huge grin.

We all stood at a workbench. I was excited to start in this new world. It smelt like my old engineering room in school.

'OK, lads, here's your first order.' Dieter came out and placed an order form on our bench. He went through it. 'Forty par cans, fifteen foot of trussing, pins, cables to accompany par can lights, spot light and stand … John, one lighting desk and power racks!' he roared down to Electron John.

'Fuck off!' answered Electron John, which normally meant OK.

Dieter left. Myself, Steve and Eoghan all looked at each other and burst out laughing. We had no idea what any of this shite was so we grabbed what we thought was being asked of us.

When the truck arrived to collect an amazingly prepped and put-together lighting rig, all there was in the middle of the floor was forty bulbs (they looked like lights on their own they were so big), a bit of scaffolding and seven plug boards.

Electron John then wheeled up his lighting desk and power racks. He stopped at our pile and just looked at us. 'Fucking idiots.' He walked back down to his electronic cave.

Dieter soon ran out in a panic and got most of the gear together himself, while pointing at stuff for us to grab. Looking out from the office was Andrew, still intensely on the phone, Bernard, still drawing up lighting designs while glancing at the crossword with AC and DC lying at his feet, and Angie, with a big smile as she waved to us from the window.

But this time, there was an added extra: Bernard had an African Grey on his shoulder. A parrot. It went by the name of Amp. The thing could talk, too.

Bernard told us that at home the parrot entertained itself by tormenting the dogs. The parrot would normally be in its cage in the kitchen. The parrot had heard Bernard calling the dogs in from the living room when he had their dinner ready. So when the parrot was bored, it would call the dogs into the kitchen.

'Here, boys, here, boys, AC, DC, your dinner!' the parrot would squawk. But there was no food for the poor fools.

Amp would do this a lot to the dogs in the warehouse. If Bernard walked out onto the floor with Amp on his shoulder, all we'd hear through the warehouse was 'Here, boys, here, boys, your dinner!' as two Great Danes came bounding out of the office, knocking over everything as they ran towards Amp's voice, dragging a light connected to a cable to its destruction.

'I need to go, I'm double parked,' moaned the truck driver who was to collect the order that we – well, Dieter – had put together. We now had flight cases full of lights and cables that we needed to load up the ramp on the back of the truck. Myself, Steve and Eoghan tried with not much strength to load them. The truck driver was furious as we piled all the flight cases in the wrong order.

There was one last case to go. I pulled it up the ramp as Eoghan pushed it. I then heard the driver screaming to Eoghan as I and the flight case entered the truck: 'Tilt it, tilt it!'

Eoghan and the driver tilted the case up on its end, wedging me into the corner of the truck. I thought it was a joke till I heard the doors close, the truck start, then move off.

What the fuck? Where was I going? I roared me head off in the back, but no one heard me. Then, finally, the truck stopped. It had arrived at the National Stadium on South Circular Road.

The doors opened and the waiting crew began to unload the truck. The case that was blocking me in now fell down in front of me. The fella who had pulled down the case to reveal me got the shock of his life.

'Whaaa? Hello … are … you … alright?' he asked, as if I didn't speak English. I'm pretty sure he thought I was a refugee.

I walked up to him and past him, as I said, 'I'm alright, are you alright?'

'Yeah, I'm alright,' he said with an open mouth.

'Well, if you're alright, and I'm alright, then we're all alright, alright?' I said as I walked off into the distance, all confident, with my arms swinging, as if I hid in trucks for a living.

Thank God it was only the South Circular Road and the warehouse was in Long Lane, beside the Meath Hospital. It only took me fifteen minutes to walk back.

Steve and Eoghan had no idea where I'd gone. I walked up to Eoghan and told him that he had jammed me into the van. He burst out laughing, as did Steve. Steve suggested that we gaffer-tape Eoghan and throw him in a skip for being so silly. We laughed. Then me and Steve stopped laughing and slowly moved in on Eoghan, gaffer tape in hand.

Cut to Eoghan being completely gaffer-taped from head to toe – I mean, he was mummified. We lifted him up and threw him into the skip in the corner of the warehouse, among wood and rubbish. A cloud of dust formed in the air as he landed.

This was to become a tradition in Lighting Dimensions.

OCCASIONS YOU WOULD BE GAFFER-TAPED AND THROWN INTO THE SKIP IN THE CORNER OF THE WAREHOUSE

1. Birthday.
2. New member of staff.
3. If your girlfriend was on her way in to collect you.
4. If it was really busy and we were asked to have every one of us ready for a big order.
5. If you were a customer who annoyed us.

Dieter once came out of his office stressed to the hilt, as we never did what was asked of us, and we were most likely costing him a fortune with all the messing every day. He stood over the skip with Eoghan wriggling in there for the umpteenth time. 'Lads, that gaffer tape costs a fortune!'

SILENCE.

Cut to Dieter in the skip beside Eoghan, gaffer-taped like a cocooned caterpillar.

How we were not sacked was beyond me. We never stopped messing on the job and barely came in on time.

THE WORK TIMETABLE IN LIGHTING DIMENSIONS

9 a.m. start … we normally sauntered in around 10 a.m.

11 a.m. small break … we would head out and get breakfast sandwiches, or muck sandwiches, as we called them.

11.15 a.m. resume work … we normally started again around 12 noon after we finished our muck sandwiches.

1 p.m. lunch … we'd head out to a pub on Wexford Street, normally Whelan's.

2 p.m. resume work … we'd roll back in around 2.30 p.m., glassy-eyed.

5 p.m. finish … only Dieter would be still there at 5 p.m. – everyone else was gone by 4.30 p.m.

6 p.m. … Dieter would be sweating trying to load a truck on his own …

BANG! 'BASTARD!'

'Don't you ever go home, John?' roared Dieter. 'If you're staying, could you help me with this truck?!'

'Firstly, I have had to move a bed into the loft here because you bastards do not pay me enough to rent even the smallest of shitholes in the area,' answered Electron John. 'Secondly, I do not load trucks, especially after I did my back in last month helping one of your useless little shits.'

★★★

'So, how's it going, son, the new job?' Dad asked as we sat in his shed, him smoking his fag while sipping on his whiskey. He didn't have his usual Perry Como playing, but he had whale noises on a tape recorder going.

'Eh, grand, I suppose – it's a job. What's with the whales, Dad?' I asked.

'The union bosses said we need to remain calm at all times, as we're still very much suffering from TCP after the gas explosion, son,' he explained.

'PTSD,' I corrected.

'Don't you start. I get enough of that from your mother. Anyway, because 60 per cent of us humans is made up of water, we are much happier connected to the sea. We should be in it, as we are it. We are literally like walking seas.' Dad was passing on knowledge he had learnt in the pub. Bollix, in other words.

'So …'

Oh sorry, not finished, more bollix to come.

'… the moon is connected to the Earth, as in the gravitational pull changes the tides. The moon is literally pulling on the seas of the Earth, just like when I have to get in and out of bed all night for a piss when it's a full moon. The moon is trying to drag the piss out of me, the way it drags at the oceans of the globe,' finished Dad, thank jaysus.

'But you're OK otherwise, Dad?' I asked.

'Well, I'm pretty sure I have vertigo now, son. It's one of the side effects of TCP, apparently,' said a man who drank whiskey and Guinness all day. I'd be dizzy too, for jaysus' sake.

CREAK!

Just as Dad said this, the door of the shed flew open. It was Mam with a tray of biccies and tea. 'He doesn't have vertigo, son. The shed is on a slant, so when your father stands up, he gets dizzy as he walks towards the wall there,' explained Mam as she placed the tray down and the cups slid to the edge of the tray. 'I don't know why I bother.'

TIMES YOUR MOTHER DOESN'T KNOW WHY SHE BOTHERS

1. Cooks a full meal that the kids barely eat. 'I don't know why I bother.'

2. Hangs out the washing on the line, then it immediately rains. 'I don't know why I bother.'

3. Mops kitchen floor, then Dad walks in in his dirty boots. 'I don't know why I bother.'

4. Makes all our lunches, including Dad's. We all grab them and leave with not so much as a thank you. 'I don't know why I bother,' said to the dog at her feet.

5. Has her fourth child in the Coombe hospital, with no Dad around again ... screams as she pushes: 'I DON'T KNOW WHY I BOTHER!'

BURP! went Dad after polishing off his last biccie.

'I don't know what I see in that man,' Mam said as she walked away with her tray.

TIMES YOUR MAM DOESN'T KNOW WHAT SHE SEES IN THAT MAN

1. When he farts watching telly. 'I don't know what I see in that man.'

2. When he wipes his mouth with a cushion after a doughnut. 'I don't know what I see in that man.'

3. **When he falls in the door after the pub, singing and cheering. 'I don't know what I see in that man.'**
4. **When he arrives down for breakfast in his white Y-fronts and vest, beer belly sticking out. 'I don't know what I see in that man.'**
5. **When he says, 'I would not, and I mean would not, go in there for at least an hour,' after he has a shit. 'I don't know what I see in that man.'**

'You're the luckiest woman alive, Eithne!' Dad shouted to Mam in the distance as she slammed the kitchen door.

★ ★ ★

Dad had stopped dropping me in to Lighting Dimensions, as he was told not to do too much driving due to his TCP – sorry, now he has me going – his PTSD, which, as we all know, didn't exist. So I had to take the hairdryer that was the Honda Vision moped in to Long Lane.

I arrived at the warehouse and could see Dieter, Andrew, Bernard and Angie all in their offices but Steven and Eoghan were missing. I guessed they were late.

'Hey, Jay, over here,' I heard a voice call. Just beside my bench was a stairs to a basement where we would store stuff. Steve and Eoghan had their heads around the door at the top of the stairs, calling me over and down the stairs. 'Look what we did after the late load in last night,' said Steve.

In the corner of the basement, they had made a full bar, with optics, beers in fridges, bottles of whiskey, vodka, you name it, accompanied by old couches that had been down in the basement for years.

'What the fuck?' I said.

'Last night, the truck dude gave us all this booze – he had gotten it from a show he was working on. He didn't drink and said we could have the lot for a hundred quid,' explained Eoghan.

Holy shit. The lads had built a full working bar. We would get away with this for a long time, as none of the bosses would ever go down into the dirt and filth of the basement.

'And look at this, Jay, we found it when we were moving stuff around last night.' Steve pulled across a wooden board to reveal an old well. 'It's a fucking well,' he said excitedly.

It was indeed an open well, and it was terrifying to look into it. Years later, when Lighting Dimensions was being knocked down to build houses, it was found and said to be a Viking well.

'How deep is that?' I asked.

'Oh man, it goes on forever,' said Eoghan.

'How do you know?' I foolishly asked.

Eoghan went over and fetched a sixteen-foot scaffolding pole. He then brought it over to the edge of the well, fed it in really slowly and dropped it. The pole banged off the sides of the well as it fell, but it just kept going. Then, I shit you not, we heard a faint splash in the distance as it hit the water.

'Whoaaa!' we all screamed.

'Holy fuck, cover that back up, lads, that's terrifying,' I said.

'Yeah, that's the sixth one we threw down there too,' laughed Eoghan.

Not a good place to be: in a basement with two mad bastards full of booze, looking down a well that you would never return from if you fell into it.

It was 10 a.m. and myself, Eoghan and Steve were already pissed, pretending to work at our bench while listening to Gerry Ryan on our massive stereo.

Dieter walked over to tell us that they needed to do a stocktake today, and also there would be a new member of staff coming in, so to please tidy up. We loved stocktaking, as we normally spent all day at it and wouldn't do any other work. Well, we never really did any work, so this would just be another way of not working.

To tidy up, I stood up on the bench, which was filthy and covered in shite. Steve handed me up the massive brush, and Eoghan held the bin at the other end. I then brushed all the contents of the bench into the bin. I literally didn't care what was on the bench, in it went, me full of whiskey dancing on said bench.

Dieter, the poor soul, then came out, saw how quicky we had tidied, and checked the bin.

CONTENTS OF THE BIN

1. Set of really good screwdrivers.
2. Three wire snips.
3. Endless washers and screws.
4. A drill.
5. A twenty-pound note.
6. Steve's pipe. 'Oh, there is it – thanks, Dieter.'
7. Order forms for later on that day.
8. A mirrorball.
9. Seventeen brand-new plugs.
10. Only set of keys to the bolt locks for the front warehouse door.

Dieter was furious but we could not stop sniggering. 'You lot were supposed to stocktake too. Now I see why our stock is all over the place: it's in the fucking bin. I also have to go and order six sixteen-foot scaffolding poles that are missing. Now, I know you lot couldn't have lost those, they're too big, so I'll ring around. They've probably been left out on a job. And stop using up my gaffer tape on your childish antics,' roared poor auld Dieter as he walked back to the Portakabins.

We stood in a line like bold schoolboys, trying not to laugh at the thought of six sixteen-foot poles at the bottom of a Viking well downstairs.

'Oh, by the way, this is PJ. He starts today, so look after him,' added Dieter, pointing to a sixteen-year-old boy standing at the warehouse door in a hoody with weird dreads hanging out of his head.

'Oh, sure, we'll look after PJ,' I said.

Cut to Dieter helping PJ out of the skip, completely mummified in gaffer tape.

PJ said very little and was really quiet for a long time, so we gaffer-taped him and threw him in the skip a lot. One day, he decked Steve in the head as we came towards him. Fair play. No more gaffing PJ in the skip.

The crew on the floor was now me, Steve, Eoghan, PJ and Electron John. Until one day …

BANG!

All the lights went out, but this time there was no …

'BASTARDS!'

Electron John was trying to build the brightest strobe ever – you know, the flashing ones that normally have one bulb. He had tried to wire up five very strong bulbs, and for this he needed a lot of power. This time, it was too much and he was lifted in the air and planted against the back wall. We rang an ambulance for Electron John. It turned out he was OK, but he was never to be seen again.

He was then replaced by Larry from Kilkenny. We all welcomed our new member of staff in ... well, into the skip ... fully gaffed.

I feel the warehouse was the start of my comedy career. We laughed and joked so much that prepping the lights and getting the orders ready for the shows were secondary to our hilarious antics. Well, they were hilarious to us, not to the bosses.

One day we decided that HAT HOUR would be introduced. The concept of this was that between 3 p.m. and 4 p.m. you had to make a hat out of anything you could. The main rule was that you could not mention or refer to the hat once it was on your head. Especially to customers, as we loaded their trucks or cars.

My hat one day was the casing of a light with a coloured sheet of lighting gel as a visor. I looked like something out of *Blade Runner*. Steve came onto the floor with a mop head taped to his head, accompanied by his smoking pipe. Eoghan had plugs all tied into his long hair by Steve. He got in a little trouble for this, as it wasn't technically a hat. PJ sported a plunger on his head with 'just been pulled out of the shitter' written on it in marker.

There was nothing funnier than loading up a truck wearing plungers, plugs, parts of lights and mops on your head, stinking of whiskey, also totally ignoring all of this while you're doing it. Oh, and we added in posh accents for no reason.

We really pissed off one angry truck driver. We would hear him saying to his helper in the truck, 'Just ignore these mad bastards. Let them load the truck and say nothing – don't encourage them.'

Again, I apologise to all the bosses and Larry for making your lives so hard while we made ours so funny. The fun never stopped. Seriously, I would say working in Lighting Dimensions was the best years of my life.

A lady once backed her car into the warehouse, opened the boot and took a vacuum out. 'OK, I'll leave that with you – it won't suck. I'll maybe collect it next week,' she said as she got back into her car.

And with us being total bastards, we didn't tell her it wasn't a vacuum-fixing place. We kept her hoover, glued all sorts of mad shit on it and taped working disco lights to it. On her return, we plugged it in and it looked like something from *Close Encounters of the Third Kind*.

The woman was in shock as we loaded the vacuum into her car and sent her on her way, telling her it was right as rain now. Would love to have been a fly on the wall when she returned to her husband and plugged the UFO in, still not sucking, of course, but turning the front room into a disco all the same.

NOTE: Could that lady return the disco lights to Lighting Dimensions, or at least to Dieter, as they are missing from the stocktake.

OTHER MAD SHITE DROPPED IN TO US

1. Very often flat tyres, both bike and car.
2. Cars driven in and left; they thought we were mechanics.
3. Hospital supplies (the warehouse was beside the Meath Hospital); we either ate or sold these.
4. Once a whole pallet of wine (thought we were Musgrave's, the cash and carry, as it was just down the road). Lorry returned very swiftly, but not before we'd stocked up our basement bar.
5. Four tonnes of bricks, which we let a truck unload. He asked if we were Chadwicks, the builders' suppliers. We, full of whiskey, sporting new hats on a Friday, said yes and told him to put them in front of Dieter's office door. The truck left, and Dieter and the bosses spent all day getting in and out of their office windows, furious.

Then came the big one. On our way into the warehouse one day, myself and PJ had found piles of magazines in a bin. They had cassettes attached to the front of them, so we grabbed a load and brought them in. I popped one into the stereo and pressed play. The song was '5-4-3-2-1' by Manfred Mann (I suggest you go find this song now to actually understand how annoying it is).

We turned the stereo up as loud as we could …

5-4-3-2-1!

… the song started, and that was basically the lyrics for the whole song. As soon as it ended, we immediately pressed play again …

5-4-3-2-1!

We played the song non-stop for three hours, again, and again, and again …

5-4-3-2-1!

Finally, Dieter came bounding out of the office. He went up to the stereo, grabbed the cassette and smashed it with a hammer on our bench, much to the dismay of four Mexicans, as we had decided to dress as Mexicans that day, complete with sombreros.

Dieter marched back into his office. We waited about thirty minutes, then …

5-4-3-2-1!

… roared Manfred Mann from the stereo. We had loads of tapes from the magazines, so it didn't matter how many were broken: we were stocked up.

Dieter opened his office door once more with his coat in his hands, got into his red Golf and sped off, to the sound of …

5-4-3-2-1!

… and four Mexicans screaming, 'Hey, gringo, why you leave us?'

CHAPTER 8
WE NEARLY WON THE LOTTO

'I need a bigger kitchen. I can't feckin' work in this matchbox,' said Mam for the millionth time.

'Sure, didn't I move the sink to the wall, Eithne,' said Dad.

Mam and Dad were sitting in the kitchen. We had all just had breakfast at the kitchen table. Dad was reading his newspaper, Rachel was reading her *Jackie* magazine, and Eithne was moving the stickers on a Rubik's cube to make one side the same colour.

SCRAAAATCH!

(You know, the sound effect they use for a needle dragging across vinyl to indicate that what you've just heard is not true?)

We never had a table in the kitchen. Firstly, it would never have fitted. Our semi-detached houses in Ludford Drive were not designed for dinner parties in any room.

Downstairs, there was a front room with a three-piece suite wedged into it. The door never opened fully because there was a leather sofa stopping it. At the back, the good room. Nobody went into it, as it was the good room. Hall with phone table. Spiral staircase installed to make room for phone table.

The front door would open and bang into the hanging light above. My dad used to shout, 'Lift it, lift the bloody light as you open the door.' No shit, if we were bringing in shopping or something, we had to open our front door slowly, squeeze around it to the other side then lift the light up into the air to open the door fully.

All Dad had to do was chop it down and maybe put a ceiling light in there. 'Do you know how much ceiling lights are?! They need a transformer, replastering … No, you can all lift the light when you open the door – sure, that costs nothing!' he'd say.

I'm pretty sure if he didn't go to the pub for a week, that would have been enough money to get someone in to fit the light. 'A week not in a pub? Sure, I've TCP, I need me pint to calm me down,' Dad would confirm … again … jaysus.

Sorry, back to eating around the kitchen table.

As I said, we never had a kitchen table. My mam would be in the kitchen peeling spuds into the sink while having a shouted conversation with my dad who was in the front room watching the telly. All the doors were left open so we could hear each other. My sister Rachel was normally upstairs in her room, door open …

'RACHEL, WHAT TIME ARE YOU GOING OUT TO YOUR FRIENDS?' Mam would shout from the kitchen up to Rachel.

'6.30!' Rachel would shout back down.

'EITHNE, WHERE ARE YOU, LOVE?' howled Mam.

'I'M OUT IN THE BACK GARDEN PLAYING WITH THE CAT!' Eithne would roar into the open kitchen window.

'OK!' Mam would roar back.

'I'M IN MY ROOM!' I'd roar before Mam would ask.

'NOBODY ASKED YOU,' Mam would shout back.

RING RING RING!

'PHONE!' Dad roars from the living room.

'I'M BUSY!' shouts Mam. 'RACHEL!'

Rachel runs down the stairs and answers the phone. 'IT'S ERIC FROM SWEDEN!' Rachel tells us all.

'TELL HIM I'M BUSY AND I LOVE HIM,' shouts Mam.

'*COUNTDOWN* IS ON BUT TELL HIM HI!' shouts Dad.

'TELL ERIC I'M PLAYING WITH THE CAT,' Eithne shouts in the kitchen window from the garden.

'YEAH, HI,' I shout from my room.

'OK, I'LL TELL HIM,' shouts Rachel. 'They all say hi.' Rachel then hangs up.

Dad walks into the kitchen. 'Is the food ready, Eithne?'

'Not yet, have a biccie.'

'What is that noise?' Dad asks as he opens the back door. 'Jesus, it's next door, all roaring at each other – you'd think they'd keep it down.' He closes the door on a very similar family to ours, communicating through their un-soundproofed house.

'I can still hear them,' Dad says as he shuts the kitchen window.

It would make no difference whatsoever – all our windows were single glazed. Open or closed, you could hear everything. Open or closed, cold still got in. The only use windows had in those days was looking in or out of.

You know that moment in movies where the camera climbs into the sky above thousands of houses, and we hear thousands of conversations, people all chatting to each other on their phones?

Well, if you did that in Ludford, you would hear families, not on the phones, just roaring from room to room … You'd hear them from space.

'Gather around, children, here it is.'

Dad was just back in from the pub with cod and chips. He had rung from the pub, telling Mam, 'Heat the plates, Eithne. I'm bringing home chips!' We had just finished eating.

'Gather around, children and mother,' he said again. Dad was leaning on the table in the good room, which didn't fit in there either and was normally against one wall with two chairs on the other side. Myself, Rachel, Eithne and Mam all looked on.

Dad had a building plan rolled out on the table. Every time Dad was in a good mood, he would order cod and chips, but our punishment was to listen to him again about …

'The side extension, kids, here it is: the answer to all our dreams.' He looked down on the plans as if he was Indiana Jones discovering where the Holy Grail was hidden. 'These plans will allow us to extend this house. Finally, we will have the room we need.'

Now Dad was on a *Braveheart* rant.

'No longer will we sit on top of each other while watching telly, no longer will we eat dinner on our laps, and when we fight, we will no longer have to go to the other end of the couch. We will have a room to run into, a door to close, and it will be, wait for it … SOUNDPROOFED.' Dad stood back with his arms in the air, expecting a round of applause.

Silence.

'Well, why won't you build it, or at least give me a bigger kitchen, Paddy? We have the money from Guinness's, your "was nearly in an explosion" compensation,' quizzed Mam.

'Eithne, I have already told you all this. If we use that money to start building the extension or your kitchen, the phone will not stop ringing, nor will the doorbell. Everyone will assume that we have won the Lotto, and we will be inundated with callers, never mind that bollix of a priest up the road!'

STUFF WE COULDN'T HAVE BECAUSE PEOPLE WOULD THINK THAT WE HAD WON THE LOTTO

1. New curtains ('You may as well write "won the Lotto" on them').
2. New car ('They'll think you've won the Lotto if you drive in here in a Ritmo').

3. **New handbag for Mam ('They'll think you won the Lotto and most of it is in that bag!').**
4. **King Charles dog ('Are you joking? They'll think we won the Lotto. I've a half-breed from Jacko in work on its way').**
5. **Haircuts for all the family at the same time ('Sure, that's Lotto-winner carry-on').**

Dad had had these plans made up for years. The side room would go along the side of the house in the driveway, not even the full length of the house, just from the front to the kitchen door. It was about eight feet wide and about fifteen feet long. Extension, me hoop.

Well, you will not believe what happened next.

I arrived in from work one day. It was summer, and a nice hot one at that. I walked into the kitchen to Mam and asked where Dad was. Over an armful of washing, she pointed to the garden.

My dad was in a suit, walking up and down the path, hands behind his back. He even had a cravat on – where in the name of jaysus did he get that?

'What is he doing, Mam?'

'I don't know, but he's asked me to make a lunch for us all outside on the good plastic garden furniture.'

(I once bought garden furniture for my own house. I told my mother on the phone and she was so excited. Was it green or white? I told her it was wooden – she lost her shit with excitement. 'Wooden? Oh Jesus, wooden garden furniture! Wait till I tell the girls at Mass.')

'He says he has an announcement for us all,' continued Mam.

We all went outside: me, Rachel, Eithne, Mam and Eric. Dad had asked Mam to ring Eric in Sweden, bring the phone out to the garden and lay the receiver on the table. The wire barely reached. Eric now always seemed to be in the shape of a phone. We had a phone for a brother.

'Please be seated,' said Dad in a weird posh accent, while wearing his suit and cravat.

We all sat down, phone receiver on the table.

'Are you still there, Eric?' Dad shouted.

'Yes,' came the muffled, confused voice.

'I have an announcement to make,' said Dad.

'Oh great,' said Mr Murphy from next door, over the hedge.

'Fuck off, Alan,' Dad said to Mr Murphy.

'Fair enough.' Mr Murphy disappeared.

We all looked on in wonder as Dad started again. 'I, Paddy Byrne ...

(yes)

have ...

(yes!)

won the ...

(YES!)

Lotto ...'

YEEESSSS!

We all jumped up in the air, screaming. I hugged Rachel. My mam grabbed Eithne and started to dance around with her. You could hear Eric whooping on the phone all the way from Sweden.

'... nearly ...'

WHAT?!

'Yes, nearly,' said Dad.

'Sorry, Paddy, what are you saying? Have you or have you not won the Lotto?!' asked Mam as we all stopped dancing.

'Kinda. I nearly won,' explained Dad.

'How can you nearly win the Lotto?'

'Well, I got five numbers out of six. We get £2,500 for that,' Dad said with joy.

We all started dancing around again, chanting, 'We nearly won the Lotto, we nearly won the Lotto!'

'Pints on you tonight, Paddy,' said Mr Murphy over the hedge.

'Fuck off, Alan,' Dad said again in a posh accent.

'Fair enough, and well done, Paddy.' Alan disappeared behind the wall once more.

Mam picked up the phone. 'Isn't that great, Eric? Your dad nearly won the Lotto! Hello? Hello?'

Eric had gone, most likely not excited by the news about nearly winning the Lotto.

'But one thing is for sure, lads,' said Dad. 'We'll be spending the money on the house. What with my compensation for TCP and nearly winning the Lotto, it's all go now. We'll just have to hide it, that's all,' explained Dad.

'A new kitchen, finally?' asked Mam.

'No, it will be the side room!'

Myself, Rachel and Eithne kept singing, 'We nearly won the Lotto, we nearly won the Lotto, we're going to get a side room, we're going to get a side room!'

Mam walked off, disgusted. I could hear her say, 'I'll get me own kitchen, the auld bollix.'

'Where's your mother?' asked Dad.

We were all sitting in the living room waiting for our dinner. It was nearly five o'clock and Mam still wasn't back.

We were watching those weird public information films that were on during the ads, insane infomercials showing ways to keep people safe. Dad especially liked the one where Grandad went missing. They had footage of a family picnicking at the side of the river. For some reason, Grandad was sitting on his own on a deck chair looking into the water. The voiceover warned: 'Do not let old people near open water without being accompanied by a responsible adult.'

Dad would burst out laughing when the camera spun around to the family having a picnic, then back to an empty chair with Grandad missing.

'Where's Grandad?!' the grandson would scream.

'Grandad has fucked off to the pub 'cause you lot are boring shites,' answered Dad, laughing at himself.

These commercials ran on our tellies for years. I reckon Dad laughed at them all, and why not? They were so over the top, the brainchild of some mad politician from Longford. Dad thought anything mad or unusual came from Longford, even though he had never been there himself.

OTHER PUBLIC SAFETY ADS

1. A nun screaming as loud as she could into a deaf child's ear to show that meningitis can cause deafness. She would famously shout 'Bawww! BAWWW!' (Dad used to sneak up behind us in the house and roar 'BAWWW!' We'd jump out of our skins, and he'd laugh and say, 'Well, you don't have meningitis.')

2. Kids playing frisbee near a power station. The frisbee gets thrown towards the power lines and a kid goes in to get it. He climbs the pylon, gets electrocuted and is flung off into the air. (Dad thought this was hilarious. He would say, 'Well, whoever owns him has a Rice Crispy for a son now,' followed by loud laughter. I suppose the way it was shot was pretty funny.)

3. We see a man falling asleep watching the telly with a cigarette in his hand. It falls to the ground and burns his

whole living room down. ('That would never happen to me. I always make sure I have me basin of water for me feet to the side so I can drop the fags in there.' He really did this, by the way.)

4. A shot of a man's hand changing gears in an old Escort. The voice says, as the man changes gears really fast, 'One, two, three – don't have that fourth pint.' (It was a drink-driving ad telling lads not to drive after three pints. I mean, they're all battered by three pints. I remember me dad coming in from the pub one evening, moaning that they had just passed a law saying you could only have two pints max while driving. 'Mother of jaysus, have you heard, Eithne, two pints max? They're trying to stop us enjoying ourselves. Soon we won't be able to drink and drive at all – how the fuck will we get home from the pub?' Notice Dad didn't ask 'How will we get to the pub', mainly because getting to the pub was never a problem, it was getting home when they were locked that was the issue. I would often hear my dad say, 'Thank God I drove home from the pub last night. I would have ended up in a bush!')

5. A kid playing near a paddling pool in his back garden. The mother goes to answer the phone, then looks out the window and sees the kid's legs sticking out of the pool, face down. ('Hey, missus, your doll fell in the pool,' Dad would howl, as they were obviously a pair of doll's legs with booties.)

BANG!

The front door closes and Mam walks in.

'Where's the dinner, Eithne? We're all starving,' Dad bravely said to Mam.

'Sure, you've loads of money now, Paddy, with your PTSD and Lotto win, you can hire a bleedin' maid.' Mam headed to the kitchen.

The following morning, the builders were to start on the side extension. Dad was, of course, up the walls, as he didn't want the neighbours all watching what was going on. So he asked the builders to arrive at 5 a.m. while it was still dark. Dad had me up to help him and the builders unload all the materials into the back garden before anyone saw us.

The truck backed into the driveway with the loudest beeping ever. Dad was pleading with the driver to shut up as curtains began to twitch around the road. It was Dad's mate Vinny Byrne – of course the builder was going to be one of Dad's drinking mates, and more than likely would be paid in large bottles of Guinness along with some cash.

Finally, we got all the materials into the back garden. Bricks, sand, shovels, cement mixer, windows. Then Vinny and Dad went back out to the front, assembled a quick bit of scaffolding, then pulled out a large piece of tarpaulin and hung it from the scaffold. This acted as a screen so no one would know what we were building. Vinny then headed off, saying he'd be back later to start with a few lads.

Dad came inside and swore us all to secrecy: we were never to tell anyone what was going on behind the tarpaulin.

Of course, this was a housing estate in Ludford, Ballinteer.

DING DONG!

'Hi, Missus Byrne, could you please tell me what's going on behind the blue tarpaulin?' Mrs Murphy asked at the door.

'Oh, eh …' tried Mam.

'It's a new swimming pool – tell her to piss off!' Dad politely shouted from the living room, much to the embarrassment of my mam.

A LIST OF DING DONGS TO THE HOUSE

1. *DING DONG:* 'My son's football went over your wall, may I go out the back and get it?' DAD SLAMS DOOR.
2. *DING DONG:* 'Couldn't help but notice ...' DAD SLAMS DOOR.
3. *DING DONG:* 'I was in the area ... ' DAD SLAMS DOOR.

4. *DING DONG:* 'My sister is very sick, and as a dying wish would love to know what is behind the blue tarpaulin ...' DAD SLAMS DOOR.

5. *DING DONG:* 'Hi, I'm Father Declan, your parish priest ...' DAD SLAMS DOOR, then immediately opens the door again. 'Sorry, only joking, Father, come in.' DAD SLAMS DOOR A SECOND TIME AS THE PRIEST ATTEMPTS TO COME IN. 'Wasn't joking, prick.'

To make tensions even higher, news was spreading that someone local had won £2.5 million on the Lotto. All eyes were beginning to land on the Byrnes.

The mystery of what was going on behind the blue tarpaulin was spreading around Ballinteer too. Dad would have been better off just leaving the tarpaulin off and letting people know. There's nothing worse than hiding stuff from the Irish. He was adding fuel to the fire with all this.

At Mass, Father Declan said that he wished Mr and Mrs Byrne the best of luck in their new venture, whatever it was, and that we would all be praying for them. The priest and churchgoers looked at my mam with beady eyes. My mam had to leave Mass early as she was being quizzed outside as to what was behind the tarpaulin.

Then, of course, my dad's nightmare came true. With the bits of information the locals had about Dad, his compensation claim from Guinness's and nearly winning the Lotto, someone had written an article.

LOCAL MAN WINS £2.5 MILLION LOTTO WHILE ALSO RECEIVING COMPENSATION FROM A BLAST HE BRAVELY SURVIVED AT WORK

That was the bleedin' headline in the local *Southside* newspaper. There was our house on the front cover, along with the tarpaulin in all its glory with a question mark over it.

'Jesus Christ, Eithne, what in the name of God did you tell people?' Dad roared from the living room.

'I didn't say a bleedin' thing to anyone!' she roared back from the kitchen.

'Well, we're bollixed now. They think we won the Lotto. I mean, why do they think that?!' Dad wondered as he stared at the headline in the *Southside*. 'Where in the name of jaysus are they getting £2.5 million from?'

★★★

'Now, lads, you're me best mates – not a word to anyone, but I nearly won the Lotto, five numbers I got, but not a word to anyone,' Dad slurred into the group at the bar.

Dad and Mam on their honeymoon in Monte Carlo in 1966.

The lads – Brian, Ciarán and Damo – all came over to me mam's house to see the beautiful Pamela before the Debs. Me, looking proud as punch, in the middle. My sister Rachel with a perm from hell was thrown in at the end.

Myself and Ken Newman at our Debs in the Sands Hotel in Portmarnock in 1989. Ken was with me in school, and in life. He has never aged, and works in Supervalu with my sister Eithne now.

Myself and Peter on holidays in Salou. Best fun ever. Dad finally brought us all there, but just kept saying we wouldn't enjoy it.

Me, my first serious girlfriend, Rachel, and my dad's best friend, Pat Reid, in Ballinteer House around 1992. Rachel was always smiling, was great craic, and had the best bounce as she walked.

Oh, *yeah* – cool Jay on the steps of Trinity College. Lighting Dimensions were providing the lights for the Trinity Ball. We installed the lights, drank and danced all night, then took them all down in the early hours.

One of many letters that my mam, pretending to be a fan of my work, sent to TV and radio stations. She once got a bus to Gerry Ryan's house in Clontarf and posted a letter through his door, asking would he please mention Jason Byrne on his radio show. Notice how Mam had misspelt 'O'Brien'.

27 Griffith Avenue
Dublin.

Dear Sirs,
We have just finished watching your wonderful programme from the children's hospital which was a great idea, and must have been wonderful for the sick children. The reason I am writing is because of this guy Jason Byrne, he really made us all laugh while we were having our breakfast. Please please can we have more of him and why is he not presenting on T.V.3, we love T.V.3 and don't even switch on R.T.E. because its boring. So go ahead give us more of this guy.
Many Thanks
The O'Brian Family.

The Swedish Wedding. Gittan, Eric the Phone, and me dressed like a car salesman, with a random Swedish child and Eithne at the front. This was 1993, I think.

No idea where this is, but pretty sure I was twelve years old, at home babysitting my sisters, while these two went on the lock again. 'Never let your children get in the way of your social life,' Dad would say. And they didn't … ever! Notice that the chairs they're sitting on were plastic school chairs, and there were clearly no staff to clear tables – it was either a Sinn Féin meeting or a shit wedding.

The beginning of the press and audition shots as I entered the world of showbiz. This was 1997. I'm pretty sure I was in agony trying to get into that unnatural position. 'Any movies for a fella that can't sit in a chair properly?'

Dad brought me to his retirement lunch in Guinness's. God knows why I was there – I was the only son or daughter to be brought. Don't know where I got the suit. In the front row at the far-left is another of my dad's good friends, Tony, or Uncle Tony to us. He even looked like a mafia boss.

Me and Mam dancing at my wedding. She was always grabbing me in the kitchen for a spin.

Myself and Dad holding my first son, Devin, in Clontarf. 2000 was the year. Dad always did this pose for the camera – the old-fashioned point.

What a pic. Ken Doherty agreed to play snooker with my dad, Paddy Mac Breen and Pat Reid for Dad's 70th. They played in Ken's private training room at the Radisson Hotel in Stillorgan. The lads had no idea where they were going or who they were meeting, till I knocked on the door and Ken Doherty opened it. The lads spent all day taking the balls out of the pockets for Ken.

Mam, Dad, Eric the Phone, Rachel, Eithne, Azita (Eric's partner from Sweden), Max, Jessica and Alex. My son Daniel is right beside me, as always, like the little puppy he is.

The Paddy Lama in his natural habitat: the garden shed, with fags, whiskey and red lemo. Surrounded by broken shit that he was always getting to. Dad used to say, 'Sure, what do I need? I have everything I want in here, there's no need to complicate life.'

'You won the fucking Lotto, Paddy?' asked a locked Pat.

'No, five numbers,' corrected Dad.

'You won five zeros on the Lotto? Holy shit, Paddy!' joined in a plastered Charlie.

'No, not five zeros, £2.5 I won,' slurred Dad even more.

DING DING DING!

'Drinks are on Paddy Byrne – he won £2.5 million on the Lotto,' roared the barman to the pub, while pulling on the last-orders bell, as he had been eavesdropping.

'I have in me bollix!' Dad roared back.

RING RING RING!

'Hello, this is St Mary's of the Weeping Wound. We are in desperate need of a new bell for our church …'

CLICK.

'Ah jaysus, I can't take this anymore, Eithne. I'm plugging out the phone and the jaysus answering machine. A bell for their

church, I'll give them a bell for their church alright!' moaned
Dad.

NOTE: Just to clarify, when an Irish person says they'll give you
what you're asking for in a certain tone, they have no intention
of giving you anything at all. As in, my dad saying 'I'll give you
a bell alright'. In fact, he means that instead of a bell he'll give
the nuns something else, normally a punch. But he would never
punch a nun.

LIST OF STUFF YOUR DAD WOULD 'GIVE YOU ALRIGHT!'

1. Can I have a new bike, Dad? 'I'll give you a new bike
   alright.'
2. Dad, can I have a fiver? 'I'll give you a fiver alright.'
3. Dad, I'm unwell, I can't go to school. 'I'll give you unwell.'
4. Terry Jones got new Levi's. 'I'll give ye Levi's.'
5. Dad, can I watch *Scooby-Doo*? 'I'll give ye cartoons.'

I think you get the idea.

Anyway, it was a nightmare for Dad. The building continued
at the side of the house. Dad still wouldn't tell people what it
was, until one Saturday morning we woke up and there were
neighbours all outside the house looking in. A storm had blown
in overnight and the tarpaulin was gone, so people could now
see the extension.

Also, that day they revealed the actual winner of the £2.5 million Lotto. Dad was delighted, but also not, as it was a neighbour on another road.

'Yes, we are so happy, we can't believe it!' said the winners as they were being interviewed on *RTÉ News*.

'Jammy bastards, I know them, they wouldn't give you the steam off their piss, but will they be happy? Look at what happened to us when people thought we won it,' said Dad.

The heat was off the Byrnes. Also, everyone now knew what Dad was building. They didn't believe he'd won the Lotto anymore, but they knew he defo had a few bob from somewhere.

By the way, during all the work, Mam was being very quiet for some odd reason. She didn't get involved at all. Something was up and I was worried.

One day I came home on me hairdryer moped from Lighting Dimensions. I walked into the house and Mam was on her own in the kitchen with some man in a suit. As soon as I arrived in, Mam was being all weird. She introduced the man to me as Tom. Tom got his coat and briefcase. 'I'll be in touch, Mrs Byrne,' he said, as he left in a hurry. I asked Mam who that was and she said he was a census man.

Could Mam have been having an affair?!

No way, literally none of our mothers had affairs in those days. They just didn't have the time for an affair.

ONLY WAYS YOUR MAM COULD HAVE AN AFFAIR

1. Get kids up for school, have an affair under the stairs while they have breakfast.
2. Kids head off to school, have an affair while hoovering, putting washes on and making the beds.
3. With all the washing on and hoovering done, have an affair while ironing the washed clothes non-stop for hours.
4. Ironing done, have an affair smelling of cat and dog while cleaning and feeding them.
5. All chores done, about to have an affair, kids all arrive home. Now work till you're dead on your feet at 10 p.m.

But what was Mam up to?

RING RING RING.

'Hello? Yes? Oh, that's fabulous news!' Mam then put the phone down with a huge grin on her face. 'I got the loan!' she screamed.

Mam had applied for a credit union loan for a new conservatory, so her kitchen could extend and be bigger.

'A new conservatory and a side room, now people will defo think something is up,' roared Dad in the living room.

'How in the name of jaysus did you find out about the conservatory?' asked Mam.

'Terry Murphy told me today, said he heard it in Mass.'

'But Terry Murphy doesn't go to Mass – none of your mates go to Mass,' said Mam.

'He does now. He's a big auld one since his wife died, drinks gin and tonic and all now,' replied Dad.

'Bloody Mass,' sighed Mam.

'Also, best of luck to Eithne Byrne with her new conservatory, and her now nearly finished side room,' said Father Declan in a packed church to a rumble and shuffle of arses on pews. The crowd were far from happy with this news, thinking, 'Who the hell do the Byrnes think they are?'

My mam didn't have a clue how he knew until she spotted the manager of the credit union, Ms Quinn, nodding at the priest.

'That bitch Ms Quinn tells that priest everything,' said Mam.

Apparently, Ms Quinn approved all the loans. She knew exactly who was applying for what and would then pass that info on to her beloved priest.

Ms Quinn was one of those spinsters that would love to be banging the priest, and I'm sure she was. She headed into confession a little bit too often, as my mam would say.

Do you remember *The Muppet Show* or *Sesame Street?* In the bit I'm thinking of, Kermit the Frog used to report on fairy tales as they happened.

One particular one was Humpty Dumpty. Here, Kermit arrives on the scene as Humpty is smashed on the ground after falling off the wall. There are king's horses and king's men all over the place. It's total chaos as Kermit tries to interview them.

With that general chaos in your head, the next part of the story's atmosphere is at least set.

The side room was finished, and all the builders had left. Now, my mam's conservatory began. My dad didn't want anything to do with it, mainly because he wasn't asked to help with the planning of it in the first place, so he let Mam organise it all.

My mam had been talking to my auntie Cora, who knew some fellas that built and installed conservatories. Now, not builders: SOME FELLAS CORA KNEW.

I remember the SOME FELLAS CORA KNEW arriving in their truck that morning. The SOME FELLAS CORA KNEW unloaded the conservatory frame over the back wall. They couldn't get to the side of the house because of the new side room, or come through the hall as the frame was too big. So they drove their truck around to the field at the back of our house. They stood on the roof of the truck and unloaded the frame into the garden, scraping and damaging it as they went.

My mam was so stressed, as she could now spot that they had no idea what the fuck they were doing.

I watched as they pulled out the old kitchen window like a protestor ripping down an offensive statue. It was all ropes and pulling and pushing and pulling. Then the SOME FELLAS CORA KNEW began Kango hammering the brickwork around where the window frame was to make a hole for the conservatory entrance. Bricks were being removed by boot. I say boot, but more shoe, as in slip-ons.

While this was happening, SOME OTHER FELLAS CORA KNEW began to mix the cement. You could see they had no idea what was going on, as they were reading the back of the cement sack while arguing with each other.

Poor Mam. Dad was due home at any moment, and there was a massive hole in the wall where the window used to be and some very dodgy brickwork in a circle outside where the frame was to sit.

Dad arrives in from work, looks around at the work and SOME FELLAS CORA KNEW.

CUE KERMIT THE FROG!

Dad starts to run around with his arms flapping in the air as if he was at the scene of a disaster that Kermit would have been reporting on.

He points at the hole in the wall. 'What the fuck is that?'

He goes over to the shit brickwork and begins to kick over the so-called solid wall. 'Who taught you how to make a wall?!'

He then looks at the frame of the conservatory thrown against the back wall with no covering or protection over it. 'Are you lot fucking thick?!'

Well, Dad then gets their tool bags, which were actually sports bags with hammers in them. He gets their Kango hammers and anything he could carry, brings them all through the hall, then fucks all the tools into the front driveway. Then he goes back in, all Kermit the Frog, grabs SOME FELLAS CORA KNEW and pushes them all out of the house.

'Now fuck off and never return here, you useless bastards!'

SLAM!

Dad then sat down, lit a fag and got his breath back.

'But, Paddy, I've already given those lads a deposit, and there's a hole in the kitchen!' cried Mam.

'It's OK, Eithne, I'll finish the job. Bleedin' cowboys,' said Dad.

And he did. Himself and his mate Pat finished off that conservatory on their own. Brickwork and all. When I asked Dad how he knew what to do, his reply was …

'You should know how to do that.'

I would have too, if Dad could have bothered his arse to ever teach me. But now we had a side room and Mam had a bigger kitchen. Well, she had a conservatory off the kitchen that would eventually never be used, as it was freezing in the winter. So the door had to be kept closed or Mam would be cooking in a snorkel jacket. In the summer, it was too hot, so you couldn't sit in it or you'd bake.

192 · Memoirs of a Wonky-eyed Man

TOP USES FOR A CONSERAVTORY

1. **In the summer, you dry your clothes in it.**
2. **In the winter, you store freezer food in it.**

It had a leak in the roof where Dad hadn't sealed it properly. It still has, to this day, a small red bucket in the apex of it to catch the rain.

People used to ask Dad what it was. 'It's character, that's what that is.'

SOME FELLAS CORA KNEW apparently went back to their real jobs – a school janitor, a council road worker and two binmen – but not till they semi-installed conservatories all around Dublin. They actually ended up on the telly on a programme called *Cowboys of Ireland*.

> DAD/KERMIT THE FROG (watching the telly): Look, Eithne, look, those bastards SOME FELLAS CORA KNEW are all over the telly. I can't take this – I'm off up to the shop to do the Lotto …

Dad stood up to leave but immediately sat back down. 'Actually, bollix to that, I'll have a cup of tea and a fig roll,' he decided instead.

There was silence and no movement from my mam or any of us in the room.

Dad jumps up. 'Right, I'll get it myself then. I have to do bloody everything!' he moaned, walking into the kitchen to look after himself, mumbling in the distance …

'Get your own tea, get your own fig rolls, go to work, build a fucking conservatory …'

CHAPTER 9
I'M NOT DOING THAT AGAIN

'But you're funny, Jay – you'll be great. You're a natural performer!' said Brian Roche's sister Louise.

Remember Brian, my good mate from the road and college who asked if everyone was alright all the time?

'Well, if you're alright and I'm alright, then we're all alright, alright?'

Brian's sister was a nurse, and she and her friend Linda were heading off to Romania to look after children with HIV, so they wanted to put on a charity event in the Coach House pub in Ballinteer.

Revelino, a great band headed by Brendan Tallon and Brendan Berry (who went on to be the booker for Vicar Street for years), were to headline the event. Other amazing talent from our road was to join in too, like Joe Dunne, the beautiful singer and musician. Mick Dolan went on to dance in Vienna, jazz ballet and the like. There was a fella who played in the RTÉ orchestra, can't remember his name, and an opera singer at the top of the road. And, of course, me. We were quite the road, Ludford Drive.

All these acts were to perform on the charity night in the back room of the pub. My job was to be the MC and do a bit of comedy in between acts. I was twenty now, and had never done anything like this in my life. Yes, I was fun and funny. But being hilarious among your friends in a pub is totally different from being funny on a stage.

Most of the great comics of the world were not the class clown. They were not funny or loud in their social groups. They were, and are, mostly reclusive, shy characters. Shy? I know, you must be thinking: how can you be shy and stand in front of a crowd?

Easy. Well, it's not easy. Some of these comics ask for a spotlight in their eyes so they cannot see the audience. This way, it feels like you're talking to a wall, and over the wall is the laughter from people you convince yourself are not there.

Many times, I've had people come up to me saying, 'Ah, Mick is hilarious, way funnier than you, he has us all in stiches at work, you should get him up on stage!' This is normally followed by Mick telling me a racist or sexist joke, and all the lads crying laughing, patting him on the back.

Well, once I got a Mick a gig in the International Bar on Wicklow Street when I was MCing. All his mates were there, echoing, 'This is going to be deadly, he is so funny.'

'Ladies and gentlemen, will you all please welcome to the stage Mick Murphy!' I screamed to a round of applause. 'I said … Mick Murphy …' Still no sign of Mick Murphy. Mick Murphy had fucked off, as he was shitting himself, and was never to enter a stage.

Little advice to everyone reading this book: if your mates say you're funny in the pub, nine times outta ten you will die on your arse on a stage in front of total strangers.

Die on your arse —————————————————————

When a room full of people simply stare at you, with no laughter whatsoever.

TIMES YOU WILL DIE ON YOUR ARSE

1. Weddings.
2. All corporate events.
3. Your mam's friend's sixtieth.
4. Your friend's fiftieth.
5. Anywhere that's not designed for comedy.

So when Louise asked me to MC, I was shitting myself. I couldn't go on a stage and make people laugh. I didn't need to be a Mick Murphy. I knew how it worked from the Braemor Rooms – I knew that being on a stage is a craft.

'But the dancing competition, Jason, you were brilliant,' said Louise.

Yes, well, Louise was right. I had indeed entered a dancing competition in Drogheda. It was the funniest, most embarrassing moment of my life. Well, OK, one of them.

Louise was studying to be a nurse in Drogheda, so Brian and myself said we'd go there for the night to visit and have a laugh. These days it takes thirty minutes for me to drive to Drogheda from North County Dublin. Back then, myself and Brian had to go into town to get a bus to Drogheda, so it took three hours or so.

On arrival, Louise told us there was a dancing competition in the nearby nightclub, hosted by a local radio station. First prize was two cinema tickets and a bottle of wine.

The dance competition was freestyle, meaning you could use whatever dance style you liked. I'd always fancied myself as a dancer. I had learnt from my mam, who was a professional ballroom dancer and made me do classes when I was younger. The lads slagged me to death, but I ended up with all the women at discos.

(This is explained in detail in *The Adventures of a Wonky-eyed Boy* – I encourage you to buy it … Just a bit of promo in the middle of the book there.)

I had a disco move I always did in the clubs. You know, where you get people to make a circle around you, and you make a show of yourself. So I gave it a go.

'Ladies and gentlemen, in association with Drogheda FM and the Odeon Lakeside, welcome to the floor, all the way from Dublin … Jason Byrne!'

The DJ howled as I spun onto the floor, wearing my thick-rimmed glasses, black and white checked shirt, chinos with slip-ons accompanied by white socks. I danced to Yazz's 'The Only Way Is Up'.

There weren't many in the nightclub that night as I spun and danced, improvising the whole thing. I looked like Woody's horse Bullseye from *Toy Story*. The music ended, I took a bow and left the floor to Brian and his sister clapping. I was sweating, with steamed-up glasses, thinking I was the bollix.

Anyway, guess what? I lost … to the only other contestant. Turns out there were just two entries. Brian could not stop laughing. I lost to a ballet dancer. This girl came on the floor and performed ballet to Led Zeppelin's 'Stairway to Heaven'. Me bollix, it was shite …

'The cinema tickets and the wine go to our ballet dancer, Aoife.' (That wasn't her name, but she danced like a feckin' Aoife.) 'A big thank you to all our other contestants!'

There were three claps in the room. All the other contestants, what was he on about? Turns out the DJ was recording himself and this soundbite would go out on Drogheda FM. He didn't want the sponsors to know the dancing competition was a shite idea, with a fella from Dublin in his Sunday best and Aoife the *Swan Lake* madzer as the only contestants.

So purely based on this, and because I was a funny fella in the pub (which is, as I explained earlier, an absolute cardinal sin), I was to host the charity night.

★ ★ ★

'Sure, I did a lot of comedy meself,' Dad told us as we sat in the living room.

'He did in his shite,' said Mam.

'Yeah, yeah, meself and Tom Flanning opened a comedy club in school after listening to *The Goon Show*,' said Dad.

More bollix from Paddy Byrne.

'Now Billy Connolly, he's a funny fecker,' said Dad. 'In fact, he's playing here next week. I'll get us tickets to that, get you prepared for your big gig.'

I was highly suspicious, as Dad had never brought me anywhere on his own ever. I mean, nowhere.

LIST OF PLACES I NEVER WENT WITH DAD ON MY OWN

1. The pub.
2. To town.
3. The park.
4. The cinema.
5. The shops.
6. The bus.
7. The front ...
8. Or back ...
9. Garden.
10. In fact, nowhere, ever, ever, ever.

It was all based on a pint. 'Sure, how am I supposed to have a pint if I'm on me own with him, Eithne?' Dad would say. But now I was twenty, I could have a pint with Dad. That was the only theory I had for him wanting us to see Billy Connolly together.

We arrived at the Olympia Theatre in Dublin. Billy Connolly was playing there for a few nights. I was so excited, as I had only ever seen him on *The Late Late Show*, with a very patronising Gay Byrne.

'Well, a very funny man, Billy Connolly,' Gay would say with gritted teeth. You may all think: What has Jason got against poor auld Gay? You'll find out later. He called Mother Teresa 'a good girl' live on air, for jaysus sake. But that's not why I don't like him.

'No, wait, not yet, son, let the crowds go first,' said Dad as we stood outside the Olympia. Dad made us wait till nearly every soul had gone in. I then went to go in, but he held me back. 'Wait for the bouncers to follow the crowd in, then we go.'

What was he up to …

'Dad, where's the tickets?' I asked nervously.

'We don't need tickets where we're going.' Dad sounded like Doc from *Back to the Future*.

Unbelievable.

'So this is a two-man job, son.' Ah, now I knew why he wanted me to come. 'When the crowd go in here, the bouncers follow them into the main area of the theatre, leaving the entrance to the boxes completely unguarded. So you go ahead of me until the bend there in the foyer. When you give me the thumbs up, I'll push open the entrance to the boxes and we'll leg it in,' he explained.

'But what if the boxes are taken, Dad?' I asked.

'This is Dublin city – no one pays for the boxes, son.'

So I went in, kept an eye out for bouncers and gave Dad the thumbs up. He pushed the door, called me and in we went. Dad was dead right: there was no one in the boxes, so we sat like royalty. Billy had already begun, so no one was watching as we slipped into the dark box.

I was at an angle where I could see Billy Connolly perfectly, but also the thousand or so faces watching him on his own on stage. This man had nobody with him. I had never seen live stand-up before. I was in tears laughing at him – so much so, I was willing him to stop talking. The whole room cried laughing and clapped all night at this genius.

I can confirm now that I have never laughed like that at another comic, ever. I love this man, everything he stands for, the rarity of him. I have never met him, but maybe that's the way it's supposed to be.

When you watch your heroes on stage, you think, Oh my God, I'm going to become a musician, or an actor, or even a sports star. But afterwards, on the way home in the car, I looked at Dad and said …

'That was the funniest thing I have ever heard. There's no way I would ever do that. He is a genius – no, no way, I will never become a comedian after seeing that. He was just amazing. I can't do this charity gig now.'

'Yep, you're bollixed, son. There's no way you'll ever be that funny. You'll most likely die on your hole at this thing,' Dad encouraged … NOT.

I was going to march over to Louise Roche to tell her that no way could I host this charity night. Billy Connolly had ruined everything. I was not equipped to do this – not even my amazing dancing to 'The Only Way Is Up' was going to save me now.

SLAM! went the hall door.

'Jesus, the rain out there is awful, but it was a lovely Mass by Father Declan. We all found out who was getting new cars, and a best of luck to three families heading off to Spain for the Easter break on sun holidays, as Father Declan nodded to Ms Quinn. Sure, you can't move on this road now without her knowing. Oh here, son, Louise Roche asked me to give you this – she was handing them out at the front of the church,' Mam said as she handed me a leaflet while taking her wet coat off in the hallway.

You know in the movies when they zoom in on a picture or a murder weapon with terrifying music? Well, imagine that's happening right now as I read the leaflet.

CHARITY NIGHT FOR THE ROMANIAN AIDS BABIES

HOST JASON BYRNE ALONG WITH MANY OTHER ACTS

HEADLINERS REVELINO

Oh, shite. It was too late. I had to host the night now.

'Isn't that nice what they're doing for the AIDS babies, Jason?' read Mam as she took the leaflet back from me. 'And you're helping them with the AIDS babies too.'

'Mam, can you stop saying AIDS babies? They have HIV, they are children with HIV!' I corrected, trying to make Mammy Byrne more PC.

'What? Sure, it's AIDS they have, love, they're born with AIDS – that's why they're called the AIDS babies,' Mam went on.

'No, Mam, they can be born with HIV, but with the right treatment and medicine, AIDS can be prevented or slowed down …' I tried to explain to my staring mother.

'OK, I'll put the dinner on,' she said as she walked into the kitchen.

'What are you on about out there?' roared Dad from the sitting room.

'Jason is going to stop kids in Romania getting AIDS by telling jokes, Paddy,' roared Mam from the kitchen.

'Oh yeah, the AIDS babies, I seen them on the news!' Dad roared back.

'Can you all stop saying AIDS babies?' I joined in, roaring.

'Ah, you'll do great at that show. We'll all be there to support you, love,' roared Mam from the freezing conservatory.

'That charity thing? Sure he's bollixed – he'd be better off with AIDS than doing that gig,' Dad finished.

★ ★ ★

God help me. I had no idea what I was doing. The only stand-up I had seen was Billy Connolly, and that didn't help at all. I'd seen that he was wearing funny clothes, so I thought, *That's it, I'll wear something funny, just to get the crowd on my side.*

The big night came. I think I had spent most of the day in the toilet. I couldn't even go into work, I was that nervous.

'What the jaysus are you wearing?' Brian asked as I stood in the bar of the Coach House, wishing I was dead.

I had gone to the shop and bought huge brown baggy stripy trousers, a white T-shirt with braces, a red beret (I know) and a pair of wellies (Jimmy Cricket wrote the L on his right wellie and the R on the left – I thought that might help). I also bought massive badges that said 'I am 1 today', 'new born' and 'my other car is a Porsche'. I'd no fucking idea what I was doing.

'I'll be recording it too so you can look back at it all,' said Brian as he held up a huge camera. This made me even more nervous.

The guest list for who I was about to make a fool of myself in front of was long. And I can tell you now, they were not the type of people you want at your first-ever comedy attempt, or at any comedy event, ever. Some of these heads had never laughed in their life.

GUEST LIST FOR AIDS BABIES NIGHT

1. Local priest, Father Declan.
2. Ms Quinn, Father Declan's Mary Magdalene.
3. Four nuns.
4. Mam and Dad.
5. Uncles and aunties.
6. All my mates from the road.
7. Past teachers of mine.
8. Lots of old people.
9. My girlfriend Rachel.
10. Even SOME FELLAS CORA KNEW.

The function room in the Coach House was like an old barn. It had a double-door entrance with steps down into the venue. It had all been done up since I was a kid, but I clearly remember playing on those steps with other kids in the eighties while our dads had pints. We played on six steps for hours. I'm laughing now at the thought of kids creating several different games from six steps.

I hate to sound like an old moan, but these days you go into restaurants, pubs and cafés, and you will see kids glued to their phones or iPads, not communicating with other kids unless it's through Snapchat. This, yes, might sound like moaning, and I hear people say, it's progress in the world, it can't be stopped. Well, my son who is now sixteen, said to me: 'Why did you let me use an iPad when we were out – you should have made me go outside and play with other kids.'

My point being, we are using the iPad as the steps. If iPads were around when I was a kid, I can guarantee you Paddy Byrne would have given us one if it stopped interference with his pint. But thank God they weren't around.

Anyway, in the room, the stage was to the right of the double doors. It was about two-foot high and roughly eight by six. Then the crowd were all down the room in front of you, some to the left side, and the bar was leaning right against the right side of the stage. So there was no escape.

'Are you all ready, Jason?' asked Louise.

'Ah, you'll be grand,' said Linda, the other nurse heading off to save babies.

'I'm shitting meself, girls – do I still have to do it?' I asked, half messing, but totally not messing. Why did I say yes?

LIST OF TIMES I SAID 'YES' BUT WISHED I HAD SAID 'NO'.

1. Rolling down the hill inside a barrel that the lads had just pushed.
2. Sitting in a trolley heading down a ramp towards the school.
3. While waiting in a bedroom in Coleraine to go to a Formal.
4. Smelling that (when your mates said, 'Here, smell that').
5. Holding this for a second (getting an electric shock when your mates said, 'Here, hold this for a second').

Before the crowd arrived into the room, we had a sound check. Revelino were testing their drums, guitars and mics, then suddenly burst into a full song. As I watched the lights changing to the beat and Bren Tallon blasting out a song, I ran to the toilet and simply wrecked the jacks, not with my mouth but with me arse.

Wreck the jacks ─────────────────────

The phrase 'wreck the jacks' in Ireland does not mean to head in to the jacks and throw toilet paper around the floor and/or splash water on the mirrors, thus leaving it a wreck.

No, in this case, you are entering the cubicle and destroying the toilet bowl with your arse contents, due to an illness OR YOUR FIRST-EVER STAND-UP GIG! You literally wreck the jacks or in some cases CRACK THE JACKS.

I then came back outside. Brendan Tallon was so good to me – he walked me to the mic to do a sound check. I was even frightened of that.

ONE, TWO ... WHUUUUUUU (feedback)

'Say something, Jason, talk!' shouted Bren.

I said a few words into the mic, but all I could hear was my shit voice booming out of the speakers all over the room. Holy shit, they were going to hear what I was about to say for sure.

'OK, guys, we're going to let them in!' shouted the bar staff.

The room began to fill. I sat with Brian, Karl, Ken and my girlfriend Rachel, who were all drinking and laughing. I looked around the room, watching as Father Declan walked in – he gave me a thumbs up. My old English teacher walked in with her husband. My gym teacher, Mr McCann, with his wife. Every neighbour I ever knew was filing into that room. Ballinteer must have been empty outside.

'How are ye, Jason, you're going to die on your arse son, best of luck!' said Alan from next door, grabbing me from behind and shaking my shoulders vigorously. Then he left.

Why do Irish people do this? I have had so many come up to me, to this day, with this weird move that they think is encouragement … well, finally I can tell you all.

IT DOESN'T HELP, AND I MEAN AT ALL!

LIST OF THINGS THAT DON'T HELP… AT ALL!

1. You're going to be shite, best of luck.
2. You better be funny, best of luck.
3. Sure, my pet goldfish is funnier than you, best of luck.
4. That's a lot of people to disappoint, best of luck.
5. Don't give up the day job, best of luck!

Yes, people still ask me after twenty-seven years in comedy.

> IDIOT: Is this your full-time job?
>
> ME: No, I'm a plumber in the day, I write my books on bits of piping, material for new shows on U-bends, radio, TV and corporate gigs all done on the toolbox. And on me break I fly to London, Sydney and Finland for shows …

SILENCE

IDIOT: Alright, I was only asking.

'Best of luck, son, remember Billy,' said Dad as he patted me on the back and he and Mam took their seats. Dad was being encouraging now – he would never knock any of his family in public. The slagging was for the house only.

'Ladies and gentlemen, welcome to Louise's ...' (said Louise) 'and Linda's ...' (said Linda) ...

They were doing that taking-turns-to-talk-into-the-mic thing 'cause they thought it was funny. As they spoke, I could feel my arse trying to drag me towards the jacks to wreck it again!

'... SAVE THE ROMANIAN AIDS BABIES CHARITY GIG!' (Louise and Linda together). The whole room clapped and cheered. Now even the nurses were saying AIDS babies all the time too.

'So thank you all ...' (Louise) 'for coming ...' (Linda).

WRECK-THE-JACKS RUMBLING AGAIN IN ME PANTS

'And without further ado ...' (Louise) 'your host for the night ...' (Linda) ...

WRECK-THE-JACKS GETTING WORSE

'COMEDY FROM JASON BYRNE!' (Both together)

The jacks-wrecking would have to wait as the whole of the Coach House whooped and cheered. Linda and Louise got off the stage, waving their arms like those inflatable tube men you see outside car dealerships.

I stood with the lights in my eyes. I couldn't see anyone. I had my list of stand-up jokes in my hand, my little bag of props. My throat began to dry up. I was terrified. They all stopped cheering and clapping.

'Hello, hello all, and welcome. I think that hand dryers in toilets are too loud – if you are an old person and you try to dry your hands, when it comes on, it frightens you, gives you a heart attack and you die. There's toilets all over Ireland with old dead people at the bottom of hand dryers …'

TOTAL SILENCE IN THE ROOM, FOLLOWED BY A FEW CLAPS AND CLINKS OF HALF-DRUNK GLASSES.

'When you walk home tonight, you will hear HOOTING in the trees, *Hoo hoo hoo.* You may think it's owls – well, you will be half-right. It will be owls in the trees cooling their chips before they put them in their mouths –' (miming an owl cooling a chip in a tree) '– *Hoo hoo HOOOOoo …*'

TOTAL SILENCE AGAIN, A BIT MORE NERVOUS SHUFFLING.

Right, this wasn't working. What would Billy Connolly do?

'You know when you do a wee with your willy, and you look down and the top of your willy looks like a smile …'

OH JESUS, PEOPLE WERE STARTING TO GET UP AND WALK AROUND.

I was now in a living nightmare. No one was laughing or even listening. They began to talk to each other to try to drown out the blue stand-up I was now doing. It was a disaster. People even began to queue for the bar. Right in front of me, there were people totally ignoring me. They were all mortified for me, wishing it would all stop.

'And now for my finale!'

I then took out a teddy bear and cut its head off with a scissors to pockets of screams and 'What the hell is he doing now?!'

As quick as flash, Louise and Linda jumped up and grabbed the mic off me.

'Ladies and gentlemen, Jason Byrne,' said Louise nervously to small claps … and …

'Genius!'

… from Paddy Byrne at the back, clapping louder than anyone.

I walked off the stage and straight out the door. In the distance, I could hear …

'So we're going to have a raffle …' (Louise) 'at the break …' (Linda) 'to collect as much money as possible for our AIDS babies …' (Louise) 'Remember, the more money, the less AIDS!' (Linda).

I stood out in the cold to get my breath back. Right then, at that moment, I realised stand-up comedy was a craft, an art form, that comics all over the world work really hard to perfect. It was literally no joke.

STAND-UP COMEDY IS NO JOKE … bet you never thought you'd hear that.

'Don't worry, son, fuck the lot of them.' Dad had come out to join me, even gave me a fag. I only ever smoked when drinking in those days.

'Holy shit, Dad, I'm never doing that again. They want me to do the raffle at the end – well, they can fuck off!' I said still shaking.

'You are going to get yourself a few pints, then get back in there and do the poxy raffle or they'll be talking about how shite this was for life. Sure, that feckin' priest in there will be dining out on this with his sideline Ms Quinn. No, you go back in. Fuck the lot of them. Don't do any of your written stand-up – you're a Byrne, son, and we are naturally funny. Use the force, Luke,' advised

Dad. 'You see, I'm not that out of touch. *I am your father* … now get in there and sort this shit out,' Dad said, while breathing into an empty pint glass, trying to sound like Darth Vader. I gave Dad an almost-hug, as he wasn't a hugger. Then headed back in.

'Got it all on tape, Jay – you did great. You should have seen the faces on our old teachers when you were talking about willies, fuck them,' said Brian.

He did get it all on tape. My first-ever gig. I sat in with Karl, Ken, Brian and Rachel and I had a few pints while some of the locals, Joe Dunne and then Revelino, played. It was a great night. I almost forgot I had to do the raffle.

> LOUISE: 'Ladies and gentlemen …'
>
> LINDA: 'Welcome back to do the raffle for the AIDS babies …'
>
> BOTH OF THEM: 'JASON BYRNE!'

Up I went. Back to face my fears head on. I looked down into the crowd and could see my dad holding up an empty pint glass to speak into it.

I picked up the bucket full of raffle tickets. I didn't think about material or anything I was going to say. And …

LAUGHTER, CHEERS, CLAPPING, HOWLING!

What a feeling. It was like a drug flowing through my veins as they laughed and clapped. I slagged everyone that won …

'Sure, Peter Mackin will love that whiskey as he can put it on his cornflakes in the morning, the auld alco.' Claps and cheers as they pointed and laughed at Peter Macken who was, yes, an alcoholic, collecting his prize with his chin on his chest.

'The beauty treatment goes to a much-needed face, battered Joan O'Brien, the state of her. Come on up here, Joan, and leave the birds you have nesting in your head at the table,' I continued.

MORE CLAPS AND LAUGHS

The raffle ended. My dad was right to push me back up there. I may never have done it again if it wasn't for him.

I first died on my arse trying too much too soon, but I loved slagging them all off, and it worked a treat. I had loads of people coming up to me after, congratulating me on a great show.

'Well done, man, you're a funny fucker, you should keep that up,' said Bren Tallon from Revelino. I never forgot that either, Bren.

LINDA AND LOUISE WORKING WITH THE ROMANIAN AIDS BABIES THANKS TO THE CHARITY OF BALLINTEER

… read a headline in the *Southside* newspaper, underneath a pic of Louise and Linda holding AIDS babies, I mean babies, on their laps in Romania.

Would I do that all again? Would I shite. I wasn't to stand on stage for a while after that wreck-the-jacks scenario.

CHAPTER 10
POOR RICHARD

'Well, I laughed at the old people dead at the bottom of hand dryers around Ireland.' Dad was giving me a lift to work on his way into Guinness's.

He was still trying to big me up after my disaster of a charity gig. Well, it was half good, half shit. Like life, I suppose. Yeah, that'd make a good T-shirt. 'Life: it's half good, half shit.'

I walked into the warehouse. Steve, PJ and Eoghan were all standing at the bench looking a bit stiff. There was no music playing or Gerry Ryan pumping through the warehouse. The lads were wide-eyed as they pointed behind me to the Portakabins. I could see Dieter, Andrew, Bernard (and AC and DC) all around a table talking to a tall bearded man in a suit. They were looking out at us as they spoke. Angie gave us a wave from her desk in the other Portakabin.

'That's the boss man from England,' said Steve. 'He's come to check on us all, a surprise visit.'

The owner of Lightning Dimensions was a fella called John Simpson. He owned a company in England called White Light, which was very successful. I'm pretty sure he was coming to us to see why we were so unsuccessful.

He walked out onto the floor. At this stage, we were all getting an order ready. John Simpson, with Dieter, headed over towards us, leaving Bernard, the dogs and Andrew in the Portakabins.

'Morning, lads, this is John Simpson. This is Jason, PJ, Steve and Eoghan,' introduced Dieter. We all said hello.

'Do you all like working here, lads? Anything that makes it difficult? Any way I could help on my end, a better working environment, if you get me?' asked John Simpson.

Behind John, Dieter was nodding his head furiously. He knew we were about to do him in for fun …

'Welll …' I began, much to Dieter's horror. Steve popped his pipe in his mouth and placed one leg onto a chair to listen to me intently. 'It's very cold in here. The lighting is atrocious and dangerous …'

'And dangerous …' joined the lads now, like a little chorus.

'Sure, PJ has to go to the toilet with a torch on his head 'cause the lighting in his jacks is broken,' I continued.

'Sorry, why does PJ have his own … jacks?' asked John.

'Toilet,' said Dieter.

'Oh yes, toilet, why do you have your own toilet?'

'Because I destroy the jacks or simply wreck it when I go. I wouldn't let another human near there when I'm done,' PJ backed up. As in backed me up – he wasn't backed up, if you excuse the pun.

'Anyway, we are working in a very dangerous environment. Just the other day, Eoghan received a very bad shock from an unchecked bare wire simply lying on the bench,' I told John.

'Could have killed me,' Eoghan agreed, wide-eyed.

'Well, that is not good enough, boys. I'm sorry about that,' said John.

He didn't know that this was one of many stunts we would pull on each other over the years. The trick was to plug a cable in, with the plug attached, of course. The other end would have nothing on it, so we would strip the wire back to copper, then we would hide the bare wire among a bit of rubble on the victim's bench. Eventually, the victim would touch those wires and get the shock of their life.

'They know the wire is there,' Dieter said with a red face like he was going to kill us.

'Sorry, they what?' asked John.

'Yes, Dieter, we what?' I asked in a posh accent, while Dieter wafted the smoke from Steve's pipe out of his eyes.

'Nothing,' Dieter retreated.

'Also, we never have the right tools, we're loading trucks with no back harnesses at all, we don't have any hard-toe shoes, no overalls, and none of us are fully qualified in electrics. This place is a lawsuit waiting to happen,' I said.

Total silence, with wafts of smoke heading into the air from Steve's pipe and lots of blinking from us all. Dieter looked like his whole world had just ended.

'Is this true?' John asked Dieter.

'No, not really, Jason may be exaggerating a bit there. This is a pretty safe place to work.'

As Dieter said this, one of Bernard's Great Danes came bounding out of the office followed by the other one, both with files of paperwork in their mouths.

'AC, DC, no!' shouted Bernard.

They turned at the lighting rack (these were basically massive stands that lights hung on before they left the warehouse), and because of the size of the dogs, they both banged into the lighting rack. It fell, starting a domino effect, and the other lighting racks fell over against each other with the loudest of bangs.

Bernard continued to try to rescue his paperwork from his dogs. John Simpson looked at Dieter, who now was a ghost of his former self.

Myself, PJ, Steve and Eoghan all stood silently, waiting for John's reaction.

'OK then, lots of improvements needed here. Dieter, a long lunch, I believe?' announced a very calm John Simpson, even though he had just found out that most of his wealth was in the hands of fools.

'This is Richard, everyone, he will be our new warehouse manager. He's come all the way from England, so let's make sure he is alright and looked after.'

We were all in the canteen at the back of the warehouse. Dieter was introducing Richard Watson, sent all the way from White Light London, where he was a manager for John Simpson. After John had seen the mess his Irish investment was in, he had sent over Richard Watson, or as we called him 'Poor Richard', with all his knowledge, to the warehouse, where he could teach the little people, the silly Irish, the ways of the lighting world.

'Morning, boys!' (Already we wanted to kill him, with his 'morning, boys' in a Cockney accent as he rubbed his hands together like Ian Beale at a stall in the market on *EastEnders*.)

'Right, anyway. So, gang, we are going to turn this warehouse around, make it the best lighting hire company in Ireland. People all over the land will know who we are. We are going to own every event – music, conferences, weddings, fashion shows, even TV. Are you with me, boys?' asked Poor Auld Richard.

We just stared at the man that John Simpson had sent to Ireland to be tortured till he left again.

'Well, are you with me, lads?' asked Richard again. 'Are we going to look after each other today?' asked Richard yet again, as Dieter rubbed his hand down his face, knowing well what was about to happen.

Dieter left the canteen, walked up to the office, got his coat and headed out for a coffee. Like the way a prison guard leaves the victim with the other prisoners cause he's been paid to do so by some Mafia boss. Dieter knew he had no control over us

'Has anyone seen Richard? It's John from London on the phone for him,' howled Angie across the floor.

'Have you checked the skip?' asked Dieter nonchalantly as he walked back in from his coffee.

Sure enough, as Angie looked into the skip, there was our brand-new English warehouse manager, gaffed from head to toe, with a strip of gaffer tape across his mouth to muffle his pleas.

Having a warehouse manager brought in from England to babysit us all didn't solve anything. In fact, it just made us worse. Those days were insane.

LIST OF INSANE ANTICS WHILE UNDER THE MANAGEMENT OF POOR RICHARD

1. Richard came back from lunch and his bike was gaffer-taped to a beam in the ceiling with a mirrorball beside it and the words DISCO BIKE taped to the frame.
2. Hat hour continued with a vengeance. No matter how often Richard tried to take the hats off us on a Friday afternoon, they just got bigger and more extravagant.
3. If Richard (or, to be fair, any one of us) wanted a cup of tea, you would most likely be swallowing tiny washers and nuts if you didn't check quickly enough.
4. Electrocutions came thick and fast. There were bare wires everywhere, even underneath the warehouse phone as Richard took a shock, sorry, a call, to his head.
5. We began to gaffer-tape people outside the warehouse. We gaffer-taped Richard to a pole outside the Meath Hospital. The guards were called, and they took him off in the squad car for questioning. To be honest, we knew the cops in the area, so we kinda requested this.

It was beginning to feel like one of those army movies like *GI Jane*, where Demi Moore would just not give up, no matter how much you punished her.

Eventually, Richard realised if you can't beat them, join them. He began to help us gaffer-tape and electrocute others, like a dirty cop accepting a bribe. It was like *Training Day* with Denzel Washington. Except we were training Richard on how to be a pro messer.

But there was one stunt that nearly killed Richard, the one we are all so proud of to this day.

Unfortunately, it was Richard's birthday. We all dreaded our birthdays in the warehouse. Richard arrived in, well aware of what he was in for. I remember him standing in the middle of the warehouse screaming, 'Let's just get this over with!' in his Cockney *EastEnders* accent.

We proceeded to gaffer-tape Richard. We put him into a flight case, locked it, then called a courier. The courier arrived and had no idea what was in the case. We told him it was to go to the Gaiety Theatre, then loaded the case into the van, with Richard inside. We could have suffocated him!

Here's the best bit: he eventually got to the Gaiety. Terry, the tech there that we all knew, opened the case, saw Richard in it, who he well knew too, then closed it back up. He called another courier and sent Richard back to us.

When we opened the case, we thought Richard was dead.

Later, we went for pints in Whelan's. Richard had earned his pints. I suppose we nearly killed him too, so it was more a relief buying-of-pints.

I decided to drive the Honda Vision electric hairdryer down to the pub, have two pints and head home. But, of course, after two pints, I wanted to stay with Richard and the lads. So I decided to walk outside, get the moped, drive it up a few metres to the warehouse and leave it there overnight. PJ came out with me and stood beside the Honda Vision. I sat onto the moped, turned the key and pressed the little red start button. The rest is a blur.

I somehow pulled the accelerator back to full power. The bike did a wheelie, except I didn't let go. I followed the moped with my feet on the ground, the moped between my legs, running with it as it went. It hit the opposite wall with its two wheels, me with two pints on me still holding the accelerator, revving. I then fell backwards, screaming, the moped came with me, and for a moment, I was on my back, legs in the air, with a moped upside down on top of me. The wheels were still turning, smoke now hurtling out of the exhaust.

All I could hear was PJ howling with laughter. A crowd had gathered, and PJ was asking them to call an ambulance. People were saying I looked OK, even though I was under a moped, but

PJ kept saying the ambulance was for him, as he didn't think he was going to be able to stop laughing. I mean, this man was so funny when he laughed. I really thought PJ *was* going to need an ambulance – he couldn't catch his breath.

All I hurt was my pride. PJ helped me wheel the now-battered moped back to the warehouse. He laughed all the way up there, about a ten-minute walk, then laughed all the way back to Whelan's pub. He just kept going over the crash again and again. PJ said I basically drove the bike up the wall and back on top of myself.

That was roughly around January. February was to come, which would mean my twenty-first birthday.

I was born on 25 February, the same day as my mam. 'Sure, you nearly fell out in the lift.' More lovely exaggerations from Mammy Eithne Byrne.

'You're going to do what?' asked Dad.

I had been summoned to Paddy's shed in the garden. Dad was asking me what I wanted to do for my twenty-first.

'I'm going to have it in Lighting Dimensions' warehouse.'

'Are you sure, son? I don't know. That's a place of work – there's no licence to have entertainment in there. But if that's what you want, go ahead. Sure, I'll throw a few bob in for food and drink,' Dad said.

He was always kind that way: he'd give you money if you asked or help you out if you were in a crisis. The only thing was, though, if he gave you money, he kinda owned you for a while.

TIMES DAD OWNED US DUE TO GETTING DOSH OFF HIM

1. I'll have that cup of tea now – sure, didn't I give you fifty last week.
2. Get the basin of water for me feet – sure, I handed you a tenner this morning.
3. Go buy me fags and the Lotto – there's a fresh twenty in your wallet because of me.
4. A small foot rub, me corns are killing me – a tenner a foot if I'm not mistaken.
5. They're just false teeth, go get them, they're upstairs in a glass on the bathroom sink – surely that's worth the fifty I gave ye.

Dad had false teeth for most of his life, by the way. When they were kids, loads of them had the teeth pulled out of their heads for no good reason at all. No fillings, they just pulled the teeth out. When Dad ate, he would take his teeth out and leave them on the table. I mean, he was the only human in the world I knew that took his teeth out to eat.

'Ah jaysus, Paddy, not again, that is gross,' Mam would say.

He was the most stressful man to have a meal with, ever. Not only did he insist on having his teeth out, he also sneezed constantly while eating.

Aaaaaachoooooo!

Bite of the steak.

Aaaaaachoooooo!

Bit of potato.

Aaaaaachoooooo!

Mouthful of peas.

Can you imagine trying to eat with that at the table?

'Ah for feck's sake, Paddy,' Mam would say again.

'I'm allergic to eating. I can't help the sneezing,' defended Dad.

He was in his bollix allergic to eating. The real story was that he was getting older, his nose hair was growing more and more, and my dad and all of his mates had never heard of grooming. Sure, my dad had tufts of hair that lived on his back for life. What was happening was that when he closed his mouth to eat, he had to breathe through his nose like the rest of us. This was tickling the hair up in his nose and making him sneeze.

'All you have to do is cut that forest that's hanging out of your nose, Paddy, and you won't feckin' sneeze anymore,' advised Mam.

'What are you on about, woman? I don't have hair up me nose. I'm a rare case, what with me TCP from the explosion in Guinness's, and now an allergy to food. I'll be over in Oxford soon as a medical mystery.'

'You're no mystery – you're a simple shite,' laughed Mam, and all of us.

Aaachoooaaaastaaardsss!

All week, we prepped the warehouse for my twenty-first party. Nothing else got done.

When Richard or Dieter came out to ask us to hurry up with orders, we had to explain that it was my birthday and we needed to prep the warehouse. Myself, Steve, Eoghan and PJ had meetings each morning, much to Dieter's anger, deciding what we would tackle next.

The plan was to have a massive black curtain at the entrance to the warehouse, just inside the sliding metal door. We would put a dry ice machine in the ceiling so it would eventually fall slowly to the ground, creating a smoky waterfall to walk through. Then this brought you into a tunnel of white curtains, all changing colour as you walked. If you looked to the ceiling, more black curtains would hang with tiny little starlights in them to make it look like the night sky.

Out the other end would be another dry ice waterfall that led you to the dance floor, which would have mirrorballs, lasers, more smoke machines and a DJ area. Then, to the back of that, we would use the canteen as the bar. It was unrecognisable, covered in moving lights and disco balls. It was the best design ever.

A monster party, and we had invited everybody. Sure, what could go wrong?

★ ★ ★

'Your father's had a heart attack, he's in hospital, I'm going to kill him!' roared Mam after putting the phone down. The hospital had rung the house. Dad had had a minor heart attack in work and was now in St James's Hospital in Dublin.

'Get your coats while I ring Eric in Sweden,' she instructed.

I got Rachel and Eithne, and all our coats, then went out to the car.

'He's had a heart attack and I'm going to kill him for doing this to me, Eric ...' Mam was still on to Sweden as I got us all in the car.

Mam drove to the hospital, moaning all the way, while at the same time telling us different ways she was going to kill Dad for nearly dying and putting the shits up her.

WAYS IRISH MAMMIES THINK ABOUT THEMSELVES

1. He has cancer – what am I going to do now?
2. He's in bed for a week with pneumonia, very selfish – I've loads to do.
3. Oh, she has six blocked arteries. That'll never happen to me – I was told I'm as fit as a fiddle.
4. Menopause, more like meno-non-stop with this one.
5. Dead! Can you believe it? Sure, that's twice the workload for us now!

'Where is he? I'll kill him ...' Mam quickly changed to her posh accent at the desk in the hospital. 'Yes, Patrick Byrne, wife of myself, Eithne Byrne, father to Jason, Rachel, Eithne and Eric, but he's in Sweden, which doesn't make a difference. Anyway ...'

'Oh, you want St James's private clinic, Cardiology. This is the public section, Mrs Byrne,' explained the receptionist.

You could see Mam was delighted being told out loud, with a queue behind us, that we were to go to the private clinic. If Mam knew this was going to happen she would have encouraged Dad to have a heart attack sooner.

'Of course, silly me,' Mam said, which she never said, as she looked around at the other people waiting.

'Oh, silly meee …' I teased.

WHACK!

'Owwww,' I said, as we walked to the private section of the hospital.

'Well, this is lovely, but I'm still going to kill him,' said Mam.

'Yes, Paddy Byrne, room six,' said the very posh receptionist in the foyer of the private section. Beethoven was being pumped through the ceiling.

'Yes, dear, and the name of the ward?' asked Mam, expecting St Joseph of the Bleeding Heart or St Bridget of the Weeping Eye.

'No, just room six, down there on the left,' pointed the very posh receptionist, much to Mam's confusion.

We pushed open the door and there was Paddy Byrne, all propped up in a bed watching telly in his private room, noshing down on some jelly and ice cream, with a garden view. It was like a bleedin' hotel.

'Ah, welcome to Lord Muck's humble abode, gang,' Dad said as we went in.

'I'll bloody kill ye, Paddy. What are you playing at? But after looking around this place, I'd love a heart attack meself …' Mam said.

She then gave Dad a hug and a kiss, which we'd never seen. Jesus, she must have really thought he was going to die, as zero affection ever happened between these two. We all gave him a hug too.

RING RING RING!

'Ooohhh,' we all went, as dad answered his own bedside private phone.

'Excuse me till I deal with this,' he said in his posh accent.

'Yes, hello, hello, Eric, yes, I'm fine, minor heart attack, nothing to worry about, thank you, yes I will, bye-bye, bye-bye now,' Dad said as he talked to our phone for a brother, Eric.

'Eric says hi to all,' he said in a regal way, while holding his hand in the air. It was soon slapped back down by my mother.

'What in the name of jaysus happened to you, Paddy?' asked Mam.

Apparently, Dad had been in work and everything was fine. Then he then got a pain in his chest, passed out and woke up in the back of the ambulance.

The door opened and a doctor walked in.

'Come on, everyone, out – the doctor has to do his work,' Mam said, bowing to the doctor as she spoke.

PEOPLE MAM BOWED TO WHEN SHE SPOKE TO THEM, FOR SOME FUCKING REASON

1. Doctors.
2. Priests.
3. Guards.
4. Dentists.
5. Anyone in a high-vis jacket.

'It's OK, Mrs Byrne, you can stay. Just a routine check-up and a chat with Paddy here,' explained the doctor.

This place was so posh. In the public hospital, whenever there was even a hint of a doctor entering the room, the nurse would usher visitors out. Under no circumstances could a mere member of the public be near a doctor, unless you were in that bed sick.

Guinness's had taken a bit of Dad's wages each week and they had us all on a family plan for VHI health insurance now. This was the first time we'd got to see it in action. I remember Dad showing me the plan they had him on. I'm pretty sure himself and Bono were the only ones in the world on it. Dad had never checked, as he never checked any finances, ever. He had the same car insurance for years. Pension, house, life insurance, you name it – he joined it once and that was him for life.

'So how do you feel now, Patrick?' asked the posh doctor in posh room number six overlooking a garden with Lord Muck in the bed.

'Not great, doctor. I feel strange, different. I've no pain at all now, but I just can't put my finger on it. Things are definitely much clearer – I can see and hear better, you know, stuff like that. Do you reckon the heart attack gave me a new lease of life, a jolt if you will?' said Dad.

'No, you're sober, Paddy,' said the doctor.

'What?' asked my dad.

'For the first time in a long time, I'd say, you're sober,' explained the doctor.

He was right. My dad entered Guinness's at the age of fifteen and was around fifty-four now. He was handed a Guinness on his lunch hour and had at least two pints, sometimes twenty-six pints, a day for the last forty years or so. He was finally sober, and it needed a heart attack to do it.

'And would you drink much or smoke, Paddy?' asked the doctor.

'Haaa!'

'Ah jaysus …'

'Are you joking?!'

'Him, drink much or smoke? Never …' My mam was the last to comment as we all fell around laughing.

'Well, the odd pint and maybe a ciggy a day,' answered Dad.

'You're going to hell, Paddy Byrne,' my mam said to a sick man in a hospital bed.

'OK, no matter. We're going to have to fit you with a pacemaker and stents too, as your heart is all over the place,' said the doctor.

'But me son's twenty-first is this weekend,' said Dad, mainly worried about the massive session he was about to miss.

'No parties for a while for you, Paddy, or cigs or drink,' said the doctor.

'Right, that's it. Gas me now, me life is over,' said Dad as the blood drained from his face.

'Well, that's just great. How in the name of God am I going to cope with all this?' Mam howled. She took out her hanky while the doctor rubbed her back, confused as to how this was all about Mam.

CHAPTER 11
GOODBYE WAREHOUSE, HELLO COMEDY

'Oh, holy shit,' I said to myself as I walked into the warehouse on the day of my twenty-first birthday. I had been dreading this all year. There, in the middle of the warehouse, stood an upright metal-framed crucifix made from trussing, with the letters JASON XXI.

I walked towards the canteen like a character from Alfred Hitchcock's *The Birds*. Slowly I walked by the bench where PJ, Steve, Eoghan and Richard stood, beaming, arms folded.

'Morning …' I said.

'Happy birthday,' said Richard, with revenge in his eyes.

Even a glance towards the Portakabins was suspicious, as Andrew, Dieter and Bernard all watched me as I walked.

There wasn't even a wave from Angie, just an eerie silence around the warehouse. The calm before the storm. I awaited my fate.

I placed my coat on the table, looked up and what looked like a crowd of zombies came towards me. Not only the warehouse staff were there, but truck drivers, regular customers and other lighting designers had all come to wish me a happy birthday. I'm pretty sure I had pranked the lot of these somewhere along the line.

They carried me out of the canteen and laid the metal crucifix on the ground. Workers and bosses all joined together to get me tied to this cross. They gaffer-taped and ratchet-strapped me to it then hoisted it upright. This thing was massive – it was a good twelve feet tall, all bolted into a heavy plate at the bottom to keep me up there.

Then the boys laid pyrotechnics underneath me and began to set them off just under my balls. They covered me in beans and other bits of goo. Then they brought me outside for neighbours and passers-by to see the great Jason, son of Paddy, being crucified.

Let's have a little think about how dangerous this was. I'm outside in the cold, basically being crucified, the exact same way crucifixions would have taken place all those years ago. Except I'm covered in beans and gunpowder.

The main cause of death in crucifixion is exhaustion and, wait for it, asphyxiation. People died from their body weight pulling down on their arms, making it difficult to breath. I HAD A COLLAPSED LUNG A FEW YEARS BACK!

I was up there a good two hours, exhausted. Thank God for Rachel Gerrard, my old girlfriend, who came along to have a birthday lunch with me. She screamed at the rest of them to take me down. I was pale as fuck – I had basically been dying up there.

They immediately took me down and couldn't have been more apologetic … Were they, bollix – they took me down alright, but they couldn't stop laughing at the thought of nearly killing me by crucifixion.

'Think of all the sinners you could have saved, Jay,' roared Bernard across the floor as I cleaned myself up and got back to normal.

It was fair enough. I wasn't angry as I had nearly killed the following:

1. **Dieter (gaffer skip).**
2. **PJ (gaffer skip, pepper down his pants).**
3. **Steve (set him on fire with joke birthday candles).**
4. **Eoghan (gaffer skip, electrocutions).**
5. **Larry (stress from us).**
6. **Andrew (a fright would do it).**
7. **Bernard (hid his *Times* crossword).**

8. **Angie (gaffer skip and even wheelie bin).**
9. **Richard (every way you could think of).**
10. **And finally, just names of victims: Paul Weldon, John Holland, Kevin Saunders, Peter Canning, Dara Toner, Yvonne, Barbara, Corrie, Ciaran Tallon, Niamh ... and all that had the unfortunate luck to pass through the doors of Lighting Dimensions.**

Oh sorry, and Robbie Fossett of Fossett's Circus, who had brought a mirrorball in to us to say it was broken and was sucking in light instead of reflecting it. I took it from him and cleaned off the thick dust it had acquired from many a year in the roof of a circus tent. I put a light on it: hey presto, it wasn't sucking light in anymore and was reflecting it off the newly cleaned little mirrors.

He ended up in the skip for wasting our time.

'The only way is up ... baby!' we all sang as we danced on the dancefloor. Workers, bosses, my mates, aunties and uncles all at a warehouse party, a mad rave. It was so funny to watch my uncles and aunties trying to dance to this music. Dad wasn't there because he was in his posh hospital room getting his pacemaker fitted.

The drink and food were flowing in the canteen. My mam kept saying it was too loud. The lights were amazing, and the smoke machines pumped all night long.

'Strip-o-grams!' roared somebody as four lads dressed as firemen walked onto the dancefloor. Everyone gathered around them, clapping, until more strip-o-grams arrived, four, eight, twelve lads dressed as firemen, then, get this, four more dressed as coppers. I couldn't believe it – the lads had surpassed themselves!

Then one of the strip-o-grams went over to the DJ and asked him to switch the music off. It was then that I released they weren't strip-o-grams: they were real firemen and coppers. Somebody had seen smoke coming out of the warehouse, thought it was on fire and called the fire brigade. Someone else had rang the guards to complain about the music pumping through the ground. Then it got worse: the cop wouldn't let us continue the music as it was upsetting the residents. She asked the barman, SOME FELLA CORA KNEW, if he had a bar licence. Of course he didn't.

The whole party went to shit. It looked like Paddy Byrne was right all those weeks ago, when he had warned me about this. But I didn't listen to his wise words in the shed.

We all ended up in Whelan's, squashed to the walls, but we still had a laugh. In fact … BEST TWENTY-FIRST EVER!

'I don't feel great, man,' I said as I lay on the warehouse floor a few days later.

'Don't be messin',' PJ said as he sat on me, thinking I was joking.

I felt really faint. PJ saw how pale I'd gotten and decided to get off me. We walked across the road to the Meath Hospital, where I checked in with a collapsed lung again.

Was it the crucifixion that had brought it on? Maybe. Or maybe the drinking and smoking and partying for years while working in the warehouse.

I lay in the bed in the hospital, a new chest drain in me, and I looked out the window and down to my right, towards the Lighting Dimensions warehouse. There, in the wind and the rain, was a man with a sign rising up into the air above the hospital wall.

It was PJ with a GET WELL SOON cardboard sign held aloft as the lads raised him about twenty feet off the ground in an electric cherry picker. The whole hospital must have been wondering what the hell was going on.

The day went on and …

'SUMMARISE, I DON'T HAVE TIME FOR ALL THIS SHITE!'

Oh yes, sorry, Niall Tubridy. I'll summarise.

I ended up having an operation to fix my lung permanently. I went back to Lighting Dimensions for another year or so and continued to have a great time. Then myself, PJ, Larry and Dieter left to start a company called Arena Lighting.

Leaving the warehouse was the saddest day of my life. I was devastated and cried a lot. It felt a bit like school, the way I had made so many friends that I had laughed and cried with for a long time.

When anyone left the warehouse, we would all stand around on different flight cases or benches and play 'Born Free' by Andy Williams, singing that person out of the warehouse for the last time. Not a dry eye in the house when we did that.

'OH, FOR FUCK'S SAKE, COME ON, COME ON!'

Alright, man, hang on.

While in Arena Lighting, I went to a comedy night with my good friend Martin Byrne, as I was still a big comedy fan.

It was in the Castle Inn in Dublin city centre. The act was an Englishman called Simon Bligh, who was a black belt in karate and a very funny man. I recently met him in the Comedy Store in London. I asked how he was, and he said, 'I've stopped trying to be famous and I'm loving life.' Good auld Simon, what a great idea. It's a pain in the hole trying to be famous.

Anyway, the MC was Barry Murphy. There was a joke competition at the break. I remember it clearly.

Barry read out: 'What's the difference between Éamon de Valera and Mary Robinson?'

I wrote: 'My mam doesn't live beside Mary Robinson.'

I thought it was just mad, didn't have a hope, but Barry thought it was hilarious. I won, I actually won the joke competition. After the gig, I approached Barry for my Foster's baseball hat and T-shirt.

Barry said well done. Then Martin said to Barry ... 'Oh, Jason would love to do stand-up.'

I would in me shite. Last time I had done stand-up was in the Coach House for the nurses going to help the AIDS babies. No way, no way!

Barry took out a blue book, opened it and began to write. 'I'll put you down for six open spots in the International Comedy Cellar. If you don't like it after that, then fuck it,' he explained.

Before I knew it, I was booked in. This was it: the start of my comedy career.

'WELL, THAT WAS PAINFUL.'

Shut up, Niall!

Stand-up comedy is an odd job to choose, especially for me. Most of my younger life, I surrounded myself with friends and work colleagues. I liked being part of a team. Little did I know that comedy was to be a lonely job. Most of the time, you're on your own, and – get this – the more successful you are at comedy, the more alone you become.

You start off in clubs with other comics, having the laugh, but you move all the time, never really seeing the same comic for long enough to befriend them. Then you begin your solo shows, where it's just you on stage. You might have a tour manager – mine is Luke Molloy and thank God for him – but mostly I'm on planes or trains, getting to the countries or towns alone. I've been doing it for twenty-five years, and to be honest, I hate being on my own.

But it's the drug, the drug of comedy, the satisfaction of making hundreds if not thousands in a room laugh at what you're saying. It's a feeling that no other trade or art can give you.

But as with all drugs, it can be dangerous. I remember Les Dennis saying to me that the entertainment world is the cancer of relationships. At the end of the day, it's hard to hold down a normal life. The audience almost own you – you're their property; you move around the world keeping others happy. It's bad for your mental health, the stress levels are massive, and it's a bollix on your physical health too, as it's non-stop on the body. As we'll see.

★ ★ ★

So I'm shitting myself again. Sorry – one thing I forgot to mention is that with stand-up comedy, you are up the walls before a show, forever. It never stops.

People always ask if you are still shitting it before a gig. Well, yes, as the audience is different every night. You have no idea who you are about to walk out in front of. Every country in the world has different humour, every city has different humour, every town has different humour, everyone in that audience has an individual sense of humour.

So how do you make them all laugh at the same time? I'm not sure, but somehow I bring them all in as one unit. No matter how rich, poor, smart or thick they are, I get them all to a level playing field, where they will pretty much all find the same things funny.

So yes, back to shitting myself. It was my first gig in the International Bar on Wicklow Street, the first place I had had a pint of lager, downstairs, at fifteen or so. A few mates came along on the night.

The comedy club was called the Comedy Cellar. It was upstairs, so they thought it was funny to call it the cellar. It was run by Barry Murphy, Kevin Gildea, Dermot Carmody and Ardal O'Hanlon.

Barry was MCing. The audience of about sixty or so was in a tiny smoke-filled room, as you could smoke indoors then. You stood out in the hallway waiting to be called or sat at the top table, if you liked, with other comics: Ian Coppinger, Kevin, Barry and the like. I couldn't sit at the table as my opening bit was a big prop.

'Ladies and gentlemen, Jason Byrne!'

Out I walked to the side of the stage, which was a doorway. I had a full set of curtains that I was holding in front of me, hiding behind them, so all you could see was my feet. People began to giggle, and the comics were loving it.

Then I sang a weird tune, like a magic-act tune. I lifted a hairband with alien antenna glued to it. I just kept singing and lifting the alien antenna in and out of view behind the curtain – you couldn't see me at all.

It was very visual alright!

I only had five minutes to do, so I then dropped the curtains to huge applause. For the other two minutes, I took out rubber hands on a pair of sticks, then used them as an extension of my own arms. Rubbing them on my face, head and chest, even nipples.

Well, the room loved it. You see, the Coach House was different because it was full of non-comedy fans. This room was full of cool, arty comedy fans, so the curtains accompanied by the rubber hands went down a scream.

Barry Murphy gave me a fiver as payment. I kept that fiver framed for years.

This was the drug I was to chase now for the next twenty-five years: always trying to better myself, looking for the bigger laugh or hit.

★ ★ ★

Dad was just home from the hospital after having a pacemaker fitted. They decided on stents and a pacemaker because dad's insides were bollixed from drink and smokes. He would not have survived open-heart surgery.

My mam had told me not to say a word to him about the twenty-first being gatecrashed by firemen and coppers. Dad sat into his chair with his cup of tea. Mam was on the couch.

'So you're going to do the comedy, the stand, the thing on stage, the gigs …' Dad was a bit all over the place, highly strung, speaking too fast. 'I told jokes, I did that, I was on stage, sure no bother to ye, Jay,' he said, all frantic.

'Are you alright, Paddy?' asked Mam.

'Yep, as good as new, new pacemaker, new heart, new me.'

There was a pause for a moment, then …

'To be honest, I feel very strange, very odd, as if me heart is going through me chest …' Dad finally admitted.

The heart surgeon did say that if Dad felt bad at all to come back immediately. So we bailed into the car, and Mam drove him back to the heart clinic in St James's. Dad went in to get checked.

Jesus, we laughed all the way home when we got him back in the car. There were actual tears in my mam's eyes as she tried to drive.

The heart surgeon told us that Dad's heart was indeed beating too fast because, and get this, they had set the pacemaker at too high a speed. Dad was walking around the house talking and speaking like a hummingbird, as if someone had put him on fast forward. They readjusted it and got his heart rate back down again.

'It's not funny. I could have had a heart attack,' moaned Dad in the car as we laughed.

'Well, you didn't, but I must say, it was a miracle to see you moving around the house at speed for once. I should have got you to mop the floors and do the dishes – you would have done that in seconds,' laughed my mam.

My dad had PTSD from an explosion he wasn't at in Guinness's, and now stents and a pacemaker. He would make sure everyone knew this.

★★★

'OK, I'm off, everyone,' I shouted around the house as people all sat in their different rooms.

I looked into the living room. Dad was in there with his shirt open, rubbing his bare chest on the TV screen.

'Eh, you OK, Dad? I'm off to Edinburgh,' I said.

Dad continued to rub his bare chest on the screen.

Mam then walked in. 'You take care of yourself there, son, and we'll see you soon,' she said as she kissed and hugged me.

'What is Dad doing?'

'Oh, he's been doing that all morning. He thinks the pacemaker is interfering with the TV reception. He's already been rubbing his chest off the radio in the kitchen, the madman,' said Mam.

'I'm telling you, the pacemaker is definitely messing with the electrics in the house. I was on the phone to Pat Reid yesterday – he said all he could hear was buzzin' on the phone. I told him, "That's me chest, Pat, the bloody pacemaker"!' explained Dad.

'OK, I'm off, see you Rachel!' I shouted up the stairs.

'See ya,' Rachel shouted back down.

'See you, Eithne,' I shouted out through to the back garden.

'I'm playing with the cat,' Eithne roared.

'See ya, Mam, enjoy all that.' I pointed to Dad. God help my mam, she literally had the patience of a saint.

RING RING RING!

'It's your brother Eric. He says good luck in Edinburgh,' Mam shouted at me as I walked out the door.

'Tell him thanks.' And off I headed to Edinburgh.

★ ★ ★

The Edinburgh Comedy Fringe Festival is a monster. It also has a book festival, food festival, theatre festival, music festival and dance festival, all running for the month of August.

There are 3,500 shows a day, in the corners of pubs, big venues, tiny venues. One year we even went to watch a fella perform a play in a car. There were three audience members at a time. You had to sit in the back seat and watch him perform in the driver's seat.

I had never been to a festival like this, ever. Sure, I'd seen music festivals while working in Lighting Dimensions, but nothing like this.

It was 1996 and I had entered the 'So You Think You're Funny?' competition. A few months previously, they had heats in Derry, so myself, John Henderson, Paddy Courtney and Bob Reilly all headed up there. The heats were hosted by Patrick Kielty in a terrifying place called the Delacroix. They didn't like us southern folk much. We all performed, scraping through with pockets of laughter, got in our cars and legged it back south. That place famously told Jenny Eclair she was going home in a box.

Anywayyy … Myself, Paddy and John had all arrived in Edinburgh. We had nowhere to stay. All I remember was meeting these really cool nurses from Ireland who put us up for the night – it was so good of them.

Our heats were to be held separately over three days. There were seven comics in each heat, and seven heats. One comic was picked from each heat to go into the grand finale.

I fell in love with Edinburgh immediately. The place was rammed with shows everywhere, people performing parts of their plays on the streets, acts shoving flyers into your hand, pleading with you to go to their shows. Total mayhem.

My heat was coming up that night, but I wasn't nervous at all. In fact, I didn't really give a shit, to be honest. I thought this comedy career wouldn't last long, that I'd be back in lighting in no time.

We waited in a tiny dressing room in a venue called the Gilded Balloon. The competition was run by an amazing woman called Karen Koren, a loud blond Scottish-Finnish woman, whose pastime was to make her staff cry. I was terrified of her at first, but went on to be great friends with the great Karen.

Seven acts, including myself, each had five minutes to impress the judges. The judges were Karen Koren herself and a lovely man called Dominic Holland.

Get this, I met Dominic years later in Edinburgh. I hadn't seen him for a while and asked him what he was up to. He said he was with his son, that his son was an actor and was playing Spider-Man. I assumed Dominic meant that his son was in some weird play dressed as Spider-Man. It wasn't until the conversation went on that I copped that his son is Spider-Man. *The* Spider-Man, Tom Holland. Amazing.

I walked out sideways onto the stage to giggles that built up into proper laughs. The reason I was walking sideways onto the stage was that I had brought a pair of mannequin legs over on the plane.

Imagine: 'Are you carrying any weapons?' 'No, just the bottom half of a mannequin, sir.'

I had a black dress on to cover my real legs, then I pulled my black T-shirt over the top of the mannequin legs. They really looked like my legs as I waddled sideways onto the stage. The judges were clapping and laughing. I then took out my rubber hands on a stick and did my thing. I sailed through to the final. Dominic, fair play to him, had said Jason Byrne for sure as a finalist.

Now the only problem was the final was not for another week. Seven acts were chosen for the final, an unbelievable line-up. Jason Byrne, Tommy Tiernan, John Henderson and Patrick McDonnell were four of the seven, all Irish. I tell you now, if there was a Comedy World Cup, Ireland would win it hands down with the comics we produce. We're the Brazilians of comedy.

'There's no way an Irishman is going to win my competition,' said Karen Koren to me as she passed me in the streets of Edinburgh. Holy shit, she was scary. She just walked on as I looked at Paddy Courtney with a 'What did I do?' face on me.

We stayed with the Irish nurses for the week. We also went to some of the weirdest stuff ever. In Edinburgh, there was no limit to what you could see.

LISTS OF MAD SHOWS I SAW IN EDINBURGH 1996

1. A double female trapeze act, where their finale was to piss into a pint glass from a height.
2. A man doing a show with a bucket on his head. He put different eyes and mouth stickers on the bucket to show how sad or happy he was.
3. A woman as a dog with depression.
4. A fella on an ironing board pretending to be a surfer.
5. A man juggling a glass jar, a ball and his baby. Yes, his real baby, like a real child, tossing him into the air. The baby loved it.

We survived by doing small club gigs for the week. The money would be spent on food and drink for us and the nurses.

The gigs could be anywhere. We ended up in caves and catacombs, doing actual gigs in the damp and dark at around 2 a.m. One night I was asked to MC. I said no bother at all. I was on the stage at 2 a.m., as drunk as the audience. I asked a guy what he did, and he said he was a cyclist. I said, 'You are in your bollix.'

He screamed, 'Do you want me to prove it?' in a heavy Scottish accent. ·

Up he got beside me on the stage, as pissed as a coot.

'That's Chris Hoy,' one lad shouted.

'Never heard of him,' I replied as Chris smiled at me.

To be fair, most of us (unless you were a cycling fan) would never have heard of Chris Hoy in those days.

I asked him how he was going to prove he was a cyclist.

As an answer, Chris pulled his trousers down to the sound of the audience, men and women, screaming at the sight of Chris Hoy's legs. It looked like somebody got the Alps and stuck them onto both of his fucking legs, they were that veiny.

Years later, when Chris Hoy was knighted, I tweeted him to say well done on the knighthood, and did he remember that fateful night all those years ago when he dropped his bags on stage in Edinburgh at 2 a.m.?

Sir Chris Hoy replied, 'I do indeed, my man, I do indeed ...'

This was only the start of the great men and women I was to rub shoulders with during my career.

'Will you lot just sit the fuck down? You're making me nervous, and no amount of pacing is going to change your fucking act. So fuck off with the shuffling and sit down,' moaned Mark Lamarr at the seven finalists as we paced backstage at the Gilded Balloon, waiting to go on stage. We sat down pretty quickly, as Mark was not a man with much patience. He sucked on his fag, checking his quiff in the mirror.

A room in the Gilded Balloon called Late'n'Live was the space we were performing in. This was to be a major haunt for us at future Edinburghs.

Karen came in to wish us all good luck through gritted teeth. She wanted one of her Scottish acts to win. But they hadn't a hope with four Irish heavy hitters about to storm the place.

Mark Lamarr walked out onto the stage to begin. The judges that night were Karen Koren, of course, and Phil Kay, one of, if not the, best improv comedians I have ever seen. A beautiful soul and total genius.

I once saw him in Dublin. He came on with a small jug of milk, poured it on a pole that was at the side of the stage, then slid up and down the pole. 'I'm trying to make cheese, for Christ's sake,' he said to the audience. He also famously does not leave the stage at the interval – he keeps the gig going while people head to the bar. I was about to perform for a hero of mine.

I can't remember the order we all went on, but I'm pretty sure I was somewhere in the middle. Out I walked sideways with my mannequin legs. The audience was in knots laughing. All the other acts had done funny stories, which were great, but here comes this skinny redhead, shuffling onto the stage with fake legs. I then did the splits with the legs, followed by a cartwheel, which of course was a disaster in a funny way. Phil Kay stood up and clapped and cheered me as I left.

'Right, you fucks, there's a bit of a problem,' said Mark Lamarr to us through a cloud of smoke and wafting hair, hating us all. 'The judges are gone nearly fifty minutes now, and the crowd are getting restless 'cause the fucking judges can't make up their minds who's won. As far as I know, it's between you, Tommy, and you, Jason.'

Holy shit, I couldn't believe it. My heart was pounding.

Eventually we all went back up on stage. Karen went to the mic. Phil was standing to the side, furious.

'And the winner is … Tommy Tiernan, by a point!' shouted Karen.

'Second, Jason Byrne, third, John Henderson and fourth, Patrick McDonnell,' said Karen, half happy, half angry.

Go on the Irish. We all won that day, I suppose. Tommy walked offstage and into the arms of an agent. I went on the piss. Holy shit, second! I was chuffed.

Years later, I found out through staff that Karen and Phil were arguing the whole time about who should win. Phil wanted me to win and Karen wanted Tommy to win. Phil would not back down until Karen agreed to say, 'OK, Tommy only beats Jason by one point.'

So that's it, that's the story of 1996. Tommy beat me by a point, but not really.

Here's the funniest bit: Karen turned to Phil before she went back on stage and said, 'Anyway, it's my competition, so fuck off, Tommy wins.'

Hello, showbizzz.

CHAPTER 12
GIGS, GIGS AND MORE GIGS

I couldn't believe what was happening to me. I thought: At any moment now, I'll be called back to the lighting warehouse. 'That's enough of your comedy bollix now, Jay, back to real work,' I'd hear the bosses call in my dreams.

'Now, be careful over there, son. They don't take to the Irish too kindly. The last time I was there, I had to sleep on the street. Every B&B had "No Blacks or Irish" actually written on the front door. It's that bloody IRA – sure, I was taken in for questioning once, dragged out of a pub in London. Locked up in a cell, stripped naked, beaten, hosed down with a high-pressure fireman's hose. Then they threw this awful powder all over me. Fucked me into a room to interview me naked, accusing me of membership of the IRA!'

Dad then took a sip of his whiskey, followed by a long drag on his fag.

I looked at him with narrowed eyes. Sometimes Dad had a tendency to exaggerate.

CREAK!

The shed door opened. It was Mam with a tray of tea and biccies for me.

'He was watching *In the Name of the Father* on Sunday and then *The Shawshank Redemption* yesterday. So don't mind all that shite, Jason, enjoy your tea, son,' Mam said as she laid the tray down on the small table in the middle of the slanty shed.

Dad had certainly experienced the awful bigotry towards the Irish in London in the '60s. But I'm pretty sure he was never called in for questioning. If he had seen a movie, he would somehow wedge that into a story that included him.

MOVIES THAT INFLUENCED DAD

1. *ROCKY* ... Once put up a punch bag in the shed – it only lasted for two days. I suppose punching a bag with a smoke in your mouth is not going to last. Told the lads he had been sparring in the National Stadium with other boxers.
2. *BRAVEHEART* ... Actually tried to ride a horse in work. The local Travelling community knew Dad well. They had a site just beside Guinness's that was destroyed in

the gas-plant explosion. Apparently, they let Dad have a go on the horse. He sat on it, no saddle, slid off into a pile of car doors.

3. *THE GODFATHER* ... Sat in his chair with cotton wool in his cheeks, thought this was hilarious till he swallowed some of it. My mam was crying laughing trying to help Dad as he nearly choked to death pretending to be Marlon Brando.

4. *RAMBO* ... Decided to bring us all into the Dublin Mountains one day – which were just behind the house, by the way – in his suit and shoes to teach us the way of the forest and how to survive if we ever had to spend the night up there. We got lost. Well, he did. I knew the place backwards from playing up there as a kid. So I guided us back to the car, as it had gotten dark.

5. *JAWS* ... Bought binoculars to bring to Spain. Mam said he stood at the edge of the water looking into the sea for the fin of a shark. He even had a whistle in case he had to call everyone out of the water. I didn't see this first-hand, as, again, we wouldn't have enjoyed the heat and were more than likely in a neighbour's house.

'They're mannequin's legs,' I said.

'They're what?' asked airport security as I tried to put my mannequin legs through the excess baggage machine, all wrapped in black sacks like half a dead body.

'I'm using them for me comedy shows in London,' I told the fella.

'What in the name of God kinda comedian are you? Do you have your jokes stuffed in there?' he said, as he pushed my fake legs through the machine. 'Hey, here's one for ye ...' he said, as I tried to walk away.

This happens all the time to comedians. Many of these guys – security guards, taximen, builders, salesmen, you name it – they think we want to hear their jokes. We don't, and this is why ...

'There was this fella from Nigeria ... He was a *bleep bleep bleep* ... his wife loved *bleep bleep bleep*, so they *bleep*ed, then a Chinese guy walks in, they say *bleep bleep bleep* to the donkey that decided to get up on the *bleep bleep bleep*, so says the dwarf to the *bleep bleep*, it's hanging in my *bleep*!'

This is always followed by ...

'You can use that tonight!' from the idiot who has just told me the so-called joke.

Firstly, it's not your joke – you didn't write it, so I don't need your fucking permission to tell it. Secondly, not only can I not tell that joke on stage, I can never repeat all that racist, sexist mayhem to another living soul ever. I mean ever. I can't even write the details into a book. STOP TELLING ME FUCKING JOKES!

… and breathe.

Sorry, it's all the stress of recalling my first journey around London gigging. I hated it – the travel, that is. Believe it or not, I'm a home boy. I don't like loads of travel; I like to stay in my own country. Walk the hills of Glendalough or stay in Clare for endless days, have pints in Gus O'Connor's in Doolin after being in the sea at Lahinch all day.

I had no idea how successful this comedy lark was going to be. Don't get me wrong, I loved seeing Australia, Paris, most of Europe, Jakarta, Hong Kong, Singapore, New Zealand, Edinburgh …

It's not so much those big countries, as you get to more or less stay in the one venue while you're there. But when on tour in Britain, it's motorway, shit weather and very little to see, as you're in one town for a day, then out again.

But first, this was London. I was on my own at the age of roughly twenty-four. I was shitting myself. The tube was terrifying – I hadn't enough money in the budget for taxis. Everyone stares at you. Well, especially me, as I was headed to my B&B in Ealing, West London, with a backpack full of props and a full set of mannequin legs in a black sack.

Nobody spoke to each other there, not like in Ireland, when anyone and everyone that sits beside you will have a chat, which is lovely. I think we may be losing that a bit as Irish people right now. I hope we don't. If you are sitting on a train with your earphones in reading this and an old person sits beside you, take the earphones out and say hello. They might only want to say hello back, or maybe have a little chat. It's not annoying and we can always find out so much by talking to each other. It also makes the environment you're in safer: if we all kinda know each other on the train, bus, whatever, then we all feel safe. It's the oddball in the corner that has us all freaked 'cause they won't speak to us.

I'm telling you now: I wish just one person would have spoken to me that day on the tube. I thought I was about to be attacked every time I sat next to someone on one of those journeys. They were all afraid of each other, not a smile among them, because it's the unknown – none of us knew who was capable of what on that carriage.

Especially the Irish boy with half a dead body wrapped in black plastic bags resting against some poles.

WOOF WOOF WOOF!

'Hang on … shuuut uuup, you twooo,' roared a very Cockney lady to two massive Alsatians who were trying to kill whoever was on the other side of the very run-down B&B door, as she unbolted around seventy-eight locks.

Oh sorry, I forgot to say …

'SUMMARISE!'

Fucking hell, Niall.

I had gotten an agent in London. Dawn Sedgewick was a great agent – she had Simon Pegg, Ardal O'Hanlon, Tommy Tiernan, Catherine Tate and loads of cool acts. And now me. This was my first visit to London. Dawn had gotten me accommodation. Well, I say accommodation …

'This way, love, this way, don't mind the dogs,' said the little old English lady, as she tried to show me to my room while keeping back the hounds. She was bent over like a Monty Python character that Terry Jones would play. 'Sorry, love, the dogs are a necessity – there's terrible people living around here, just terrible. Best not to go out at night in this area,' she warned, sounding like Peggy from *EastEnders*.

Don't go out at night! That was all I'd be doing. Jesus, I just wanted to get back home to Ballinteer, to my dad in his shed, to me toast and jam in the boxroom supplied by Mam, with me sisters and Eric the Phone.

The room was awful. There was wallpaper peeling off the walls and one of those old metal-framed beds with sheets and a mattress that had been used for all sorts over the years. There was a three-bar heater in the corner that the lady said not to use, as gas just came out of it that could kill me. The window looked out onto a wall.

The en suite was, I shit you not, a toilet in the corner of the room. No walls or a door, just a toilet with a sink beside it. The carpet hadn't been cleaned since … eh, oh yeah, NEVER! It was like a prison cell.

This was all finished off with a black and white TV. The first thing I saw when I switched it on was snooker, our own Ken Doherty who would go on to win the World Championship the next year, 1997. But I was trying to watch the coloured balls in black and white.

GO ON, KEN!

'Ah, fuck's sake, Jason. Summarise, I really don't have time for fucking asides,' says Niall Tubridy.

I was so miserable, lonely and sad. This was not exciting. Then horror struck. I heard a group of people arrive in the other room. They had Cockney accents and there was lots of laughing, shouting, the noise of equipment being set up. The walls were paper thin. In fact, I'd say the wallpaper was the wall.

Then it started … sex noises. But not just sex noises. *Guided* sex noises.

'Put that in there, maybe raise your leg a bit, love. Right, now you join them!'

Oh Jesus, they were making a porn movie. My first night in London, and I'm put in a porn hotel.

I gathered up the fake legs and props. I crept by the porn-movie room in case a door flung open and someone asked me to join in with my mannequin legs.

I got to the massive front door with the seventy-eight bolts. Then the old lady appeared behind me with her dogs on either side of her.

'Are you going out there in the dark, son? I wouldn't do that if I was you,' she warned me as if we were in *Halloween* the movie, Part Fucking Terrified. I just ignored her and went out into the London night. It was around October, so London at night in the autumn. It was a scary place. I was really uncomfortable walking up dark streets with a map. There were no phones then, you see, so I had to use A–Z maps. If someone saw you using one of these, you lit up like a target, so I used to hide in gardens while I checked out my map so no one could see me.

Such a shite existence. I hated this. Where was my warm, fun warehouse? My bed in Mam's house? Irish people? I was going to die there, I knew I was.

But I never did.

Well, until I turned up at one of my first-ever gigs in London. The dreaded Up the Creek in Greenwich. Little did I know that this was the hardest club in London to play, if not the world. I thought maybe Dawn, my agent, had booked me in here to give me hair on my balls or something. Start hard, not easy. I had already been booked into a bleedin' porno B&B; now I was about to face the toughest crowd ever. They were famous for being the best hecklers in the world.

The night was hosted by the great Malcolm Hardee. I loved Malcolm. He's gone now – he drowned while using the dinghy he used to move to and from his floating restaurant called The Wibbley Wobbley. He was most likely hammered. I like to think of Malcolm singing to himself as he went down to Davy Jones's locker, holding a lit fag above his head; the singing fading all the way, the lit fag the last thing above water, all ending in a quiet sizzle.

But on this night, he was alive and well, doing a great job as MC. The crowd loved him. This was their church, and if they didn't like you, they would let you know.

I don't know who was actually on when this famous line was spoken, but rumour has it there was a comic on one night in Up the Creek that started with 'I'm a schizophrenic …'

One of the audience members replied …

'Well, why don't you both fuck off?'

This is what you were dealing with. They were not only annoying, they were funny and annoying, sometimes funnier than the comic. They were also famous for calling Malcolm back on if you weren't doing well. They would jeer, MALCOLM … MAL … COLM … MALLLCOOOLLLMMM, until they all joined in to boo off the comic.

Another famous one was TAXI! They would shout to have a taxi called for the act if they were shite.

This club was not for open spots or new comics like me: this was for Jack Dees and Jo Brands, tough comics that could handle it. Not little Paddy redhead and his fake legs.

'Ladies and gentlemen, you pack of pricks, welcome to the stage, all the way from Ireland, the wonderful Jason Byrne!' screamed Malcolm as I passed him on the stage, entering with my fake mannequin legs that had gone down a storm in Edinburgh.

I got to the mic and began to do the splits to total silence. There was just a sea of angry London faces wanting to kill me. I then dropped the legs, reached for my rubber duck, fake rubber hands and giant cards and …

'MALCOLM!' shouted one guy.

'Oh no, wait, wait,' I remember saying into the mic in a panic.

'MALLL … COLLMMM,' shouted another.

'No, I'll just – just wait, this will be funny!' This made it worse.

'Anything is funnier than this,' shouted a voice in the corner.

Soon enough …

'MALCOLM, MALCOLM, MALCOLM, TAXI, FUCK OFF, MALCOLM!'

The whole room had turned on me. Malcolm returned to the stage. Then, embarrassed, I gathered up my props while trying to drag my fake legs off the stage. I will never forget the words that came out of Malcolm's mouth next.

'Jason Byrne, everybody …'

'BOOOOO!' screamed the room, laughing at themselves.

'I thought he was great. You're a pack of cunts. He's a genius – he's coming back next week,' announced Malcolm as he winked at me and gave me a thumbs up.

The crowd went mental. 'Fuck off, no way' was heard all around the room.

Turned out that Malcolm was a massive Tommy Cooper fan, the famous prop magician comic. He loved what I did with my props, thought it was very different and fresh compared to the other comics at that time.

Malcolm pleaded with me: 'Come back now and face your fears, son, or you'll never come back.'

This sounded like advice from my dad. Maybe Malcolm was my English Paddy Lama. Malcolm and Dad never met, but if they had, I'd say that would have been one of the great meetings of our times. Both loved drinking, both loved smoking, both did what they wanted all the time and didn't give a bollix about anything.

Well, fair play to him. I came back the following week. Malcolm told me to slow down and not to panic, no matter what, to enjoy it and they'd love me. I did all this and I stormed it. The crowd at Up the Creek loved that I had the balls to come back so soon and was brave enough to try it again. They respected that. They thought I was mad to do so, but they respected me for doing it.

Thank you, Malcolm, for your sound advice. I've used this throughout my life, and it has helped me so much. Face your fears, and if you fail, get back up and go again, no matter what.

That night, London was good to me.

'Oh Jesus, yes, yes!'

'Mind his balls on your cheek, love – I can't see your eyes.'

'Sorry. Yes, yes, bang me!'

Oh yeah, except for my porn hotel.

★ ★ ★

Home at last. After nearly two weeks of terrifying gigs in London. I was back home in me lovely safe house in Ballinteer, where the only violent thing that happened was children knocking on your door and running away.

I was in bits. I had aged around ten years while experiencing the real life of a travelling comic.

LIST OF TOUGH GIGS I HAD JUST DONE IN LONDON

1. Up the Creek (we all know about that).
2. The Bear Pit (and it was).
3. Balham Banana (no MC, I walked out to silence).
4. The Walnut Tree in Kent (I did a gig in the corner of a pub using the tannoy announcement-system thingy as a microphone, fellas with pints just staring at me).
5. A gig in ... can't remember the name of the club. All I remember is the MC singing happy birthday before each act. We all died on our arses as the crowd just wanted to keep singing happy birthday.

The phone rang. It was my agent, Dawn. She said that RTÉ wanted to do a documentary all about myself, this up-and-coming comedian.

'Jaysus, I'll do it indeed – I'd better get the hair cut. But first, let's celebrate!' said Dad, after I told him the TV crew would like to interview himself and Mam as part of the documentary. So off he went to the pub to tell them all and celebrate, without us, as usual.

'Oh Jesus, I wouldn't know what to say. Sure, what would I say? I've nothing to say – why would those people care about what I've to say? Sure, I've never said anything in me life in front of a camera. I'm not a great talker, I hear you say,' said Mam.

The big day arrived. A full TV crew with sound, lighting and a director all set up in the leaky conservatory.

'Here, you better be paying the bill for those massive lights, or we'll need another bleedin' mortgage,' said Dad to the director.

'Oh, absolutely, Paddy, you just send us the bill for the lights and we'll cover it,' replied the unfortunate director.

LIST OF BILLS RTÉ GOT FROM MY DAD

1. ESB bill for two months.
2. Food bill for sambos and tea.
3. Petrol costs to come from Guinness's.
4. A day's wages, as he took a day off.
5. Per diems for fags and whiskey, to calm his nerves.

DING DONG DING DONG DING DONG

'Ah, lads, come in, come in. They're here, RTÉ is here, you lot take a seat in the sitting room, we'll be with you soon,' said Dad.

The doorbell was going on and off all day with odd fellas turning up with banjos, fiddles, squeeze boxes, even the spoons. What the jaysus did Dad tell the lads in the pub?

'So I had a friend called Pat Dunne – meself and himself started a radio show right here in Ireland. We got a load of valves, wired them all together with a microphone and started Radio PaddyPat. Not too sure who was listening to us, but pretty sure we were the first back then,' Dad told the crew.

'OK, Paddy, that's great, but maybe a bit more about Jason, growing up and all,' pleaded the director, as they interviewed Mam and Dad in the conservatory, which was freezing. Mam said nothing. She had nothing to say, as she kept telling the crew all day long, sitting in her massive fake-fur coat.

'Oh right, em ...' Dad continued.

'Can we stop for a minute? There seems to be some interference with the sound,' said the director.

'Pacemaker,' Dad told them.

'Sorry?' asked the director.

'I've a pacemaker, pretty sure that's interfering with your equipment,' said Dad in his official I-can-solve-your-problem-with-my-high-intelligence voice.

Dad then got up, went to the TV monitor, lifted his shirt and began to rub his left tit off the screen.

Mam explained, 'He does this to everything, rubs his man boob off tellies, radios, even pedestrian-light buttons. He thinks his pacemaker interferes with feckin' everything when it does nothing of the sort.'

Dad continued to walk around, rubbing his left boob off all the equipment, asking if that had changed anything. Of course it hadn't. While this chaos was occurring, my dad's mates kept trying to come in and out of the conservatory to see if RTÉ were ready yet.

'Ready for what?' the crew would ask as Dad ushered his mates back into the front room, closing the door.

Look, a tiny break here. I know people reading this may find all this very funny but are questioning the truth of this story. This all really happened. This is why I'm a comedian. Not because I'm funny or a great writer. Because this mad shit never stopped happening around me. My dad was a walking Del Boy, always getting himself into all sorts of shit, shit that I would just have to pass on while on stage. He really rubbed his man boob off

RTÉ's equipment. 'Now, I'd pay me TV licence fee to see that,' I hear ye all say.

Anyway.

'Right, it's not your pacemaker, Paddy. We can continue.' The director settled the matter.

'OK, well, I first started in Guinness's …' continued Dad.

'Ah, for jaysus' sake, Paddy, will you shut up,' said Mam with nothing to say. 'I'm so proud of our Jay – what he has achieved is amazing. He's the funniest fella ever,' she said proudly.

'Yep, he's been on *The Late Late Show*,' Dad interrupted.

'Tell us about that, Eithne.' The director tried to rescue the conversation.

'Well, we couldn't believe it. There we were, myself and Paddy, about to sit down and watch *The Late Late Show* with Gay Byrne on a Friday night,' said Mam.

'A pile of shite, by the way,' said Dad.

In Ireland, it is customary when you hear anyone say *The Late Late Show* to reply with 'a pile of shite', even if you're enjoying it.

'Paddy,' said Mam.

'Well, it is, full of boggers and Holy Joe auld ones,' answered Dad.

'Anyway, we were both sitting there, waiting for Bill Murray to come on, then, holy moly, out of nowhere, there was our Jay asking Bill Murray a question,' Mam said proudly.

'Wearing my shirt and tie. We had no idea he was there,' added Dad.

★ ★ ★

And they hadn't. No one knew I was going on *The Late Late Show*. This was the first time I was to see the inside of a TV studio. I had gotten one audience ticket from a mate of mine that was working on the Kilkenny Cat Laughs Comedy Festival.

Bill Murray was here to play the festival. I too was playing it for the first time ever. I robbed a shirt and a tie from my dad, got the bus to RTÉ and queued up with everyone outside. But for some reason, I decided to become this odd character, a geek. I stayed in character in the holding bay. No one wanted to talk to me – they were too busy sipping on their free glass of wine.

Then we went into the studio. Wow, it was amazing. I was on *The Late Late Show* … set.

'Pile of shite!'

Shut up, Niall.

The actual show that had had Bono, Mother Teresa and Bishop Eamonn Casey on it. This place wasn't a studio, it was a church, and the church prayed to Gay Byrne. The people around me (boggers and Holy Joes, Dad was right) didn't give a bollix who was on: they were here to see their god, Gay.

He came out before we went live. I thought the two old women either side of me were going to start crying with excitement over seeing their god right in front of them. Gay did a routine with the audience that he had been doing for years. A fella with a headset and a script told people when to clap and laugh.

Then Gay said, 'So we're going live in a few moments. We have Bill Murray on the show tonight ...'

You could see most of the people in the room had barely left their towns to go to Mass, never mind to the cinema to see Bill Murray. They had no idea who he was.

'If anyone has a question for Bill, pop your hand up and we'll get to you as soon as we can. OK, OK, let's go.' You can just hear his voice as I type this.

The music pumped into the studio, the word LIVE lit up every-where, and out came Gay Byrne to massive applause. He said hello, there was a bit of chat, and then he brought out Bill Murray and his brothers onto the set.

I PUT MY HAND UP IMMEDIATELY.

What the hell was I doing? Holy shit, what was I doing?! It was like I was taken over by the spirit of *The Late Late Show* …

'Pile of shite, Lord hear us, Lord graciously hear us,' say you all.

Gay Byrne began the interview as soon as Bill Murray and his brothers sat down. All the while my hand was waving all over the place. Gay Byrne could see it at the side of his eye. Even Bill looked up. The old women beside me just wanted to die with embarrassment, but there was more to come.

'Fella at the back with … eh … the tie and glasses, do you have a question for Bill?' Gay asked.

My heart was thumping in my chest. I mean, what the hell?! This was Bill Murray on live television, ye mad yoke.

'Yes, hello, Gay, question for Bill. So myself and my friends have been working with a few possessed humans. Then we moved onto a few possessed animals, cows and the like, anyway, my question for Bill is … have you ever seen a ghost and were you frightened?'

Jesus, I have never been so scared. I had actually gotten on live telly and said this. The Ghostbusters' actual catchphrase was: 'I ain't afraid of no ghosts!'

Bill looked at Gay. He thought it was a set-up. Gay looked at Bill, as he thought it was a set-up too. The fella on the floor with the headset didn't know what to do.

SILENCE.

Then …

'We were in Roly's Bistro earlier, a waitress came up to us, we ordered our food and she disappeared,' said Bill.

Well, the clapping couldn't have been louder. The fella on the floor with the headset was jumping up and down in front of us all to clap as if Bill was a genius. I mean, what an answer. Gay laughed and clapped, hoping there would be no more questions from the mad chap at the back in his dad's clothes.

'We then got a phone call from a pub near RTÉ. It was Jason, asking us to collect him. He said he had been on *The Late Late Show* (pile of shite). I said, I know, you nearly gave me and your mother a heart attack as we watched ye,' dad told the crew.

The stories went on. I jumped in and was interviewed with my parents and it went really well. My mam ended up saying loads for someone who had nothing to say.

The director wrapped, ending the interview after about two hours. This meant my dad's mates had been in the front room drinking with their instruments for two hours.

Out they came …

'When are we starting these auditions, Paddy?' asked one holding a fiddle.

'Auditions?!' said the director.

Apparently, when Dad had gone to the pub a few days earlier to celebrate the announcement of the RTÉ interview, he told his mates to bring along some of their instruments to show how good they were to the fellas from RTÉ. He told them they might get on the pile-of-shite *Late Late Show*.

The director tried to explain to my dad and the lads waiting that he had no power and these auditions would not be happening, that the crew and himself had had a long day.

My dad was full of whiskey, as were the lads with the instruments.

Cut to the funniest piss-up I have ever seen in Ballinteer. Dad had persuaded the crew to stay, got them all hammered, and they pretended to the lads they were auditioning them for the pile-of-shite *Late Late Show*. Lads with fiddles, banjos, accordions, about eight of them in total, all jammed into the front room, full of drink, with cameras on tripods recording nothing.

After that day, my dad was a hero in the pub. All the lads told everyone that Dad was a shoo-in with RTÉ. We never saw any of those lads on the pile-of-shite *Late Late Show*, not even Mick on the spoons, who even played them on his teeth, the mad bastard.

I was to appear on *The Late Late Show* the following year. Gay Byrne did not recognise me. He introduced me and brought me out in front of the boggers and Holy Joes. I walked out with my rubber hands on a stick. The boggers and Holy Joes had no idea what I was doing. I'm pretty sure I heard one of them saying 'I think he's a Protestant' as they stared at me in silence on live telly.

When I was done dying on my arse, the man with the headset on the floor did a mild clap, which the audience copied. Then Gay Byrne came out and said:

'Jason Byrne, no relation.' THE PRICK.

COMICS THAT HAVE DIED ON *THE LATE LATE SHOW* AND ARE TOTAL GENIUSES

1. Me, of course.
2. Tommy Tiernan (his Lamb of God routine).
3. Dylan Moran (said he hadn't seen this much blue rinse since the local denim factory blew up).

4. Rich Hall (well, I'll take the silence).
5. Johnny Vegas (famously said: 'I used to think I was funny till I came on this show').

The Late Late Show: a pile of shite, even when you're enjoying it.

CHAPTER 13
AAAND ...
ACTION!

'The comedian? The comedian?' a punter said to me in Dublin airport while I waited to go to Edinburgh.

'Yes,' I said, as proud as punch, as I put my hand out for a handshake.

'Is that him over there?' The punter pointed past me to Dave Allen, who was sitting on a chair waiting at the gate. Dave Allen, one of the best stand-ups – well, sit-downs, on a chair telling jokes with a fag and a whiskey in his hand. He put the Irish on the map and was amazing at slagging off the Church. 'May your God go with you, whoever he is,' was his sign-off line. He was my dad's favourite, by the way, next to Billy Connolly.

'Oh yeah, that's him,' I said, embarrassed.

CRINGE!

And did I go over to one of my heroes to say hello? Nope, and I have regretted it ever since.

OTHER TOP ACTS I STOOD BESIDE BUT WAS TOO AFRAID TO SAY HELLO TO

1. Michael Caine (the legendary actor) ... waiting beside me in the BBC Radio reception, only him and me. He nodded at me and probably wondered why I wasn't saying hello ... idiot.
2. Michael Palin (from Monty Python) ... in a queue in the airport on his way around the world. He was inches from me and I never said a word ... idiot.
3. Jarvis Cocker (from Pulp) ... in a cobbler's in London. I was getting laces for my Docs, he was in there waiting on shoes. Only a nod again ... idiot.
4. Gazza, as in Paul Gascoigne (footballer) ... at a play in London – well, *The Book of Mormon*. He was two seats away. Say hi to one of the greatest footballers ever, Jason? No ... idiot.
5. Bob Mortimer (as in Vic and Bob) ... at a club, watching us do a set. I sat beside him at the bar, inches from him ... idiot.

I had been on the telly once or twice now, what with my RTÉ documentary and an appearance on an Amnesty gig that we all did in the Olympia. I had asked for the orchestra pit to be filled with mattresses. When the MC called my name, I walked straight out, past the mic, and fell into the pit.

Can't do that kinda thing now because of insurance and the like ... No, you can't do that now because I could have died jumping into an orchestra pit.

'Alright, Jason! There he is.'

Finally, I was getting recognised. It was good fun when someone knew your name on the street, especially in Edinburgh.

'Hey, you're Gay Byrne's son!' a fella once shouted at me in Edinburgh.

'I'm not,' I said.

'You are,' he said, in his strong Scottish accent.

'Alright, I am,' I replied to get rid of him.

'Told you.' He wanders off, fag in mouth, tracksuit flapping.

Another favourite in Scotland – and I've had this in Ireland too – 'Hey, Jason, I'm going to see you tonight!' roared at me by a fella on a bike across the street.

'Oh great, thanks,' I foolishly answer.

'You better be funny!' The man cycles off, laughing to himself.

The best heckle I have heard was in Edinburgh. I had popped along to see a certain comic (no name, but famous). In the middle of the show, a Scottish fella stood up in the aisle, put his back to the comic, stood rigid facing the room and shouted …

'Utter shite!' as he stamped out of the room, chanting, 'Utter shite! Utter shite!'

The recognition I was getting was from a TV show called *Edinburgh or Bust*. For the full four weeks of Edinburgh, Channel 4 was following me and five other comics around the festival, as it was our first solo show in Edinburgh, to see if we'd sink or swim. It was on once a week during the festival. So the whole of Edinburgh was watching the programme.

Most people told me they watched it 'to see if we could see our hoose on de telly'. They weren't interested much in the acts.

If you want to see it, go online and you'll find all this insane stuff.

Let me just quickly recap: Edinburgh. Festival running the whole month of August. Roughly 3,500 shows a day. You are only one of them across hundreds of venues. Around 250,000 people come into the town each week. There are posters every-where. Acts are doing well, playing to full rooms, which could be anywhere from a ten-seater to a thousand-seater. Acts crying also, while they mostly play to one or two people a day. This place will break you if you can't handle it. Many a comic has fallen during the festival, never to return.

SILENCE FOR THE COMICS OF '97 ... LEST WE FORGET.

Cue bagpipes.

'BASTARD, FUCK OFF!'

'BOO!'

'SHITE!'

We were in Late'n'Live at 1 a.m. on a Sunday morning. The peak of the festival. This was the room where I had done my 'So You Think You're Funny?' competition the previous year. It was now a late-night club where all the comics hung out. It was sweaty, there was no air, and the crowd was always out to get us.

Channel 4 was there to film me doing my thing on stage that night. Just before me was Puppetry of the Penis, Frendy and Simon, two new lads from Australia. They came on stage naked, with only a cape and sunglasses, where they did what they called Dick Tricks. They had cameras facing their cock and balls which were then projected up onto a big screen. They would bend their genitals into different shapes. Their most famous was The Hamburger, which was their cock wrapped around one of their balls, then squashed down.

Now you get the idea. This was what I had to walk onto. This was a stage where I watched Johnny Vegas sing well into the wee hours of the morning with the crowd, refusing to leave the room. Johnny, that is. The crowd loved him.

I watched Russell Brand get beer glasses thrown at him as he teased the crowd. Jimmy Carr came on one night in a full white suit and was screamed at for five minutes. Jimmy didn't move. They all tired themselves out shouting at him. Then he said, 'Are we all finished now? If so, I'll begin,' just like a headmaster with unruly children. They loved him for it.

I had to walk out to that type of crowd.

But this time it was being filmed for Channel 4 … Everyone would see this.

Michael Smiley, now a very successful actor, was MCing. He left comedy when he got new teeth. He introduced me. I was, of course, terrified – I was still a relatively new act, this was my first Edinburgh, my first Late'n'Live. I gathered up around five pairs of rubber hands on sticks. The props were falling as I tried to get to the mic, sweating, as I could feel the crowd waiting to devour me.

I got to the mic, looked out, raised one pair of my rubber hands and …

'AHHH NOWWW NOOO, FUCK OFF!' one Scot shouted, then another, then another.

So I did, I fucked off, without a word spoken into the mic. Didn't even get the chance to die on my arse. I just died.

I thought my career was over after they aired that on Channel 4, but it wasn't. I was the talk of the town; my venues were full.

'Let's go to the mad bastard with the rubber hands,' they'd say. Did they? Oh, they did.

Channel 4 even convinced me to return to Late'n'Live, to do the gig again. I agreed, like the mad bastard I was, just as Malcolm Hardee and Dad had taught me. This time, I stormed it.

Thanks, lads.

I've been going back and forth to Edinburgh since 1996. I have never missed a year. It's like a training gym for comedy: it will chew you up and spit you back out if you're not careful, but if you stand your ground, rewrite the stuff that didn't work and keep getting up in front of these lunatics, it will make you the best comic ever.

★★★

'What in the name of Jesus Christ happened to you, boy? I told you to mind yourself in Edinburgh – you look like you've lost about eight stone!' moaned John Boorman, the director. Yes, I said John Boorman, director of *Deliverance*, *Excalibur* and soon to be the director of *The General*.

I had gotten a part in the movie starring Brendan Gleeson as the General, Martin Cahill, a gangster from Dublin. They were making a movie about his life (the gangster, not Brendan).

Dawn, my agent, was also an acting agent. As comics, we tend to do everything: write books, do radio, host galas, act, do TV in all sorts of ways.

I had been sent to a warehouse in Dublin. The door opened and there in the middle of this massive space was John Boorman, watching me as I walked in. He invited me, in a very posh accent, to sit down. I had some bollix on me then. Who he was didn't faze me. He asked about what I was up to, then told me about the film.

Finally, John asked, 'Which part would you like to play?'

'The General,' I answered.

John laughed a lot and told me that Brendan Gleeson had the part. 'How would you like to play a journalist?'

I said alright. We both stood and shook hands. He liked me – there was no reading, he just gave me a part there and then.

I walked back to the door, and halfway across the warehouse, John shouts, 'Look after yourself in Edinburgh, young man – I need you back in one piece,' while wagging his finger at me.

I turned and smiled.

But I hadn't listened. I had literally just returned from Edinburgh, where I had been sharing a flat with Tommy Tiernan. We had eaten nothing but lemon and honey in water for food, and the odd pizza. We were up all night drinking at parties and doing late gigs.

LIST OF PARTIES AT EDINBURGH ON THE LAST WEEK

1. Channel 4's 'So You Think You're Funny?' party (where myself and Tommy handed Peter Kay his new award for winning the comp – he said he was going to buy a new Ford Escort). Free drink all night.
2. *The Daily Telegraph*'s Critic's Choice party (Alan Carr had just won it). Free drink all night.
3. BBC New Writers party (one of the lads walked up to me with a helium balloon tied to his willy while I was talking to the head of the BBC. No one noticed till he walked away with two drinks in his hands, balloon still very much attached to said willy). Free drink all night.

4. **Universal Pictures party (myself and Tommy were doing shots through an ice sculpture: the lady would pour the drink down through the naked body of a man, and the booze came out his ice willy. Thank God we have no photos of that, 'cause that's how you drank it). Free shots all night.**
5. **ITV party (a free bar for four hours. I'd say the worst TV shows ever were commissioned on those nights).**

I had lost a stone. I was in my twenties, but now looked around fifteen. The character I was playing was supposed to be in his late thirties.

'Ah, he looks great, John.'

'Who's this, please?' John asked his crew.

'I'm Paddy Byrne, Jason's dad. I'm looking after Jason,' Dad said.

Dad had given me a lift to St Patrick's Cathedral. We were filming beside it. Dad had parked up, and as we got to the security guard, we both got passes. Dad was officially on the set as Jason Byrne's minder.

'OK, well, get him back into wardrobe, and make him look older, for Christ's sake. We're losing light,' shouted John Boorman.

A woman grabbed me to whisk me away to wardrobe.

'So I knew the General, Martin Cahill, personally. I drank with his crew here in Dublin ...' I heard Dad say as I left him with John Boorman, who was looking at my dad as if to say 'Why is this man talking to me?'

Soon I returned in old clothes all puffed up to make me look older.

John then asked if I had seen the real footage of the journalist stopping Martin Cahill in the street in 1998. It was on a programme called *Today Tonight*. Of course I hadn't – there was no internet then so how in the name of God would I have seen that footage? But you can see it now if you look for it online.

Cut to the weirdest moment of my career. I was brought into the Iveagh Flats, old buildings that were right beside the set. We knocked on the door of one of the flats.

A lady answered in her dressing-gown, again with an Alsatian dog roaring barking in the background. It must be a thing with older women living on their own, like my London porn-hotel landlady.

BARK BARK BARK!

'Ah come in, love, they're all here. I'm Rita. I'd get you a cup of tea, only the dog will get out of the kitchen and rip your heads off – hahahaha only joking,' she said in her best Dublin accent, as the shadow of the dog could be clearly seen jumping up on the glass of the kitchen door. He would have killed us all if he could have got in.

BARK BARK BARK!

There on the settee was Brendan Gleeson, dressed in the Mickey Mouse T-shirt that the General famously wore, and Seán McGinley in full threads too. I had never met them before. I said hi and the lads were lovely. Then the PA put a tape into the video recorder.

I squeezed in between Brendan and Seán. The three of us looked like schoolboys on a couch.

'Are you making a documentary or something? Loads of hoo-ha out there,' said Rita. She had no idea who any of us were.

BARK BARK BARK!

'We are, missus, it's about Martin Cahill,' answered Brendan. 'You probably knew him.' Brendan winked at me and Seán.

We then watched the footage. I got the idea. The reporter had doorstepped Martin Cahill, asking him had he robbed the famous Beit paintings. It was a massive robbery in Ireland, where the General had broken into the stately home of Sir Alfred Beit, robbing eighteen paintings from his collection.

'OK, places, everyone,' shouted John Boorman.

We were now back down on the street. They had buses, cars, bikes and people running to make it look like a busy street. This was for real, a massive movie set. I was really shitting myself. What had I got myself into?

Brendan and Seán were to come out of a building, and I was to run up to them through the busy street to doorstep Brendan. John Boorman sat on a crane that hung over the scene.

'Action!'

'Good luck, son!'

'Cut! What was that?' asked John.

It was only Paddy Byrne shouting from behind the camera.

'Quiet that man,' shouted John.

'Sorry,' Dad said, as he gave me a thumbs up.

'Action, and cue rain,' shouted John once more.

Rain, they made it rain, from huge hoses either side of the road. All the extras began to move, a bus was driven past, and the cars moved up and down. Brendan Gleeson and Seán ran out of the building. Brendan had his hand up to hide his face, a trademark of the General. I ran up and stopped them. This was it, my big moment in front of the best actors ever and an Oscar-winning director …

'Are you the General? Did you rob the BEE-IT paintings?' I asked.

'What?' said Brendan as he stopped moving, taking his hands down from his face.

'Cut! What did he say?' shouted John from the top of the crane.

The rain stopped like a sad water fountain giving up on life.

'Did you just say BEE-IT paintings, Jason? It's Beit, BEIT, pronounced bite!' roared John. 'OK, places,' he roared once more.

The rain started again, all the extras began moving, the buses, cars and so on.

'Aaaand … ACTION!'

'Are you the General? Did you rob the BEE-IT paintings?' I said again. I don't know why.

'CUT! CUT! CUT!'

Brendan Gleeson burst out laughing. 'He's going to kill ye, Jason,' Brendan said, as John Boorman's crane came down to earth. He disembarked and walked quickly over to me, all red-faced. The whole cast and crew looked on as John Boorman grabbed me by the shoulders and shouted into my face ...

'BITE BITE BITE, MAN, IT'S FUCKING BITE, STOP SAYING BEEE-IT!'

He realised he was dealing with a total novice. 'Rain, places, please, everyone,' John roared through gritted teeth. Rain, buses, cars, bikes, cast, crane all moving ...

'Are you the General? Did you rob the Beit paintings?' I said.

'CUT!' roared a relieved John Boorman.

Brendan and Seán both gave me a hug and the whole street clapped and cheered, even Rita from her balcony above.

'Well, ye made a bollix of that, son. But not to worry, you still have the stand-up,' encouraged Dad.

I did, but many more acting jobs were to come. My brain wasn't a fan of the one-liner.

'Can you run around backwards for a week?' asked Graham and Arthur, the writers of *Father Ted*.

I, of course, said yes. I was now about to be in the funniest and most important sitcom of its time, *Father Ted*! It was to be the last series. The lads were going to wind it up, having no idea that Dermot Morgan was to die shortly afterwards.

The episode was 'Escape from Victory', and I had got the part as the ref in the All-Priests Five-a-Side Over-75s Indoor Challenge Football Match. All I had to do was run around in a gym in Ennistymon for a week, then head to London for one line.

'Wait a minute, Ted, are those fake hands?' was the line, but as you'll find out, that was not the line that famously went out over the airwaves.

The day before I was to leave for Clare was Dad's retirement lunch in Guinness's. I had to get into a suit and head into town with Dad.

Dad drove in, of course; I still didn't have a car, only the moped. We walked through the famous James's Gate entrance and into the Guinness Brewery. The place was massive. We then walked into a weird-looking canteen. Then into a room at the back.

There was one long table in a beige room that looked like a boardroom from the seventies. There were old pictures of Guinness's on the walls, and the table had a miserable white paper cover with plates, knives and forks all set out. Mr Stint from the waiter course would have been furious.

Behind the head of the table was a blackboard. Written in chalk was 'Happy Retirement Paddy Byrne and Dan Ryan'. In shitty chalk. Guinness's must have been retiring these lads all week.

Dan Ryan walked in with about ten other men, who were old workmates of my dad and Dan Ryan. Finally, their manager came in. We mingled and I was introduced to them all. We then had a turkey dinner, served by one of the dinner ladies from the main canteen. Maureen was wiping the snot from her nose as she dropped the full plate in front of whoever was next up on the blackboard.

After dinner, the manager stood up for a small speech. It was here that I was to find out what Dad had been up to for the past couple of years in Guinness's. Mainly bollix all, from the sounds of the manager.

'I think this is the first time I've seen Paddy Byrne in about a year. He's a hard fella to track down in here,' said the manager, as all the lads laughed while Dad went slightly red.

After the sad retirement lunch, the names were rubbed off the blackboard and new ones written up by the dinner lady.

We headed to the Guinness's workers' bar, where the manager asked me if I would like a tour of Guinness's. He also asked my Dad if he would like to go.

304 · Memoirs of a Wonky-eyed Man

'Sure, why would I want a tour? I've been here since I was fifteen, for jaysus' sake.' Dad ordered another pint for himself, determined to get every last drop out of Guinness's before he left.

Five generations of Byrnes in Guinness's, and I had never properly seen the inside of this place. It was like a little village. There were actual Georgian buildings in there, with train tracks for little trains to transport the kegs from warehouse to warehouse. Steam was billowing out of giant vats. I saw inside a brew house. What a place – and Paddy Byrne couldn't be arsed ever bringing any one of us around for a tour.

'Sure, you wouldn't enjoy yourself, you'd be bored,' he'd say. More like we would be in the way of his drinking routine.

The day ended in a local pub with a very embarrassing moment for myself. All of Dad's mates were going around in a circle, taking turns to sing a tune. I was shitting myself. I didn't know any songs, so when it came to my turn they all stared at me.

'The auld triangle, goes jingle jangle ...'

Then total silence. Me, red-faced, as that was the only line I knew from the song. All these men waited for the rest ... but there was no rest.

My dad clapped and got all the others to clap. 'He was never much of a singer, were ye, son?' he laughed as they continued to sing other full songs.

★★★

'OK, and action!' roared the director on the set of *Father Ted* in the London studios.

We had all just finished filming in Clare. It was my first table read, so it was daunting. I was with Ardal O'Hanlon (Dougal), Pauline McLynn (Mrs Doyle), Frank Kelly (Father Jack) and Dermot Morgan (Father Ted).

I remember the first time I met Dermot. He walked over to me as I sat at the table, threw his leg up on the table with his balls in my face and said, 'A bit of young blood – welcome to the crew, son.' Well, that was enough to break the ice. We all howled and they welcomed me in with open arms.

In Clare, I'd run around the gym dressed as a ref for a week. We had old actors playing the footballing priests ...

'SUMMARISE, MAN!'

Jesus, OK. As I said: about a week to film, stayed in the Falls Hotel in Ennistymon, partied every night, had the best craic ever, wanted to be an actor forever, then went to London.

'GOOD LAD!'

Now, as the ref in the gym, all I had to do was run and blow a whistle, so I only had one line that I had to say in London on the set. Father Ted had fake arms hanging either side of his coat and was using a remote control under his jacket to control Jack in his wheelchair on the pitch.

By the way, the fake arms that Ted was sporting came from myself. Graham and Arthur were huge fans of mine and loved my fake hands routines, so they asked if they could use the fake hands for Ted. I then ended up in that episode. Amazing, really.

One line, lads. I can tell you now, having only one line in a movie, play or whatever is way worse than having monologues to do. You'd be warmed up with all the monologues. Also, I have a Jason brain that never likes to do what it is told, as you read earlier, with the BITE/BEE-IT/BEIT paintings.

Now, the line in the script was: 'Wait a minute, Ted, are those fake hands?'

'Action!'

I was to run into a dressing room, which was mocked up in the studio in London. All the interiors were in this studio – the famous living room, their bedrooms, the hallway and so on. But this dressing room was only built for this scene. There was also a live studio audience watching it all.

Again, a whole crew was waiting for me to run on and deliver my line so we could all get home.

Dermot (Father Ted) stood in the dressing room with fake hands sticking out of the ends of his jacket, flapping either side of him as he turned. Ardal (Dougal) stood beside him. I came running in. 'Wait, those hands, are a minute, there.'

'Cut – what did you say, Jason?' asked the director.

'Oh sorry, that was my first go. I haven't actually said anything all day. I'll get it right now,' I apologised.

'OK, places, everyone … and action,' shouted the director.

'Haha, I knew it, wait a minute, they look like you have fake hands hanging there, out of the coat,' I said, for some reason.

'Cut. Jason, the line is: "Wait a minute, Ted, are those fake hands?" OK?' the director reminded me.

'Yep, got it, let's go, no probs,' I reassured a now getting-pissed-off cast, crew and studio audience.

'Look, fake hands!'

'CUT!'

'I knew it!'

'CUT!'

'Well, well, well …'

'CUT!'

'Fake hands in a jacket are not allowed.'

'CUT!'

'Father Ted, as I live and breathe.'

'WHAT? CUT!'

'Look, Jason, we haven't got much time. Just say the fucking line.'

An hour or so had passed and there had been many attempts to say the correct line at this stage. I will never forget the next part. I ran out and said:

'Wait a minute, those are fake hands!'

'Cut, couldn't give a fuck, that will do, next scene. Jason, fuck off and thank you,' screamed the now exhausted director.

My brain is just a law unto itself. This was not the only time it was to take over on TV.

TOP EMBARRASSING MOMENTS ON TV, NEAR TV OR IN MOVIES

1. Told Professor Green live on *Sunday Brunch* on Channel 4 that I loved his album *Ill Manors* so much that I ran to it every day and it really helped me with my mental health. He said it wasn't his album, it was Plan B's.

2. Cooked with Marco Pierre White. I was told to go to the kitchen to get a steak. I came back with a tuna steak, thinking it was meat.

3. After a *Live at the Apollo* show I told Alison Steadman (*Gavin & Stacey*) that she was amazing as the mother in *The Royle Family*. She said she had never been in *The Royle Family*. I thought she was Sue Johnston, who would be much older than her.

4. Was on *Soccer AM* with Example, the singer. I knew him as Elliot in a previous life when he had worked for Universal's comedy department. He was in the green room with me before we went on air, but I had no idea he was Example. He said to me he was in music. I thought he was a PA for someone and said good on him that he was now a PA. Then he came out onto the set as Example. I have never been redder.

5. I was in *Alice in Wonderland* with Gene Wilder as the white rabbit's gardener. My partner on the day was Paddy Joyce, James Joyce's actual nephew. I spent all day telling stuntmen and a guy dressed as a rabbit who James Joyce was, as none of them knew him. I messed up me lines (SURPRISE SURPRISE) and walked all over a

giant carrot patch, causing a huge delay in shooting that cost a lot of money to repair. But I brought home Gene Wilder's autograph for Mam and Dad.

6. I went for an audition for a milk ad. Everyone in the audition room was fabulous and good-looking. When I walked in to the casting agent, she looked at my picture, then at me, then at my picture (in which, by the way, I looked like a model, because my dad had sent off my headshots to a mate of his that I think took George Clooney's head and put my eyes on it, thus confusing every casting agent in London). I didn't get the part, needless to say.

7. Auditioned for *Alexander*, the Colin Farrell and Oliver Stone flop. I didn't get the part because the casting agent said I should have been dark-haired, in my forties and able to ride a horse. I said I could ride a horse (a lie), but she still wasn't impressed. She then asked me to tell a joke down the lens to Oliver Stone. I told it, and it was so rude she opened the door in silence. I left, with the door slamming behind me.

8. I was in the movie *Killing Bono* with Robbie Sheehan. The director asked me to improvise the scene. Robbie shat himself as I completely made it all up. This suited me really well, but not Robbie, as he had no idea when to deliver his line.

9. Told Noel Edmonds he owed me an Evel Knievel from *Swap Shop* when I met him backstage at the Royal Variety Show. I had sent him one to swap for a Stretch Armstrong. He said he had no idea who I was and to fuck off.

Maybe my brain is best suited to the stage, the free-flowing madness, the space – it needs space. The chatter in my brain is insane. All directors and writers of my future work, just tell me roughly what you want me to say and I'll remember it. But put words down on a page to learn and I'm bollixed.

'Maybe I'm dyslexic?' I asked.

'Naw, you just had too good a time in school. You're just thick,' answered my therapist.

CHAPTER 14
'I'VE HAD YOUR MA!'

'Your father has had a stroke!' Mam screamed at me down the phone. Dad had turned seventy and decided to start smoking again. He had given up smokes when he had his first heart attack all those years ago. But in true Paddy Byrne fashion, as soon as he turned seventy …

'Ah sure, I'm nearly dead now, I may as well enjoy meself.' Of all the things the doctors told him to stay off, he went back to the poxy smokes.

LIST OF TIMES DAD WAS ON THE WAY OUT

1. Whenever you left him at the door ('You'll be lucky to see me next week').
2. Peeling potatoes on his plate ('My blood pressure is going through the roof trying to peel these. I'll be dead into me dinner soon').
3. Walking to the shops for the Lotto ('I'll be in a ditch if you're looking for me').

4. **Going for a check-up ('I'd say they'll keep me in and I'll never be home').**
5. **Going to bed ('I'll be dead in the morning like me auld dad').**

'I swear to God, that man has been dying since I met him,' Mam would sigh.

But this time, I drove over to Mam's as fast as I could. I got into the house expecting to find Dad literally having a stroke – the face drooping, dead arm, unable to walk – with all the symptoms.

Instead …

'You can't even have a stroke in peace in this house.' There he was in the corner of the room, sitting up. It looked like nothing was wrong with him. Of course, a fag in the mouth.

I walked over to him. 'Are you OK, Dad?'

'I would be, if your mother would stop moaning at me. As I said, you can't even have a stroke in peace,' he repeated.

I was so confused. Who told him he had had a stroke? Well, apparently, he couldn't read his newspaper too well, saying that he could only see half the lines on the page. And he was missing his mouth a bit when drinking his tea.

So he went to the Guinness's doctor – who, by the way, was about as useful as the workers were. It was like your best mate having a go at medicine.

That doctor had a look at Dad, said he wasn't happy with what he was seeing and then sent my dad to an optician to check his eyes. The Guinness's doctor is literally beside St James's Hospital. The wankbag sent my dad to an optician in Dundrum, a good forty-minute drive away. There, the optician looked into Dad's eyes and said, 'You've had a stroke, Paddy. You need to go to a hospital.'

So what was he doing here in his house?

'Dad, we need to call an ambulance,' I said to him.

'No, no ambulance, you can drive me in. I don't want everyone looking at me as they put me into that thing.'

'Jesus Christ, Paddy, you're having a stroke!' said Mam in a panic.

'Will you leave me to die in peace, woman?!'

Dad sat in the front seat of the car, as I drove them to the hospital, smoking. There were no signs of the stroke getting worse. 'Well, I've had a good life, Eithne. We never let the kids get in the way of our social life – no offence, son. But it looks like this is it,' he said, in the most laid-back manner.

'I'll kill ye if you die on me! Step on it, son.' Only a mammy could say such a thing.

★ ★ ★

At this point, I'm around forty. I've hopped forward a bit through my career and life here. For me to drag you all through my twenty-five-year career as a comic would be entertaining, but we'd need Trinity Library to stock all the stories. So I'll …

'SUMMARISE!'

OK, Lady Di had just died in 1997. I went to Dylan Moran's wedding the day she was being buried in London. He rang and advised us to leave early as there were dead princesses all over London (you can just hear his voice as he said this).

I remember me dad coming down the morning after Lady Di died. I was still living with Mam and Dad. Dad sat on the couch with his porridge, all hungover. He looked at us all and said …

'Jaysus, can you believe Pavarotti killed Lady Di?'

'What?' my mam said in total confusion.

'Pavarotti, the lads were telling me in the pub last night, he killed poor Lady Di,' he continued.

316 · Memoirs of a Wonky-eyed Man

'The paparazzi, ye gobshite, not Pavarotti! I swear to jaysus, I wish some prince would come and whisk me away from this shite,' Mam said, taking the empty bowl out of a totally confused Paddy Byrne's hand.

MY BONO STORY – YES, WE ALL HAVE ONE.

My phone rings in my pocket.

'Jason Byyyrrrne.' I hear a voice singing my name.

'Who is it?' I ask.

'It's Bono, Jason, Bonooo.' He just kept singing everything. At first, I didn't believe him, but his voice is so distinctive. It was really Bono.

'Jason, I need you to do me a favour ... Jason Byrne' – he sang my name each time – 'I need you to perform at Gavin Friday's sixtieth. He loves you as a stand-up, says he needs you!' (All sung.)

After a twenty-minute phone call, with Bono telling me how good I am as a stand-up and that Tommy Tiernan always recommends me, I then asked him: will there be a stage, lights and a mic? The gig was in the Devlin Hotel, Ranelagh, and the do was in the restaurant. I told him I was worried about gigging in a restaurant, as people wouldn't be listening – they'd be pissed.

'No way, man, you'll knock the ball outta the park!' Bono replied. 'And of course there'll be a stage and lights.' He finished the phone call by singing 'Goodbye Yellow Brick Road'. The line went dead.

Cut to me arriving upstairs at the Devlin. I walked into the room and stood to the side. Panti Bliss was singing happy birthday to Gavin Friday, along with Bono and The Edge, Neil Jordan, all of The Corrs, Jim Sheridan … You name it, they were there. I looked around the restaurant and people were sitting all over the place. There was not a stage in sight. Where was I to perform? This was going to be a disaster.

'Happy birthday to youuu …' they all sang and clapped along with Panti as Gavin blew his candles out. Then the loveliest man ever, Guggi, Bono's best friend, walked up to me. He was MCing the night. Guggi handed me the mic and said to stand just in front of the bar and perform from there.

What?! I went red-faced, pale-faced, and some trouser action even started.

Guggi said not to worry. We stood in front of the bar while people chatted and laughed, some still singing. I could see Bono waiting beside The Edge at their table. Oh God, I was about to die in front of an Irish god. Many Irish gods.

'Ladies and gentlemen, please welcome … Jason Byrne,' howled Guggi.

The room fell silent. Each and every one of them turned in their seats and faced me. I couldn't believe it – the respect was amazing. But of course it was. Every one of these musicians, actors, you name it, had been in shite situations in their past careers. Busking, acting in crap theatres, gigging to drunks not listening … they knew that to stand in front of a bar and try to do stand-up was near impossible.

I held the mic to my mouth and looked around at their expectant faces …

'Hi, I'm Jason Byrne, but looking at Gavin Friday's face right now, and the fact that Bono booked me, I think you were meant to book Ed Byrne, Bono!'

Huge laughter. 'Sure, not to worry, nobody here is called by their right name. Bono is Paul, The Edge is David and Gavin is bleedin' Fionán Martin Hanvey, which is even weirder than Gavin Friday …'

That was it: I had them. For half an hour they laughed and clapped. I finished to huge applause and Guggi took the mic back.

I watched as The Edge ran towards me. He hugged me and said, 'Bono is some bollix for doing that to you, man.' I told The Edge that he had promised me a stage. The Edge laughed out loud. 'That fucker has never ordered a stage or a light in his life – he wouldn't even know where to start.'

'OK, OK, OK,' I hear from behind The Edge. Bono grabs me, kisses me on the neck, holds both my cheeks, looks me in the eyes and says, 'You knocked the park out of the ball – you're coming with me.'

I sat with Bono for a good hour and we only spoke about our dads. Bono said he'd love to meet mine. I said it would be an anti-climax, as my dad would most likely not jump up and down; he'd just say, 'There you are now, Bono, will ye have a whiskey and red lemo and a fag?'

To be honest, this story is much funnier spoken out loud. Hopefully I'll get to do this book on audio too.

'Jesus Christ, anything is better than that monologue of bollix. SUMMARISE, I SAID!'

Alright, Niall, take it easy.

A SUMMARY OF THE AMAZING SHIT JASON HAS ACHIEVED

1. Had a drink on my own with Jude Law at the Hay Book Festival. I walked into a dressing room after my gig at around 10 p.m. and Jude Law was sitting on his own, sipping wine after his Q&A. I said, 'Hello, Jude Law.' He asked me my name and then said, 'Hello, Jason Byrne.' We sat and talked for a good two hours until our cars

came. I stood up and said, 'Goodbye, Jude Law.' He replied. 'Goodbye, Jason Byrne,' and off we went. Lovely, lovely man.

2. Also at the Hay Book Festival, I met Stephen Fry, Jon Snow (the newsreader) and Christopher Hitchens, who famously wrote a book criticising Mother Teresa. They were all in a shared dressing room and I asked what they were doing. Stephen said, 'Oh, we're having a debate on blasphemy – what about you, Jason?' 'Oh, best you don't come into my show then, Stephen.' I cowered before such greatness.

3. Also received a signed book of poems from Seamus Heaney, who was at Hay too. I said I'd love to see his reading. He said, 'I wouldn't – there's other poets on with me and they're dull as fuck.'

4. Was on *Countdown* with Richard Whiteley. I met him in Edinburgh, and when he asked me to come on *Countdown*, I did. I gave out biscuits whenever a contestant won a round. They didn't know what to do, as they took it all very seriously. I was in Dictionary Corner. The lady gave me a word, 'dugout', and I pretended to have created the word from the letters. When asked what it meant, I had no idea. I thought it meant to dig yourself out of something. It in fact was referring to a canoe carved from a tree. Jaysus!

5. Did a gala with Joan Rivers in Montreal. She called me on to 2,000 people as Greg Giraldo (who has sadly passed since). I came on and said I was Jason Byrne. All I heard from the wings was 'Hang on, hang on, cut,

stop, whatever'. Joan walked back onto the stage, put her arm around me and said, 'I shouldn't be doing this, Jason, I'm too old. I mean, look at me. I'm hardly recognisable with all the work that's been done on me. I'm an old fool. You go to the side of the stage and we'll try this again.' I walked to the side of the stage, she introduced me correctly this time, and I stormed it. I was invited to her dressing room afterwards, where I laughed all night. What a lady.

6. Was close friends with Nicholas Parsons, one of the longest-running presenters on radio and TV. He walked up massive steps every year to see me perform at Edinburgh. When he was ninety-five, I said to him, 'I can't do this till I'm ninety-five.' He then said to me, 'My dear boy, if you stop or retire, you will simply die. Your body will think it has no purpose.' The following year, he stopped working for a few weeks, as he broke his arm, I think, but then shortly after died. I loved him and miss him a lot.

7. Wrote for Lenny Henry in his house in Reading. While I sat there, Dawn French walked in. I said hi, and she asked what we were doing. I said writing sketches. Dawn said, 'But he's not even funny, Jason. You'll have your work cut out for you.' Lenny then replied, 'Why don't you and Jennifer go and dress up as *Braveheart* with stakes through your chests – that's funny, isn't it?' There was lots of laughter that day between us all and the show went on to win a Golden Globe.

8. Won a Sony Gold award for my BBC Radio 2 show *The Jason Byrne Show*, all thanks to my amazing producer Julia McKenzie.

9. Was on *Live at the Apollo* on the BBC many a time. In fact, that's how people know me in Britain: 'You're that bloke with the special eye.'

10. Sang with Leo Sayer on stage in Edinburgh with a host of comics all roaring 'You Make Me Feel Like Dancing' till 2 a.m.

11. Was on the *Graham Norton Show* with Geoffrey Rush, Gwyneth Paltrow and Lady Gaga. I stood backstage waiting to be called on with Geoffrey and Gwyneth. Gwyneth then looked at me and Geoffrey and said, 'We're fucked – he'll only want to talk to Lady Gaga tonight,' and she was right. When saying goodbye, I said 'I'll see you later' to Lady Gaga. She stood there confused as to why I'd be seeing her later.

12. Played snooker with Ken Doherty and our all-time hero Alex Higgins. I was doing a hidden-camera show for RTÉ called *Anonymous* where Ken dressed up as a priest. He was to play snooker with Alex to try to trick him. As soon as Ken bent down to take his shot, Alex asked, 'Why is Ken Doherty dressed as a priest?' Alex knew Ken's snooker style and spotted him immediately. We then played snooker later that night with Alex, full of pints and weed (Alex, not us). The night ended with Alex saying 'I fucking hate priests'.

I also performed on two Royal Variety Shows and met Charles and Camilla. I shook Charles's hand and asked him if he was going for a pint later. He said, 'I won't, but she will,' while pointing at Camilla. Camilla said, 'Oh yes, where are you going?' Hilarious.

Met Homer Simpson in Kilkenny, did a sitcom for the BBC that flopped, became massive in Paris, Finland and Australia, have stayed the biggest-selling act in the history of the Edinburgh festival since it started ...

FX: SLOW HAND CLAP.

CLAP ... CLAP ... CLAP... (slowing down) ... CLAP

'Are you finished?' says Niall Tubridy.

'Yes.'

'Thank fuck for that. That, my friend, was painful.'

'Well, I don't know. The doctors tell me I'm a miracle,' Dad said as we collected him from the hospital after a week of observation. He was lucky. He had had a mini stroke that didn't develop into anything larger. Doctors told him to ease off the drink and totally cut out the smokes.

When we got home, Mam said, 'Straight up to bed, Paddy, to rest.'

'Feck that, all I've been doing is resting in a bed in hospital. I'm off out to me shed for a smoke and a whiskey before I have another stroke!'

Unbelievable. Dad never did, never would, never had, never ever did anything anyone told him. He did as he pleased. The meaning of life according to Paddy Byrne was: 'couldn't give a bollix!'

Around this time, Dad decided to go to a few of my events. I'm not sure why, but I think it was because he had looked at death a little in the face and thought: holy shit, I'd better start to get involved a bit. I had two boys at this stage, Devin and Dan. Dad even began playing football with them out in the back garden. I mean, who was this man?

An appearance on *The Late Late Show* came around again. This time, it wasn't with moany Gay Byrne, who never asked me back, or Pat Kenny, who never had me on. No, it was the man that is Ryan Tubridy – a great fella with a great sense of humour, thus why he would always get me on.

Dad, Mam, Dad's best pal Pat and his wife Maureen all came to the studio. This was to be a huge turning point in my career. I brought them all into the green room. There was Pádraig Harrington and Stephen Fry with their PAs, friends and relatives. Dad couldn't believe he was meeting the great Pádraig Harrington. He was a fan of golf – well, Pat and himself would follow the golf in the pub when Pádraig was doing well, as it involved drink.

They told Pádraig that they watched every swing of his, which was a lie, then turned to Stephen Fry. Dad said he loved all the stuff he did. Dad had no idea what stuff he did and didn't even know who he was.

Stephen said, 'Thank you, Paddy, for being a fan of my stuff,' and turned to me with a raised eyebrow.

I have met so many great men and women in that green room, but my biggest and proudest moment was meeting Paddy Hill and Gerry Conlon, men put in prison for crimes they did not commit. I sat with them after my piece on the show. Gerry Conlon looked at me with those deep black eyes and asked, 'What do you do, Jason?'

'I'm a stand-up comic, Gerry,' I answered.

Never will I forget this …

'Fuck, I would never do that, no way would I be able for that,' said Gerry, while Paddy laughed.

I then said, 'But you spent fifteen years in a prison for something you didn't do.'

Gerry then looked at me. 'I'd rather do fifteen years in prison than do stand-up, son – fucking hell, that's brave.' Gerry thumped Paddy Hill and they both laughed.

We drank with them all night.

★★★

'How much is that, love?' Dad asked the lady at the bar in the RTÉ green room.

'It's free, love,' answered the bar lady.

Well, you couldn't have said sweeter words to my Dad …

'It's free, Pat – the drink is free. Well, tell you what, love, fill that glass up with whiskey and Pat will have the same.'

We were all called out of the green room. The show was about to begin. Dad and Pat said they would follow us, but they never did. They never came into the studio, instead just saw bits of the show on the screen in the green room and got locked for free.

This was the show where my 'be careful what you wish for' happened. I brought out my Mammy Blinds. I held up a set of metal Venetian blinds and pushed my fist through them. I explained to a crying laughing Ryan all about how your mammy hadn't time to come outside to scold you, but instead belted her fist through the blinds and knocked ferociously on the window.

It was a hit. Everyone in Ireland was watching that night and my gigs sold out. Except every time someone came to my gigs, they'd shout …

'Do the blinds, are you going to do the blinds, I brought me family and I told them you'd do the blinds!'

So the blinds stayed in the act for longer than I would have liked.

My mam was famous at Mass.

> FATHER DECLAN (from the pulpit): And well done to Eithne Byrne, for her famous rapping-through-the-blinds-on-the-window routine that her son told us all about on *The Late Late Show*.

Oh, she was outside Mass for hours as the famous mammy of Jason Byrne, answering all the questions about blinds.

'Yes, yes, that was me, yesss, I know, very funny, yesss, *Late Late*, yesss, met Ryan, yesss, RTÉ green room, yesss very proud, yesss …'

Dad had to pretend to everyone that he had seen it, but he and Pat were in bits by the time I got on and don't remember it at all.

'Yes, son, very funny with the thing on the *Late Late*. They're all talking about it in the pub tonight,' he said, after coming home from hours of lying in the pub to other auld fellas about my appearance.

★ ★ ★

Getting to Australia and New Zealand was an amazing achievement for me. I appeared on the Melbourne International Comedy Festival Gala on TV there – feel free to google it, there's years of it.

I brought a cardboard box onto the stage and put a bloke from the audience in it. Then I dragged him around while he sat in the box making car noises.

Well, the next day it aired, and the Aussies were ringing the ticket office to ask them if they had any tickets to 'the Irish guy with the box'.

That's how I became famous in …

1. Australia, 'the guy with the box'.
2. Britain, 'the special eye fella'.
3. Edinburgh, 'your man with the rubber hands'.
4. Ireland, 'that eejit with the blinds'.
5. Roscommon, 'the fella with notions'.

I would spend a lot of time with Des Bishop in Melbourne as we both gigged. You know Des Bishop, the fella that does the immersion bit, from New York but lives in Ireland, but has now gone back, kinda.

Anyway, each Monday myself and Des would hit the Great Ocean Road just outside Melbourne and head to a beach called Lorne. Now, Des is an amazing swimmer. I've watched him swim out to sea so far that he disappears. I, however, like to stay in my depth with my head above water.

'For fuck's sake, Jay' was a mantra of Des's.

While I've been writing this book I've realised, firstly, I'm shit at spelling as the spellcheck has lit up as I typed. Secondly, I know I'm good at comedy, but I seem to be better at injuries.

Par exemple … I once was bursting for a poo – a shite, if you will. I ran in to the toilet, pulled my trousers and jocks down, sat down too quickly and me knee fell off. Well, the cartilage ripped. I was then stuck on the loo with my leg locked. I had to walk off the loo in a sitting position, then stand up really quickly to bang my knee back into place.

I mean, who rips their knee on the jacks? Me, that's who!

Anyway, Des made me get a wetsuit …

'What do you mean he made ye?'

If you knew Des, you'd know.

'Get a wetsuit, Jay, we're going surfing,' Des announced as we looked into a raging sea.

Australia is great, but everything tries to kill you there. Wildlife, sea life, the sea. Australia hates humans – we do not belong there.

I got a wetsuit and a boogie board – you know, a tiny surfboard to lie on instead of standing on. Des, of course, didn't get any board: he was going to 'body surf, brooooo …'

I mean, you have to have a body like a fucking surfboard if you want to do that. A lot of us do not have that type of body and would simply sink, but this man could use his body to actually surf.

'Jump through it, jump through it, bro,' roared Des at me in the sea.

'Yeah, mate, dive through this fucker,' said an Aussie swimming beside us.

A massive wave was coming at us. Everyone was ready to jump through it, but I was terrified. It looked like the end of the world coming at us.

SMASH!

Everyone jumped through the wave – everyone except for Paddy idiot here. I totally panicked and tried to jump over the wave but the wave grabbed me and spun me around like a washing machine. I couldn't stand up, I thought I was going to die. The wave bashed me around like a ragdoll, boogie board smashing against my head as I tumbled. Then, after what felt like a lifetime, I surfaced, having no idea if I was further out to sea or back inshore.

I tried to plant my feet, and thank God, the wave had washed me ashore. I stood up.

'Bro, your fucking arm!' screamed Des.

I looked down to my left. My arm was completely dislocated. The boogie board that was attached to my arm had acted like a lever in the water, and my arm was now pulled fully out of its socket. Then – I don't know why – I turned into a man from Galway. A lot of people do strange things when they're in shock. Des said I sounded like I was from Connemara.

'Oh Jesus, Dessie, me arm, me arm, Dessie!' I screamed in my new Connemara accent.

I still had the wetsuit on, but my arm was out of the socket underneath.

Des could not stop laughing. It was more the accent he was laughing at, but you know, when one of your mates is in an accident, your first instinct is to laugh.

'Is there a doctor here?' Des ran up and down the beach like something out of *Baywatch*, asking everyone on the beach if they were or knew a doctor. It was April in Melbourne, during their autumn, so the beach was not full.

Eventually, we found a couple that drove me to a local doctor. We arrived at his surgery, which was closed as he was having his lunch. He saw me and didn't panic at all, as he was used to dislocated-armed surfers.

'Me arm, doctor, oh Jesus, Dessie, me arm, Dessie,' howled the now Connemara man.

Des had his face in a towel, trying not to laugh out loud.

The doctor opened my wetsuit. I could now see my arm swing out of its socket. He gave me painkiller stuff to suck on, then simply and gently popped my arm back into its socket like I was Brian O'Driscoll, our great rugby captain, before going back onto the pitch.

Now the thing about stand-up is that, not only is it the hardest, scariest job in the world, but no matter how ill you are or what's going on in your life, you still have to perform, unless you're nearly dead. It's not like a real job, where someone can stand in for you. It's just you and only you. You are the show.

LIST OF TIMES I HAD TO PERFORM EVEN THOUGH I WAS BOLLIXED

1. Had pneumonia, had to gig even though I couldn't hear myself talking and had a fever of 40°C.
2. Got a concussion in Cork City Limits Comedy Club. There was an archway behind me on the stage covered by the backdrop. While on stage, I thought it would be funny to jump through the backdrop, but I went to the side too much and ran at the wall as fast as I could. Did the rest of the gig in black and white.
3. Went on *The Late Late Show* the day my father-in-law, Eddie, died.
4. Did a show the day my best friend's girlfriend took her own life.
5. Got five stents, had a tiny break, went back on stage dangerously too soon.

And now, here I was in Australia with my arm in a sling. I wasn't exactly sure of the damage – I wasn't covered for a scan over there, and it would have cost thousands. I still wasn't well, they should have sent me home, but there were still three weeks left of the Melbourne Comedy Festival.

'Naw, Jason, you'll be alright,' said the promotors as they dragged a mattress onstage and left it beside my mic. 'If you faint with the pain, fall onto the mattress,' they advised. This is no lie: they dragged a mattress out for me to fall on. They are tough fuckers over there, but this was insane.

I did the full festival with what I thought was just a sore arm. Got to Dublin and went in for an MRI scan. I had ripped every muscle in my rotator cuff, 360 degrees of muscle, as the arm went full circle to come out. I had also broken bone where the muscle had pulled away from the shoulder, taking a fragment of bone with it.

I'm pretty sure I shouldn't have been gigging that year, but it was good material. I told the crowds what had happened, all about me turning into a fella from Connemara, nearly dying in a tidal wave.

Meanwhile, Des was telling the same story in another room, how Jason Byrne dislocated his arm in a two-foot wave.

Apparently, that's all it was. Des said you don't measure the wave from the ground, it's from the surface up. 'You, bro, nearly drowned in a puddle,' laughed Des into his coffee.

'Oh Dessie, oh Dessie, oh Dessie,' is all I have to say to make that man laugh now.

Despite this, I still go back to Australia. It's a beautiful place to gig.

'No, no, no, I couldn't go to one of your gigs, son, 'cause of those bastard hecklers. Me nerves are still at me since that explosion in Guinness's' – which he wasn't even at. 'The TCP will always be there.'

I was back in the shed with Dad. I had a Vicar Street gig in Dublin that night and was trying to convince him to come along.

CREAK!

The shed door opened. It was Mam with tea and biccies. She looked tired.

'Are you OK, Mam?' I asked.

'I'm knackered, son. This fella here has had me up all night with going for wees every five minutes,' she explained.

'It's the full moon, Eithne,' said my dad.

'Ah, not the moon again, Dad?' I said.

'Oh Jesus, don't, Jason, just don't,' warned my mam. She sighed. 'You see, this is the man I married, a feckin' fool. He's two-thirds Guinness, more like, that's why he has to get up all night. The moon, me arse. I'm off to get ready.' She laughed at her moon/arse connection.

I too had to head, as Vicar Street was that night.

The place was packed. There were over a thousand people in, and I was about to go onstage all on me lonesome. Mam had come in with Cora (remember Cora? She was the auntie that always knew a group of fellas to do jobs) and my uncle Michael.

Mam was great at going to my gigs. I would always hear her laugh first, and also hear her telling people to shut up if they were talking during the set. She loved it.

Anyway, I was onstage in Vicar Street, and about twenty minutes in, there's a heckle from the balcony on my left.

'I've had your ma!' the heckler shouted.

People went, 'Oooohhh!'

I dealt with it by saying, 'Well, you alone may have had my ma, but most of us in this room have had yours!'

There was a huge round of applause. That shut him up. Then I heard a little bit of raucousness up in the balcony, like a stumble followed by some heavy mumbling. It soon stopped.

The show was a total success – people loved it. I sat backstage in the small green-room bar after. My mam came in with my auntie Cora and uncle Michael. Mam seemed a bit weird as she hugged me. 'Well done, that was so funny.'

Then who appears behind her, only Paddy Byrne. 'Son, well done,' he said as he came stumbling in. His tie was over to the side, and he had a whiskey in his hand and looked slightly dishevelled. Mam looked angry with him and there was a weird air about it all.

'Well, I finally made it in to see you, son,' said Dad.

'Yeah, none of us knew he was coming, but boy did they know he'd arrived,' said Mam through gritted teeth.

What was going on? But we all sat down, had drinks, and that was the end of it.

A few weeks later, I was talking to my uncle Michael at a cousin's wedding. He had a few pints on him. 'Now, your mam told us all not to tell you,' he began.

This is a major Irish trait: when we are told not to tell someone something, we just have to get it off our chest. Which was what was about to happen.

'You know that night in Vicar Street? Well, none of us knew your dad was coming. He sneaked in to one of the balconies to watch you. When that fella shouted, 'I had your ma,' your dad was sitting right beside him,' Michael told me.

'Oh Jesus Christ,' I said, while rubbing my face.

'Anyway, just after that fella shouted that, your dad grabbed your man, pulled him onto the steps and started decking the head off him. The bouncers had to drag your dad off him, as he nearly killed the fella. I mean, of all the people to sit beside, the comic's dad. And not only his dad, fucking Paddy Byrne,' laughed Michael.

I looked over at my dad at another table. He looked at Michael and knew that Michael had told me the story. Dad could see the look on my face. He held up his Guinness and cheered me. I cheered him back, so proud of what he had done.

He, of course, was not allowed to any other gigs ever again; my mam had barred him.

So be careful who you're sitting beside when you decide to heckle the comic. You may be pulled aside to have the shite beat outta ye by a disgruntled relative or friend.

Go on, the Paddy!

CHAPTER 15
SEE YA, DAD

'I'm just up in Rachel's, Mam – I'll be over soon.'

It was the morning of 23 February 2020 and I had just finished two nights in Vicar Street, Dublin. I was doing the Ballinteer visit: Rachel first, then down to Mam and Dad.

Mam sounded quite odd on the phone. 'By the way, your dad says he can't get out of bed. It must be his back or something – he's rolling from side to side but can't sit up. Yep, defo his back. The doctor injected steroids into his spine earlier.'

I told Mam I would be right there. I left my son Daniel with my sister, because I had a feeling that Dad was in a bad way. I could hear it in Mam's voice. The doctors had warned Dad again and again and again that if he did not give up smoking, at least, never mind the whiskey tipples in the shed, he would most definitely suffer a severe stroke. The smoking alone was blocking his arteries, and he already had a pacemaker and many stents. So it was just a matter of time.

As I drove there alone, I felt that it was time, that this was it. No more Paddy Byrne.

I was up with Dad only the week before. He was sitting on the couch with his legs spread out in front of him. His back was hurting him and he was in a lot of pain. Again, because he was such a high risk, they couldn't operate, so they were to inject him with steroids the next day.

Dad always had something niggling wrong with him. He insisted that it was old age. I can tell you now, my dad had gout because of drinking, so his feet and toes were always sore. He never went walking, never moved his joints. He only moved his right arm to his face with a Guinness in his hand. His lower back was sore because of a lot of sitting on bar stools.

But there was no telling my dad. 'Sure, you have to have a laugh, son. You can't be watching every move you make or you'll drop dead with the stress.'

I suppose, as usual, Dad was right and also dead wrong. Most of his mates had passed away now. A lot of them would have been seen walking in the parks with their wives, and Dad said that's what killed them. He had a great time, living the way he wanted. No one was going to ever tell this man what to do.

In the living room, my mam was sitting across from my dad in a huff. No doubt he had just said or done something horrendous.

'Are you alright, Mam?'

'The Sky man has just left, and I'm mortified, son, mortified!' she replied.

'What? Sure, I thought it was his job,' said Dad.

A few days before this, I had been in the house, and Dad was shouting down the phone at a robot, a Sky TV robot.

'One, Paddy, yes! Yes! No! I don't fucking know! Ah, ask me bollix!' Dad hangs up. 'I can't understand this poxy thing, son. I need to talk to a real person. The Sky box doesn't work anymore,' Dad sweated.

I looked down at the telly. Sure enough, the box wasn't working. We needed to get a tech out to the house. I calmly took the phone off my dad, rang Sky, did the 'one, yes, no, Patrick Byrne, address' routine, and a technician was on his way.

This all sounds normal, until we all found out the real reason for the need of the Sky man.

Dad had a huge flatscreen TV in the good room. It was broken, and Dad had had the back off it for months. He was twiddling with this wire and that, but had no idea what he was doing. He had electrocuted himself more than once, and left Mam in a blackout for a good few hours one day. Dad never threw out anything – he was a bit of a hoarder.

LIST OF STUFF DAD NEVER THREW OUT

1. Old school copybooks belonging to us.
2. A multitude of clocks in the attic.
3. Receipts going back years. I even found one for my first-ever eye test.
4. Nuts and bolts in jam jars, and fuses.
5. Shredded paper in black bags. He had actually bought a shredding machine, shredded the paper and kept the shredded paper. Why? 'Because anyone could get those shreds and piece them together at the dump and steal all our info,' Dad would howl. Yeah, sure, they were dying to get their hands on those five Isle of Man coins he had in a safe.

DING DONG!

Dad opens the door and lets the Sky man in. The Sky man heads to the Sky box and tells Dad that it's not broken at all, that the cable that should be feeding into the telly is gone. Dad apparently acted all dumb. The Sky man fixed the box by plugging in a new cable.

As he was packing away his tools, my dad brings him into the back good room to where the old TV was standing with the back off it.

'I'll give you an extra fifty if you fix this for me, son' were his actual words.

'I don't fix tellies. I just install Sky,' the man told my dad.

'What? But you're a telly man, son – surely you know how to fix tellies?' asked Dad. 'No? Oh right, well, you may as well have this back then.' Dad opened a drawer in the good room and gave back the cable he had taken out of the back of the Sky box.

The man left in total confusion.

'That eejit there, son, took the cable from the Sky box, hid it and told us all the Sky box was broken, so an engineer would come out here. Your dad then cornered him and it was only then that we realised what Paddy was up to. He only wanted the Sky man to fix his silly TV, and in the meantime, we've had no telly for a week!' howled Mam from her chair.

'Ah well, I tried, didn't I? No harm done,' laughed Dad.

Again, no wonder I do stand-up. This man had such a neck on him. You have to give it to him, he didn't give a bollix.

I ran up the spiral staircase. Well, it was a half-twist staircase that my dad had bought off a fella in Guinness's to make more room in the hall for my mother's phone table, all discussed in my first book, *Wonky-eyed Boy*.

My mam was standing at the end of my dad's bed. I looked down at Dad. He was reaching frantically with his right arm, waving it about as if trying to grasp at anything. His right leg was kicking the covers off him. His whole left side had gone and his face had drooped completely. This was the massive stroke the doctors had spoken about.

'It's his back, Jay, defo his back,' my poor mam kept saying. She was in shock, trying to make it as if it wasn't bad at all, denying what was happening to my poor dad.

'The rugby had started so I got worried because your dad should have been up, but I thought maybe he was sleeping again. I came in here at around 2 p.m. and found him like this,' said Mam.

You see, Mam and Dad slept in separate rooms, due to the fact that Dad snored and would roll about in the bed after a few whiskeys. Before they had the separate rooms, Mam was often found buried under Dad of a morning. So she had no idea that Dad had suffered a massive stroke sometime during the early morning. There was no telling how long he had been like this.

Fight or flight, they say. I'm good in these situations. I just remain calm, separate myself from the person or situation that is happening and deal with it.

I told my mam to hold onto Dad's waving hand. He was looking at me with his good eye as the other one kept closing. I could see that he knew what was going on. He kept saying, 'There you are, Jay, there you are,' from one side of his mouth.

I rubbed his forehead and said it was OK, to just try to relax.

I rang the ambulance, described what had happened and told them it most likely a stroke. I don't know who that lady was on the emergency line that day, but she was an angel. She kept me on the phone the whole time, asking me questions about my dad, how he looked, how his breathing was, until the ambulance lads arrived, all with total empathy and calmness.

'Right, let's have a look at ye, Paddy!' said one of the ambulance men.

I brought my mam out of my dad's bedroom as they worked on him. I then stood in the doorway in case the lads needed answers to questions about his meds and such. There were three of them, pulling his pyjama top open, sticking ECG pads all over him. Dad continued to reach with that right hand, and one of the ambulance men held his hand the whole time.

They were wonderful with him, slagging him, asking him if he would have had better pyjamas on him if he knew visitors were coming. It was manic in there, but they kept the humour up. Dad would have loved this, as did I. It's an amazing trick to keep everyone's mind off the inevitable. Humour literally is the best medicine.

'We're missing the rugby because of you, Paddy Byrne,' roared one of the ambulance men, making sure Dad was responding.

And he was. It was heartbreaking to see him trying to smile, even though only half his mouth could lift up due to the stroke. Paddy Byrne was still in there. He always had the strongest brain I had ever known – not necessarily academic, but just fucking strong. It was going to take a lot to kill off this fella.

'We'll never get a stretcher down that thing,' one of the ambulance men said as he surveyed the spiral staircase.

Cut to a very funny situation in a very serious moment. Three ambulance men, two at the back, one in front. They had put my dad in one of those ambulance folding chairs, with straps around his chest and legs so he wouldn't fall out of the chair as they tried to bring him down the spiral staircase.

'Holy shit, Paddy, where did you get these stairs from?' slagged one of the ambulance men.

'He put this thing in himself, got it off a fella in Guinness's,' I told them as I watched them struggle with Dad's dead weight on each corner of the steps, panting and wheezing as they went.

'Well, you're going to have us all in the back of an ambulance at this rate, Paddy. We're all bollixed hauling your arse down it,' puffed the ambulance men.

There were hysterics at this. I even saw my dad trying to acknowledge the comment as he half-smiled at them, his right eye smiling too.

'Here, son, I made an overnight bag for your dad. His slippers, glasses, fresh PJs and his crossword are all in there.'

I hugged my mam, as she clearly was in shock. She had no idea that Dad most likely would never return home again.

My sister Rachel arrived and stayed with my mam while I jumped into the back of the ambulance. Dad lay on a stretcher and I sat beside him. I held his massive cooper's hand. It was squeezing back for dear life, as if Dad just didn't want to go, as if that hand was his only grip on life. It was strong, I'll never forget it.

'You're doing great, Jay,' said the ambulance man to me.

It was only when I realised that someone else had taken over from me that I felt sick inside my belly. My dad was dying.

As we pulled off from the road for the last time, the siren went on. I could see my dad's good eye open wide. He was most likely thinking: 'Ah, for jaysus' sake, the whole road will be looking at us now.'

I could go on a bit more about my career.

The many more appearances on TV, the shows all around the world that still keep going to this day.

The big changes in my life.

But I think it is fitting to keep going with the Paddy Byrne saga, as it's very much part of me anyway.

'Yes! Thank fuck, we have most certainly heard enough from you, you gobshite. More Paddy, please, but while you're at it, summarise!'

Thank you, Niall Tubridy.

When we launched the first book in this series, *Wonky-eyed Boy*, we did a book launch in the Sugar Club in Dublin. My whole family was at it, including Dad. He loved all the attention of being my dad, but afterwards, when I had to sign the copies of the book, people were asking if Dad would sign their books too. A new line was made so Dad could sign copies of *Wonky-eyed Boy* for them. They were asking if he loved the book, and he kept saying it was the best book he had ever read. He never read it. I mean, never. Dad would only read a newspaper and do the crossword.

So here's a final, unforgettable Paddy Byrne story. I used to tell this very tale in my stand-up.

One day …

'"One day", Jesus Christ, why don't you start with "Once upon a time" and kill us all off now, you useless shit, Jason!'

Just ignore him, guys.

One day I was on the phone to my niece in Sweden, Amanda. She was our first gay in the family, and we were very proud of her. We wondered how Dad would take it, but as he was non-religious and basically didn't give a shit about most things, I didn't think it would be an issue at all.

'Amanda likes women? Sure, so do I, fair play to her. I like women, Amanda likes women, we all like women.'

Fair play to him.

Amanda told me on the phone that she had a new partner and that her new partner was transgender. This was a good few years ago, when we were only learning about the wording and meaning of being transgender.

I, of course, pretended I knew exactly what she was talking about and told her I was delighted with her new relationship. Amanda then told me that her partner liked to be referred to as 'they' or 'them'. Again, I went along with it all and pretended I knew, doing the Irish thing. 'Oh, I know that, of course, what else.'

Amanda continued with the chat, telling me that herself and themselves were coming to Ireland for Christmas to visit Nana and Grandad.

I made sure: 'You're saying that yourself and your transgender partner are coming to visit my mam and dad. As in Paddy and Eithne.' Amanda said yes.

Holy shit, I wasn't going to miss this for the world. I had a gig on the day Amanda said she was coming, but I cancelled the date. No way was Dad going to get this right.

The day came and I made sure I was up at the house nice and early. Dad had a couple of whiskeys, as he always did when someone new was coming to the house. He said it would calm him down. At the same time, poor Mam was trying to coach Dad in what to say.

'No problems, I'm a man of the world, Eithne, a man of the world. I am versed in these things,' Dad announced, holding his whiskey glass high in the air like some sort of aristocrat in a smoking jacket, leaning against a massive open fire in his mansion.

The Swedes pulled into the driveway. I sat on the couch in the sitting room, front row in a venue that held only one person.

'They're here, Paddy. Now, I told you what you had to say to them – do not mess this up,' Mam said through gritted teeth at a now-hammered Paddy Byrne.

'Bring them in, bring the Swedes in, I am ready,' said Dad.

The door opened. Amanda ran in and hugged Dad. 'Oh, it's great to see you, Grandad. I missed you so much,' she said.

'Ah, welcome back to Ireland, Amanda, love you loads,' said Dad.

Then in walked Amanda's partner. Her partner held their hand out. Dad took it to shake and said …

'Ah, Dave, nice to meet ye.'

SILENCE, ACCOMPANIED BY OPEN MOUTHS.

'You fecking idiot, Paddy, I told you to say "they", not "Dave". I'm so sorry, he is a total gobshite,' said Mam to them.

They then ran out of the room. Amanda followed them and I stayed on the couch. I knew this was to be a day full of mishaps. There was no way Dad was going to get this right. Our mams and dads in their late seventies and eighties are being asked a lot – they just can't keep up with the technological and cultural changes. It's just too fast for them and the goalposts keep changing. But, like Dad, they do their best.

'Jesus Christ, Paddy, I can't believe you called "they" Dave,' Mam said again.

His face went red. He hated my mam pointing out embarrassing moments to him, and he hated upsetting people, so he got frustrated with himself. Well, things just got funnier as my dad was about to utter one of the best lines in comedy ever, and he never even wrote it down or remembered saying it.

'I don't know what to say anymore, a Michael is a Michelle, a Henry is a Harriette, a Susan a Seán. I'm eighty years old and I'm sorry, I'm sorry if I get it wrong, but it's impossible to fucking keep up, willies for boobs and fannies for willies, and ...'

HERE IT COMES, EVERYONE, THE LAST BIT OF GENIUS TO COME OUT OF PADDY BYRNE'S MOUTH ...

'Anyway, I thought a transgender was a truck that turned into a robot!'

I howled laughing at this. Dad ran outside to go to the pub and Mam sat with her head in her hands. This man was something else.

I was in my partner Tracy's house, in the centre of Dublin. My dad was in St James's Hospital. It was roughly 11 p.m. and I had been told to go home by the nurse and get some rest. It wasn't far from the hospital, and they said they'd ring me if there were any changes.

Just a couple of hours previously, my sisters Eithne and Rachel and Mam had been sitting around my dad, with Eric the Phone checking in from Sweden now and again.

Mam was holding Dad's good right hand, and he gripped her back intensely. He was totally out of it, but still that Paddy Byrne would not let go. They had given him a lot of drugs to stop him jumping and leaping around the bed. They had the scan results, and as we thought, he had suffered a massive stroke that had completely floored him.

After many hours, I convinced my family to all go home and that I would sit with him. The nurse said Dad could be like this for hours or even years, there was no telling. But he was never going to recover from this stroke.

Mam and my sisters all left. Now, it was just me and Dad on our own. I took over hand-holding duty. I read the *Herald* newspaper to him, as he loved that. Then, just to annoy him, I read excerpts from a mindfulness self-help book. He hated these, so I slagged it off for him as I read.

A nurse entered to check his vitals and such. She shouted, 'Hello, Paddy, how are we?'

Dad woke up, looked at the nurse and said, from one side of his working mouth, 'I'm OK, I'm in St James's Hospital, my name is Paddy Byrne, I was born in 1939.'

This was amazing. He had had a massive stroke, but still that stubborn brain of his could not be killed off. The nurse pointed at me and asked, 'Who's that, Paddy?'

Dad looked at me from his one good eye. 'That's our Jay – are you OK, Jay?' Dad said, amazingly.

I said I was. I squeezed his hand, and he fell back into his comatose state.

These were to be the last words he ever spoke.

The nurse said he was stable enough for now, but I really should go home and get some rest. So I did.

BUZZZZ BUZZZZ BUZZZZ

'Can you come in? Your dad has had more strokes,' the doctor said on the other end of the line.

I got in the car with Tracy and rang my sisters to get Mam. It was around 10 a.m. This was it, I supposed.

I walked into the hospital room. My dad's brother Tom was there with his wife Harriette, my dad's sisters auntie Joan and auntie Collette, and my cousin Laura. Mam arrived in behind me with Rachel and Eithne.

Dad looked bad. He was no longer reaching for life with his right hand. He was dying. His breathing was very odd as we all watched.

I had never seen anyone die. I had no idea how it worked, but thank God I was there. Suddenly, Dad began to cough. The nurse, a lovely man, came in and said that this was it. My mam and sisters left the room – they couldn't watch.

The beautiful nurse told us to talk to him, to tell him it was OK to go, that we would help him get there. I stood on one side holding his hand as my aunties Joan and Collette held his other hand.

Dad continued to cough and splutter. I just kept saying, 'It's OK, Dad, it's OK, we're all here … you're doing amazing.'

Then he completely stopped breathing and the fight was over. I watched the life leave my Dad, his whole body deflating like air leaving a lilo. My dad would have thought this was bollix, but you could feel the energy leaving his body. A warmth went by us and then it was cold. I'll never forget it. Was it his soul? His spirit? Or simply energy leaving the body?

'Or the window that was open behind you, son?' I could hear Paddy laugh as he said this.

He lay there in the bed. He looked tiny, nothing like the big man from Guinness's with his shovel hands. Life had literally left every part of him.

But thank God I was there when he died, that he didn't collapse in the middle of the street and die surrounded by strangers. It was a privilege to be with my dad at that moment.

Paddy Byrne was gone. Well, at least for now.

At his wake in the pub, the whole bar was lined with men mourning. I remember one of them grabbing me and saying, 'Your dad wasn't just a man, he was a character, and when a character leaves our lives, it's so much harder. God bless him, Jason, we will miss him so much.'

It was true. My dad was one of those characters that said and did what he pleased. He was always kind to everyone, making them laugh or cry, depending on if he liked you or not.

There was more laughter than tears at Dad's wake, as people remembered him fondly. He would have preferred that, as he hated people crying in front of him. 'No whinging and crying, do you hear? Laughter only, son,' he'd say.

EPILOGUE

A standing ovation. People have tears in their eyes, from laughter and sadness.

I take my bow as Paddy Byrne in Edinburgh. The Paddy Lama. I come backstage and slowly become myself again.

You see, my dad's body died on that bed that day, but he never left us. He is alive today; his memories, his consciousness. These things cannot die when you die.

'If you do not continue to talk about someone when they die, they die twice.' Dad would always say this to me.

So we have all kept him alive. I've done it by writing this book, by performing a play as him. By simply talking about him.

After the play, two little old Irish women came up to me. You could see they had misery in their knickers. They said, 'We're so sorry about your dad, but I bet he wouldn't have wanted to be around for all this Covid stuff, no pub and having to stay in.'

I couldn't help it, I just became my dad, looked at them and said …

'I'm pretty sure he would have preferred to be alive, love, than dead.' I then laughed as I walked off, leaving the two miserable old women open-mouthed.

'Nice one, son, pair of auld ones,' he would have laughed.

Paddy Byrne. The man that didn't give a bollix.

ACKNOWLEDGEMENTS

Here we go again, another wonky-eyed book. I'd like to thank my mammy, Eithne, and my daddy, Paddy Lama, for giving me this wonky eye and bad genes in general. Without this highly malfunctioning body, this book would never have come to fruition. But especially Dad, who passed on the best ever and worst ever advice to me.

Thanks, of course, to Rachel the sister, Eithne the Mistake and Eric the Phone, and everyone else named in this book.

To the amazing Gill staff – Sarah Liddy, Aoibheann, Sheila and everyone else who had to sit through the bad grammar and spelling mistakes.

My sons, Devin and Daniel, and the sweet little Roisín, who I love and adore so much. Even with their ketchup stains on the couch and their 'Dad, there's no milk' chants, not forgetting Roisín's 'That's not right, Jason.'

Lastly, my gorgeous Tracy. Always there for me, always loving, and without her guidance and support, I'd be nothing.

Now enjoy the book – laugh, cry, or use it as a doorstop.

Love you all.

Jason, the Wonky-eyed Man.